MODERNIST WOMEN AND VISUAL CULTURES

VIRGINIA WOOLF,

VANESSA BELL,

PHOTOGRAPHY

AND CINEMA

MODERNIST WOMEN AND VISUAL CULTURES

VIRGINIA WOOLF,

VANESSA BELL,

PHOTOGRAPHY

AND CINEMA

Maggie Humm

Rutgers University Press
New Brunswick, New Jersey

For Rodger

First published in the United States 2003
by Rutgers University Press
New Brunswick, New Jersey

First published in Great Britain 2002
by Edinburgh University Press
22 George Square, Edinburgh

Library of Congress Cataloging-in-
Publication Data and British Library
Cataloguing-in-Publication Data are
available upon request.

ISBN 0-8135-3265-5 (cloth)
ISBN 0-8135-3266-3 (paper)

Printed in Spain

CONTENTS

LIST OF FIGURES

PREFACE AND ACKNOWLEDGEMENTS

Sometime around 1920 Picasso famously declared 'I've discovered photography. Now I can kill myself. I've nothing else to learn'. By contrast, the domestic photographs of Virginia Woolf and Vanessa Bell teach us a great deal about gender and modernism (Baldassari 1997, p. 17). Photography is a tool which Woolf and Bell used, not simply as a documentary device but as a means of crossing the border between the visual and the unconscious. Yet one of the interesting things about domestic photography and the related art of cinema journalism is that these are very marginalised theoretically within criticism about modernism. This is despite the fact that most modernist women writers and artists, like most middle-class women in the 1920s and 1930s, owned 'vest-pocket Kodaks' and developed photographs throughout their careers as well as writing about other visual representations such as cinema. Domestic photography must have had a profound, if not necessarily acknowledged, influence on modernist women's thoughts about life, art and writing.

Yet from Adorno and Horkheimer on, criticism of modernism relies heavily on the avant-garde 'story': a disdain of popular culture as well as a disdain of the new consumers of popular culture (predominantly female) (Adorno and Horkheimer 1973). This has been at the expense of a more adequate consideration of the potential of the 'domestic' arts to imagine new visual possibilities for women in the context of individual and familial formations. In my research on Woolf's and Bell's photo albums, I found that (although different in type) they amounted to a contrary cultural formation, in which particular representations of family and friends were a source of psychic and aesthetic imaginaries. The technologies of modernity – photography and cinema – were then an incentive to, and a medium for, border crossings in this special sense.

Modernist Women and Visual Cultures takes up these issues of border crossings in modernist women's work. Chapter 4 deals specifically with the film *Borderline*, involving the modernist women writers H. D. and Bryher; and the book in general develops the interest in border crossings within the humanities that the topics of some of my other books suggest, for example *Border Traffic* (Humm 1991). The risks of border traffic, of going beyond the boundaries of a particular discipline, mean that I can only focus on modernism in an eclectic way; but Virginia Woolf herself, the main writer considered here, had an abiding interest in the margins of modernism. As David Bradshaw points out, Woolf's short stories bring readers 'face to face with the marginal and marginalised', and explore aspects of experience which Woolf's 'traditional peers' would regard as 'too ephemeral to be worth writing about' (Bradshaw 2001, p. xi).

Modernist Women and Visual Cultures owes a great deal to the kind invitations of scholars around the world who invited me to give papers at conferences and universities. An invitation to Rutgers University Institute for Research on Women as a Distinguished Visiting Scholar in 1998, by Marianne DeKoven, then director, enabled me to join a very lively group of theoretically informed scholars. I am grateful to Professor Manuel Barbeito at the University of Santiago de Compostela and to Koen van Daele, co-ordinator of the Sixth International Festival of Contemporary Arts, City of Women, Slovenia, for inviting me to give plenary and keynote papers; and to respondents at: the Seventh International Congress on Women, Tromso; the Fourth European Feminist Conference, Bologna, and the ATHENA organisation; the Tenth and Eleventh Annual Virginia Woolf conferences in Baltimore and Bangor; the Transformations Conference and ESRC Seminar Series, Institute for Women's Studies, Lancaster University; the Frontiers of Memory conference, Institute of Education, London; and the Literature of the 1930s conference, Anglia Polytechnic University, Cambridge.

I was honoured to be invited to give the Third Annual Virginia Woolf Birthday Lecture, Keynes Library, by the Virginia Woolf Society Executive and to be a Visiting Fellow, School for Advanced Study, University of London, both in spring 2002 (Humm 2002).

Like all scholars I am indebted to the curators and librarians who allowed me to explore their collections, and for permissions. In particular I would like to thank Victoria Lane, Tate Gallery Archives;

Jeremy Crow, Society of Authors, on behalf of the Virginia Woolf Estate; Karen Kukil, Associate Curator of Rare Books, Smith College Library; Annette Fern, Harvard Theatre Collection, Houghton Library, and Michael Dumas, formerly of this library; Elizabeth Inglis, formerly University of Sussex Library; as well as staff at the Berg Collection, New York Public Library, the Marx Memorial Library, London, and the BFI Library, London.

My thanks to the Bedfords for showing me Talland House, St Ives.

I am especially grateful for British Academy conference and small grants, an AHRB Research Leave Grant, and British Council support for my visit to Slovenia.

A section of Chapter 1 appears in *Woolf Studies Annual*, 8, 2002. Versions of Chapter 2 appeared in *Virginia Woolf in the Age of Mechanical Reproduction*, ed. P. Caughie, New York: Garland, 2000; *Transformations: Thinking Through Feminism*, eds S. Ahmed, J. Kilby, C. Lury, M. McNeil and B. Skeggs, London: Routledge, 2000; *Virginia Woolf Out of Bounds: Selected Papers from the Tenth Annual Conference on Virginia Woolf*, eds J. Berman and J. Goldman, New York: Pace University Press, 2001; and *Virginia Woolf Bulletin*, 1, January 1999. A version of Chapter 3 appears in *Literary Modernism and Photography*, ed. P. Hansom, New York: Greenwood Press, 2002. A version of Chapter 6 is to appear in *Signs*. Part of Chapter 7 appeared in *Feminism and Autobiography: Texts, Theories, Methods*, eds T. Cosslett, C. Lury and P. Summerfield, London: Routledge, 2000. I am grateful to the editors of these volumes for their very helpful suggestions.

For many of my publications, including this book, I have been lucky to benefit immensely from the expertise, exemplary editing and friendship of Jackie Jones, deputy managing director, Edinburgh University Press, to whom I give heartfelt thanks.

Finally my thanks go to colleagues and students at the University of East London for their vibrant discussions; to Mary Evans and Helen Taylor for their invaluable support; to Julia Watson for her guidance; to Shiona Saunders for her excellent word processing; to Andrea Rossi for the *Close Up* photography; to Dan and Male for listening; and most of all to Rodger for his visual expertise, and encouragement with this book and in everything else.

The author and publishers would like to thank the following for granting permission to reproduce material in this work:

> The Harvard Theatre Collection, The Houghton Library, Cambridge, Massachusetts, USA, for the photographs from Virginia Woolf's Monk's House Albums.

> The Mortimer Rare Book Room, Smith College, Northampton, Massachusetts, USA, for photographs from the Leslie Stephen Photograph Album.

> The Tate Gallery Library and the Charleston Trust for photographs from Vanessa Bell's Albums.

> The BFI National Library for the photographs from *Close Up* and *The Cabinet of Dr Caligari*.

> The Society of Authors on behalf of the Virginia Woolf Estate for photographs from Virginia Woolf's *Three Guineas*.

Every effort has been made to contact copyright holders for their permission to reprint material in this book. The publishers would be grateful to hear from any copyright holder who is not here acknowledged, and will undertake to rectify any errors or omissions in future editions of this book.

1

MODERNISM, GENDER, PHOTOGRAPHY AND VIRGINIA WOOLF'S 'PORTRAITS'

INTRODUCTION

Issues of vision and specularity haunt modernity. Late nineteenth- and early twentieth-century scientists, natural philosophers and artists set about appropriating visible and 'invisible' worlds through new technologies of vision: through photography, stereoscopes, X-rays and cinema (Jenks 1995). Modernity witnessed a transformation in the production of the visual more profound than the discovery of Renaissance perspective. According to Jonathan Crary in *Techniques of the Observer*, capitalist modernity effectively demolished classical vision by separating the spectator from the optical devices such as the camera obscura which, hitherto, carried the look of the spectator (Crary 1990). What late romanticism and modernism celebrate, Crary argues, is the eye's independence from the technology which earlier defined the act of viewing. In turn, twentieth-century modernism is obsessed with issues of visuality. And in the major years of modernism, the first decades of the twentieth century, new vocabularies of vision were transforming literary and cultural texts.

Descriptions of acts of observation are a major trope in literary modernism. For example, James Joyce makes the concept of parallax (how the same phenomenon looks different from alternative angles or perspectives) a structuring device in *Ulysses* (Joyce 1922). In the first six chapters of *Ulysses*, the same day in Dublin is seen from the two perspectives of Leopold Bloom and Stephen Daedalus (Schwarz 1997). Virginia Woolf concerns herself both with visible and 'invisible' vision, with what contemporary physics was recognising in Einstein's theories of space-time, as kinesis, that is the flow of differing perspectives (Beer 2000). In addition, Einstein believed that logical structures such as language were always preceded in the brain by a kind of 'combinatory play' of signs and images much like the memories experienced by Woolf's narrators (Eisinger 1995, p. 177).

While the camera, to some extent, utilises Renaissance perspective, it was photography which verified Einstein's theories when Alfred North Whitehead photographed the 1927 eclipse, an event to which Woolf returns again and again in her work (Dalgarno 2001; Goldman 2001). Although the photograph of Einstein hanging in Woolf's Monk's House is dated 1951 (after her death), Einstein's relativity theory, Bohr's atomic theory, and wave and particle theories informed Woolf's milieu while she was writing her first fictions (National Trust 1995, p. 12). And later, in 1930, the year Pluto was discovered, Virginia and Leonard bought a telescope, and may have visited an exhibition of astronomical photographs at the Royal Photographic Society in 35 Russell Square, while Virginia was looking at 57 Russell Square as a possible home (Woolf 1980b, p. 295; Dalgarno 2001).

The production of new representations of cognition, of new ways of seeing and knowing the world, became the common project of the modernist writers Woolf, Joyce and Richardson as well as modernist artists, such as Picasso and Braque in their Cubist periods. Although Jane Marcus claims that Woolf's references to a 'language of light' derive from the mysticism of her aunt Caroline Stephen, new visual processes such as photography equally had a major impact on Woolf's work (Marcus 1987, p. 129). The creation of new technologies of vision, particularly cinema and photography, shape modernity's epistemologies. Henri Lefebvre, echoing Woolf's famous statement 'on or about December 1910, human character changed', argues more dramatically that such change was created by absolute changes in visual and social epistemologies (Woolf 1978a, p. 96; Lefebvre 1983). 'The absolute sovereignty of modernism is ushered in around 1910', Lefebvre claims, 'by a rupture with the classical and traditional vocabulary' (Lefebvre 1983, pp. 5–6).

Where, as Erica Hirschler suggests, many male Impressionists 'sought to emphasize the style's basis in optical theory' precisely to discredit 'the feminine' characteristics of Impressionism, such as the prevalence of domestic subject matter, modernist epistemological doubts that Impressionism or naturalistic narratives could accurately reflect the world gave impetus to new representations of cognition, such as stream of consciousness in the novel and 'multimedia' works like Woolf's *Orlando* and *Three Guineas* (Hirschler 2001, p. 83). A growth in domestic photography in these decades, with the development of celluloid roll films and hand-held cameras, encouraged artists and the general public alike into new ideas of 'transitoriness and reproducibility' (Benjamin 1972, p. 21).

Bloomsbury's favourite philosopher, G. E. Moore, encapsulated this issue of epistemological and cognitive uncertainty about materiality and sensation, in a modernist play with classical conventions of vision. In what he modestly called a 'quite uninteresting' essay, Moore argues that 'we can and must conceive that blue might exist and yet the sensation of blue not exist' (Moore 1903, p. 435). What Moore's speculation pinpoints is the gap between our modes of cognition, the socially agreed designation 'blue' for a particular material hue, and our subjective experience. Moore additionally argues that material objects, things which we see, can only render evidence of their existence in a similar fashion as our sensations, and that 'either exists *may* be false' (Moore 1903, p. 453). This difficulty of seeing and knowing informs both Moore's philosophical enquiries and Virginia Woolf's visual texts, particularly her short fictions like 'Blue and Green' (Woolf 2001b).

In 'Blue and Green' Woolf uses the term 'blue' like Moore's theory of sense-data. 'It's night, the needles drip blots of blue. The green's out' (Woolf 2001b, p. 33). Discarding the narrative convention that colour represents emotions, Woolf uses 'blue' to show that perception is not dependable and the meaning of the story is not transparent. While Moore's monistic values of radical individualism, the subject of a devastating critique by Woolf's friend J. M. Keynes, seems at odds with Woolf's socially informed pluralism, yet, in general, Woolf's fictions do highlight the importance to vision of transitory processes as well as the problem of a world that often seems to behave in a different way from our common-sense view of it (Anderson 1993; Levenson 1999). Woolf paraphrases from Moore's *Principia Ethica* in another short story, 'A Society', and there are several photographs of the philosopher in Woolf's photo albums (Bradshaw 2001).

Modernist Women and Visual Cultures explores these new ideas and practices in the domestic photography of Virginia Woolf and Vanessa Bell and in the cinema writing of Woolf, Colette, Richardson, H. D., Bryher and other modernist women and men. In thinking about how to analyse gender issues in relation to visual modernism, it is difficult to hold to a dichotomy between feminine and masculine modernisms.

Beginning with art historian Linda Nochlin's doubt that gender alone can account for stylistic similarity, feminists have been alert to the limitations of defining cultural phenomena in terms of gender distinctions (Nochlin 1988). However, the continuous focus of many women modernists, rather than men, on domestic photography needs some examination if the links between such representations, gender and modernism are to be explained. Women were drawn to photography from the introduction of the medium in 1839 because photography involved an easily acquired skill and fewer barriers to participation in the arts (Rosenblum 2000). And despite differences of education, location and sexual orientation between modernist women, there seem to be similarities in the way in which seeing differently impacts on how women negotiate issues of the subjective, spectatorship and professionalism in their writing.

This book looks at writing and visual modernism, utilising ideas about vision in the writings of the contemporary artist and psychoanalyst Bracha Lichtenberg Ettinger, modernist criticism, semiology and the photographic studies of Barthes, Benjamin and others, as well as biographical readings of the work of Woolf and Bell. I follow a cultural studies approach, aiming to reconstruct private forms of representation in order to reveal new angles of vision on gender and modernism, because, as Lisa Tickner argues, 'both the heterogeneity and what has been called the "ecology" of modernism have been largely purged from the history of the period' (Tickner 2000, p. xiii).

The book's seven chapters share the assumption that, in their cinema writing and domestic photography, modernist women explore gender issues in a perhaps freer way than in their better-known work; and the book asks what such an exploration can tell us about gender and modernism. In a germinal phrase, Susan Stanford Friedman argues that modernist women wrote 'a modernism of the margins' (Friedman 1987). Starting from this highly productive theme, I aim to show that evaluation of the *marginalia of the margins* – ordinary but marginalised cultural artefacts such as photo albums and 'image/texts' – can help us rethink modernist aesthetics. For example, women modernists, much more than men, incorporate everyday and maternal experiences into their visual aesthetics. They were devotees of Kodaks, reflecting a modern world in which women were 87 per cent of the film audiences and active domestic photographers during the 1920s (Nava 1994). Other studies of visual and literary modernism have tended to look at common techniques, or modernist forms such as the Cubist cinema, or specifically at the artistic 'collaborations' of Virginia Woolf and Vanessa Bell (Schwarz 1988; Lawder 1975; Gillespie 1988). None studies the commonalities to be found in 'ordinary' domestic photography and cinema culture and writing. It is such a study which crucially enables us to step outside the canon into 'domestic' and 'popular' culture.

Virginia Woolf continually experiments with features of vision, radically reframing the visible world in her 'image/texts' – texts which display a concern for visual themes and images – as well as in her domestic photography. She often constitutes identity in terms of memory pictures, such as the narrators' differing memories in 'Portraits' (Woolf 1989). Other modernist women writers were also engaging in highly articulate and self-conscious ways with new images of external/internal realities and gender. The work of the poet H. D. is also about issues of cognition and the visual. 'Notes on Thought and Vision', as the title suggests, is a philosophical disquisition about consciousness and sight in which H. D. describes gendered epiphanies which are almost maternal in origin (H. D. 1990a).

What Elizabeth A. Hirsch accurately describes in '"New Eyes": H. D., Modernism and the Psychoanalysis of Seeing' are the new ways in which modernist women theorise subjectivity in terms of images (Hirsch 1986). Hirsch argues that modernist women address the increasing specularity of culture, as well as modernity's visual objectification of women, by interweaving the objective with the subjective in visual images which, while acknowledging the material primacy of objects, do not privilege materiality at the expense of the psychic. For example, H. D.'s imagist tableaux utilise processes of recollection and association. Hirsch's argument matches my own focus on modernist women's socio-psychic representations. By examining a range of image/texts – Virginia Woolf's 'imagistic' short fictions, the photo albums of Woolf and her sister Vanessa Bell, as well as the cinema journalism of Woolf, H. D., Richardson and others – we can pinpoint new gendered features of modernist memories and self-identities.

The more popular practices of domestic photography and cinema reviewing can produce complex aesthetic constructions, even if these are fragmentary and marginal. I would argue that modernist women's private obsession with photography might represent an attempt to explore forms of representation outside the objectifications of masculine modernism.

Rather than reading canonically, that is, assuming that key modernist motifs can only be richly represented in generically distinct forms – as, for example, in an Imagist poem – I prefer to trace modernist women's textualised memories in a continuum of photographic referents. My feeling is that, rather than choosing to represent authentic authorship in any purist way, modernist women delighted equally in domestic photography and imagistic writing. Such a broad and rich modernist realm conflates high with low visual cultures.

Throughout the modernist period, photography is equally embedded in high and popular culture, although it took some time for photography to be displayed in museums. For example, the first photography exhibition at the Museum of Fine Art, Boston, was not until 1901 (Hirschler 2001, p. 56). In the interwar years many modernist photographers, including Man Ray and Moholy-Nagy, undertook commercial and industrial work alongside their experimental and avant-garde projects (Sichel 1999). By the time of post-war exhibitions by John Szarkowski at the Museum of Modern Art, New York, a 'snapshot aesthetic' could even be promoted institutionally (Eisinger 1995). In the MOMA catalogue, the critic Nathan Lyons described this aesthetic as characterised by blurred and imbalanced compositions and unusual perspectives (Lyons 1966). But, as Eisinger points out, this vernacular aesthetic soon became a 'new kind of formalism' in the way in which Szarkowski wished to detach 'photographic history from social reality' (Eisinger 1995, p. 225).

Modernist photography is conventionally characterised as encompassing 'the choice of unconventional themes, a preference for close-ups and other unusual angles, attention to effects of light, and experimentation with media' (Rosenblum 2000, p. 125). Although by the 1980s domestic photographs were being read as formal aesthetic objects – for example, in the work of Tina Barney – in the modernist period family images cannot be characterised in the terms which Rosenblum outlines. Domestic photography, therefore, occupies an odd conceptual space in any account of modernism, because its formal properties often match those of high art yet carry the pregnant burden of the psychic Imaginary in unique ways. An authorial self is often surprisingly dispersed in those texts. For example, Woolf's photographs are often careful, close-up or medium-shot portraits rather than snapshot 'reportage', which immediately suggests some kind of authorial identification, yet the portraits are set into unconventional album sequences. These often contain an excessive repetition of motifs, for example, an overrepresentation of domestic objects such as armchairs and windows, which suggest the ways in which the gendered psyche might be manifested.

But it is the range of Woolf's image/texts which makes her career a very powerful example of modernist women's constant turn to the visual as a means to establishing a more inclusionary modernism. Woolf evokes memories, connecting past to present, through visual images, both in her photo albums and in the epistemologically more complex work, *Three Guineas*. In Woolf's writings, visual images play a constitutive role, creating a surface aesthetic, while at the same time images are clues to multiple and repressed femininities. In *To the Lighthouse* much of the narrative weight of the novel is sustained by images which act as visual analogues to plot developments (Woolf 1927). In Woolf's domestic photography, her heavy reliance on the repetition of particular domestic objects reveals her emotional, psychic investment in memories of her mother and her childhood home, Talland House, St Ives.

PSYCHOANALYTIC THEORY

The contemporary post-Lacanian psychoanalyst and artist Bracha Lichtenberg Ettinger similarly focuses on aesthetic reconstructions of maternal memories, in what she terms the 'matrixial gaze' (Lichtenberg Ettinger 1994a):

> For the matrixial gaze, it makes no difference if the materials
> of artwork come from with-in, as source/origin, or from
> with-out [...] the with-in-visible matrixial screen is a web
> into which subjectivity is woven in different ways in art – by
> trauma, by phantasy, by desire. It is in between us, it is a veil
> spread between joint traumas, fractions of phantasy from out
> into the inside and aspects of painting in-to the outside. On
> the screen's interlaced threshold, a feminine gaze diffracts.
> (Lichtenberg Ettinger 1994a, p. 109)

Bracha Lichtenberg Ettinger lays bare the psychic mediations which lie between the maternal Imaginary and external objects, and which are

7

visible in artistic representations. Photographs, which Lichtenberg
Ettinger uses as a primary artistic medium, she suggests, reveal a special
relationship between the I and the Not-I, between invisible, matrixial,
intra-uterine memories and the external world. 'The emotional and
mental conductivity of an artwork may reflect on far away matrixial
unconscious events' (Lichtenberg Ettinger 1994b, p. 59).

With the metaphor of the matrixial gaze, the title of her major
book, Bracha Lichtenberg Ettinger makes domestic photography into a
palimpsest source of the maternal. In her art she reworks photos using
Xeroxed memorial images of people long dead in concentration camps.
Her works *Matrixial Borderline* and *The Eye of the Matrix* are montage
tableaux which resemble, in part, snapshots assembled in photo albums.
For both Lichtenberg Ettinger and Woolf (as I shall show in Chapter 2)
the maternal is present as an experienced 'affect' in their photographs.
By incorporating a visual prehistory of matrixial references into their
photography, both Lichtenberg Ettinger and Woolf create trans-genera-
tional memories.

Post-Lacanian feminism is an umbrella term applied to the work
of a number of contemporary psychoanalytic thinkers, including the
French feminist Luce Irigaray as well as Lichtenberg Ettinger. Its premise
is that Lacan creates in his writing an impossible binary between phallic
language and the maternal body that feminism needs to go beyond
(Campbell 2000). As Jan Campbell suggests in *Arguing with the Phallus*,
'the symbolisation of the daughter's imaginary in terms of the mother
remains an impossibility' for Lacan, whose concept of an Imaginary is
based 'entirely on a masculine and phallic morphology' (Campbell 2000,
p. 110). What post-Lacanian feminism offers instead is a more positive
way of understanding both the Imaginary and the maternal, for example,
in the notion of an experiential *figural* unconscious. Lichtenberg
Ettinger's theorisation of the Imaginary recreates a lost maternal object
and lost matrixial relationship in painterly, poetic and photographic
images. This does seem to offer a way of conceptualising imagery and
narrative which can make available a female Imaginary *in* the symbolic.

Griselda Pollock argues that the maternal haunts our aesthetic
subjectivities, not like Lacan's mastering gaze, but as 'a borderline
awareness' (Pollock 1994a, p. 78). Where 'strategies of representation
in the visual arts, from painting to photography and film, have been institutionalised to lure our gaze and suture our desire to that which the

culture wishes to fix us', Pollock argues, 'Lichtenberg Ettinger's method permits a glimpse of another kind of vanishing point, a matrixial gaze', which is 'distinct' from the usual 'confrontation between practice and popular cultures' (Pollock 1994a, p. 78). The characteristics of such a method resemble Woolf's modernist experiments: a use of fragmentary images, interruptions of linearity, traces of the Imaginary and intricately worked surfaces. Lichtenberg Ettinger's 'use of found photographs', Pollock suggests, is a means of 'allowing elements of their feminine but invisible body specificity and the fantasies to which it gives rise' the possibility of signification (Pollock 1994a, pp. 78–9).

In the Lacanian symbolic 'woman' is identified only as the unknown, the *objet à* of archaic sensuality lost, as it were, when we enter the symbolic, but in Lichtenberg Ettinger's photographs, Pollock argues, the *objet à* 'may in art achieve a borderline visibility', particularly in art's excess (Pollock 1994a, p. 79). So that, rather than reading modernist texts primarily in terms of surface colour or line, it is excesses in art which can reveal elements of feminine subjectivity. In this way the matrixial is not placed in opposition to, or anterior to, the phallic but opens up the symbolic field to a feminine dimension. Lichtenberg Ettinger argues that psychoanalysis has invested the Oedipal stage/structure 'with cultural priority', and 'Lacan's idea that the unconscious is structured like a language shifted too quickly to the idea that the unconscious is structured like a verbal language and by the verbal language' (Lichtenberg Ettinger 1992, p. 201). In opposition, art can create differences in the transmission, destroy it and posit new symbols in traces of subjectivity, descriptions which 'indicate and elaborate traces of an-other Real' (Lichtenberg Ettinger 1992, p. 196). As Pollock suggests in one of her many rich accounts of Lichtenberg Ettinger's work, while 'this theorisation has many facets and radically realigns the way we think about the process of making and seeing painting, at the same time it offers a radical contribution to the theorisation of femininity, not as the other of masculinity' (Pollock 1995, p. 131). In *Virginia Woolf and the Languages of Patriarchy*, Jane Marcus suggests that Woolf similarly utilises birth images, for example, in *A Room of One's Own*, which Marcus calls 'a vaginal creative space' – Woolf's response to a phallocentric culture (Marcus 1987, p. 75).

A tangential contemporary reassessment of the maternal function in psychoanalysis is provided by another post-Lacanian psychoanalyst,

Jessica Benjamin. She agrees that the maternal is not unrepresentable in the symbolic (Benjamin 1998). Rather, she argues that the maternal is present in, and mediated by, the symbolic in 'formal elements – such as timing, kinetics, distance and closeness – that later enter into speech' (Benjamin 1998, p. 27). These post-Lacanian analyses revise Freud's account of the maternal. In 'Childhood and Concealing Memories', Freud describes the maternal memory as something screened off, unavailable to conscious perception (Freud 1938). To him, memory of the maternal can only involve the reproduction of something lost and irretrievably past. He suggests that maternal memory is only a trace of a past that has never been 'present', that it is the act of forgetting, not memory itself, which is the core experience of modernity (Krell 1990). Feminist post-Lacanian psychoanalysis, more positively, considers maternal mnemonics to be material elements in symbolic representations.

These contemporary feminist psychoanalytic reflections match many modernist women's attempt to capture more fragmentary representations of the feminine such as the maternal in marginal art forms, including photo albums and cinema journalism. Such composite image/texts both expose and resist a conception of modernist purity via their autobiographical traces. I want to suggest that domestic photography and cinema journalism, visual cultures on the margins of modernism and outside the canon, share something of Lichtenberg Ettinger's 'becoming threshold', a space of contradiction and change 'between being and absence, memory and oblivion, *I* and *not-I*, a process of transgression and fading away. The metamorphic consciousness has no center, cannot hold a fixed gaze' (Lichtenberg Ettinger 1992, p. 201).

Woolf's obsession with the memory of her mother, 'of living so completely in her atmosphere that one never got far enough away from her to see her as a person', was a shaping power in Woolf's life and art (Woolf 1985, p. 83). Her close attachment to mother figures, particularly her sister Vanessa and friends Ethel Smyth and Violet Dickinson, recreated for Woolf this pre-Oedipal attachment which is unique to women, who, unlike men, 'reproduce' their mothers (Chodorow 1978). Woolf recovers the dead mother in writing and photography by transforming loss into fictional images and photographic frames. In some senses this work of nostalgic retrieval is a defining feature of modernism itself. As Perry Meisel argues, modernism constantly recreates 'the loss of something primary that it wishes to regain' (Meisel 1987, p. 229).

CRITICAL MODERNISM

While post-Lacanian feminism does help us to re-vision the masculine specularity of modernism, one intractable problem remains: the difficulty of categorising and periodising modernism itself. One of the earliest uses of the term 'modern' in relation to literature is by Virginia Woolf herself in 'Modern Fiction', where she claims that 'the modern practice of the art is somehow an improvement upon the old'. Woolf's essay was chosen by Mark Schorer as a significant introduction to his collection, *Modern British Fiction* (Woolf 1994c, p. 157; Schorer 1961). Other critics choose a later date for the beginning of critical constructions of modernism. Astradur Eysteinsson suggests that Edmund Wilson's *Axel's Castle* (1931) is the first critique to define modernism, while Takei da Silva privileges Stephen Spender's *The Struggle of the Modern* (1963) as the first 'in-depth analysis of the modernist spirit' (Eysteinsson 1990; da Silva 1990, p. 5). Borrowing the term 'modernism' from architecture, the American critic Harry Levin was the first to utilise it in literary criticism, but by the time of Peter Faulkner's *Modernism*, published in the same year as David Lodge's *Modes of Modern Writing* (1979), the term was already being used to describe a canon of writing (Levin 1966; Faulkner 1977; Lodge 1977).

If the trajectory of the term 'modernism' is unclear, equally there is no broad critical consensus about modernism's historical periodisation. Michael Levenson suggests that Anglo-American modernism took place between 1910 and 1930, while da Silva more expansively claims 'the last two decades of the nineteenth century and the first three decades' of the twentieth century (Levenson 1999; da Silva 1990, p. 5). Malcolm Bradbury and James McFarlane's influential *Modernism 1890–1930*, as the title suggests, has a slightly narrower compass (Bradbury and McFarlane 1976). Perhaps for this reason, the relationship of modernism to modernity and the distinction between modernism and modernity are equally unclear. While not adopting a purely reflectionist paradigm, Marshall Berman nevertheless claims that modernism is the dialectical counterpoint of modernity because modernism is marked by modernity's new visual technologies (Berman 1982). Rather than following Berman's mimetic model, Eysteinsson suggests that modernism is itself a crisis within modernity because features of modernism highlight the flux of modernity's discursive

11

systems, for example, its urban rhythms (Eysteinsson 1980).

In the 1970s this issue of a canonic crisis became the project of feminist critics of modernism. Kate Millett's attack on D. H. Lawrence in *Sexual Politics* pioneers a contemporary feminist concern with gender asymmetries in modernism (Millett 1970). Feminist critics focused on the patrilineal ownership of modernism, in which experimental writing was designated as the exclusive practice of James Joyce, D. H. Lawrence and T. S. Eliot (DuPlessis 1985). Most feminist critiques utilised an insider/outsider paradigm, focusing on how the literary canon selected mainly men and relegated women writers to the position of outsider (Benstock 1989). This segregation becomes almost a cause for celebration in Susan Stanford Friedman's crucial essay 'Modernism of the "Scattered Remnant"', in which Friedman persuasively argues, as I have suggested, that H. D.'s writing, as well as that of other modernist women, is part of a gendered aesthetic, 'a modernism of the margins, a modernism based on an identification with those left out of the cultural mainstream' (Friedman 1987, p. 218). Shari Benstock's analysis of modernist women's 'support services' in *Women of the Left Bank* adds a fuller historical context in her account of the contributions of women magazine editors and publishers (Benstock 1986).

This modernist feminine alterity, the view from the margins, Rachel Blau DuPlessis argues, was marked most of all by an aesthetic blurring of art and everyday experience (DuPlessis 1985). A similar investment in the alterity of women's writing informs Marianne DeKoven's significant account of gender and modernism (DeKoven 1989). In *Rich and Strange*, and her other work, DeKoven argues that modernist women's 'differently inflected' writing, while not entirely an écriture féminine or women's writing, nevertheless stems from 'the inherent doubleness of modernist form', which is 'precisely what allows the expression of feminist content at all' (DeKoven 1989, p. 36). Rather than attempting to subvert the canon, DeKoven pierces the naturalising linearity of the canon to suggest a more interrogative model of gendered writing, one which Julia Kristeva, in her analysis of masculine modernism, characterised as a disruption of traditional symbolic significations by maternal processes (Kristeva 1980).

The problems of an insider/outsider paradigm are highlighted in Rita Felski's *The Gender of Modernity* (Felski 1995). Rather than accepting that modernist women are outsiders, Felski focuses on the often contradictory connections between the feminine and modernity evident in demonised and idealised figures such as the prostitute. By looking at modernity's mythologies of femininity, feminists made a politicised scrutiny of the deep structures underlying modernism's surface effects. 'Woman' as trope, or allegory, is also a central concern of Alice Jardine's *Gynesis* (Jardine 1985). In the book's 'Preliminaries', Jardine asks a key question: what are the implications of modernity for feminism? Jardine answers by suggesting that 'gynesis' or 'the putting into discourse of "woman" [...] as intrinsic to the condition of modernity, indeed the valorization of the feminine, woman [...] is somehow intrinsic to new and necessary modes of thinking, writing, speaking' in modernity (Jardine 1985, p. 25).

What defines modernity, Jardine suggests, is the exploration of female spaces, including 'the female, differently maternal body' (Jardine 1985, p. 34). Art is crucial to this enterprise because any problematising of 'woman', which is the core of gynesis, immediately involves rhetoric (metaphor, metonymy). Jardine's account of modernity is a striking corrective to a simple binary of patrilineal modernism/marginal women. She demonstrates the extent to which the defining terms of modernity depend on the feminine. For this reason, while the reclamation of a feminine modernism will always remain a crucial part of a feminist project, feminist strategies continue to articulate with wider social configurations.

As a sociologist, Anthony Giddens focuses on spatio-temporal rather than on literary transformations in cultural experience. Yet writing signifies here too. In *Modernity and Self-Identity* Giddens claims that modernity's construction of personhood and self-identity depends on a surface exteriorisation of 'modernity's reflexivity' (Giddens 1991, p. 2). Because interpretative self-history is at the core of self-identity in the modern era, according to Giddens, autobiographical cultural products (among which we could include photo albums) both shape and reflect the subject of modernity. In this sense, the modernism/modernity binary would not be merely reflective, but rather modernism's autobiographies, for example, could both constitute and display central features of modern society.

Autobiography, tautologically, involves a gender imperative. Following Giddens, one way of conceptualising modernism would be to focus on self-reflexive gendered memories (what Bracha Lichtenberg

Ettinger calls the matrixial gaze) in cultural products such as domestic photography. Of course this focus on representations of consciousness and on the self's existence in time is a key trope of modernism, at first conceived as an artistic resistance to the contemporary (Fokkema 1984). Other tropes include modernism's fascination with non-linear chronologies, associative imagery, fragmented multiple perspectives and a spatial aesthetic (Boone 1998; Eysteinsson 1990). The syntactical features of modernism are frequently characterised as provisionality (the notion of relative endings) and new metaphorical representations of sexuality, which, in photography, Nancy Armstrong describes as a severing of the generic line between public and private locations of the female body (Armstrong 1998).

VISUAL MODERNISM

Finding the unconscious optics which shape the visual artefacts of this moment of modernity was the project of the three key critics of modernity and the visual: Siegfried Kracauer, Walter Benjamin and Henri Bergson. In *From Caligari to Hitler* (1947) and his essays collected later as *The Mass Ornament* (1994) Kracauer argues that cinema provides a key source of insights into the status of subjectivity in modernity. Like Woolf, Kracauer often visualises subjectivity by means of everyday objects and states of mind such as 'boredom', as well as urban spaces, for example, in 'Farewell to the Linden Arcade' (Kracauer 1994). Cinema plays a key role in modernity because cinema is *the* institution which can best represent the masses. But Kracauer is himself fixed by his historical moment, in debt to a specific gender ideology. While he sympathetically understands that 'stupid and unreal film fantasies are *the daydreams of society*, in which its actual reality comes to the fore and its otherwise repressed wishes take on form', he does not include working-class women's daydreams within such an Imaginary (Kracauer 1994, p. 292). In his essay 'The Little Shopgirls Go to the Movies', Kracauer claims that shopgirls watch films merely for identificatory sensations: 'the little shopgirls want so badly to get engaged on the Riviera', and also find it hard 'to resist the appeal of the marches and uniforms' in military film (Kracauer 1994, p. 299). His dismissive response to women cinema audiences is completely at odds with Dorothy Richardson's cinema writing, for example, and her empathy with working women's everyday cinema-going (see Chapter 5).

In 'The Work of Art in the Age of Mechanical Reproduction' and 'A Short History of Photography', Walter Benjamin describes those photographic representations which lie beyond conscious perception. 'Photography makes aware for the first time the unconscious optics, just as psychoanalysis discloses the instinctual unconscious' (Benjamin 1972, p. 7). By capturing gestures and details, photography can expose features of individual psyches beyond the social moment. The availability of photographic reproductions, Benjamin argues, inevitably destroys the notion of art's singularity as well as art history's concomitant carapace of an autonomous aesthetic. What we see exposed in photographs, he suggests, are minute details or mnemonics of our unconscious, very like the details which Virginia Woolf describes when watching *The Cabinet of Dr Caligari* (Woolf 1994b) (see Chapter 5). While studying the photographs of the Russian formalist Alexander Rodchenko, Benjamin learned about the power of serial photography of everyday life. But, unlike Siegfried Kracauer's, Benjamin's sense of everyday life and contemporary mass formations was pessimistic and philosophically abstract (Hansen 1995).

These key issues of the representations of modernity were very current in intellectual debates from the beginning of the twentieth century, due, in no small part, to the impact of Henri Bergson's writings. Bergson's preoccupation with the relation of time, memory and the visual became a major theme in modernism. As if presaging G. E. Moore's refutation of idealism, Bergson argued in *Time and Free Will* (1889) that time could be photographically spatialised: 'immobility is but a picture (in the photographic sense of the world) taken of reality (duration by our mind)' (Bergson 1949, p. 16). For Bergson, inner reality, duration and the qualitative intensity of visuality are all more important indices of subjective vision than quantitative and physical time (Burnwick and Douglas 1992). In this sense memory is not the preservation of a Freudian lost past but a site where past and present interact in visual representations which are constantly being modified. A Bergsonian sense of the permeability of past and present in visual imagery marks Woolf's photo albums and visual fictions, although Clive Bell was later to claim 'I doubt whether Virginia Woolf ever opened a book by Bergson' (Kumar 1957, p. 1) (see Chapter 2).

But it was through Roger Fry's exhibitions, writings and lectures that the English public and Bloomsbury in particular were introduced to visual modernism. Fry's interdisciplinary engagement with a broad spectrum of artistic genres, including painting, literature, crafts and stage design, matched Bloomsbury's critical interest in a range of cultural expressions. Fry, together with Clive Bell, invented a new aesthetic terminology, 'significant form', in which modernism could be described and evaluated (Tillyard 1988). Fry and Bell had taken the concept of significant form to define art's objective and formal properties from A. C. Bradley's 1901 lecture 'Poetry for Poetry's Sake' (Bradley 1959, p. 19). Yet as Christopher Reed argues in 'Through Formalism: Feminism and Virginia Woolf's Relation to Bloomsbury Aesthetics', Fry's formalism always contained an element of doubt and he was openly committed to some of the counterculture values which Woolf espoused (Reed 1993). For example, Fry became interested in poetry's subversive power while translating Mallarmé and, following the publication of *To the Lighthouse*, which Woolf originally intended to dedicate to Fry, Woolf felt 'you have I think kept me on the right path, so far as writing goes, more than anyone – if the right path it is' (Woolf 1977b, p. 385). Woolf's admiration was shared by the general public, two thousand five hundred of whom flocked to hear Fry speak in the Queen's Hall (Falkenheim 1980). Woolf enjoyed Fry's expertise during their trip to Greece and discussions with him about art and literature during the formative years of her visual writings. The dust-jacket for Woolf's story 'The Mark on the Wall' was produced by Fry's Omega Workshops, and Woolf's high admiration for Fry culminated in her agreement to write his biography after his death in 1934 (Quick 1985).

Yet Fry diverged from Woolf in his view that a spectator's perceptual experience of a work of art largely depended on form and balance within the art piece, not on contextual associations. 'The question of where and when a work of art was produced has only a subsidiary interest. It in no way affects the aesthetic emotion which the work arouses' (Fry 1996, p. 225). In addition, Fry held to a hierarchy of media with oil painting at the summit, as well as to the view that the quality of art was most evident in pattern, colour and the sensuous particularity of materials (Prettejohn 1999). His modernist paradigm appears antithetical to Woolf's simultaneity of perceptions and associative interpenetrability of past and present, for example, in her autobiography 'A Sketch of the Past' (Woolf 1985).

During the years in which many women, including Woolf, were battling in print and on the street for greater visibility in public, professional and creative life, Fry dedicated himself, for example in 'The Grafton Gallery', to 'cutting away the merely representative element in art to establish more and more firmly the fundamental laws of expressive form' (Fry 1996, p. 87). Great art was immured from social values and contexts. For example, Fry judged Rubens' greatness to depend on a 'self-contained' artistic unity and declared 'we cannot imagine its being continued outside the limits of the frame' (Fry 1996, p. 43).

The palimpsest, elegiac aura of Woolf's evocation of her mother as Mrs Ramsay and the determining matrixial motifs in Woolf's photo albums sit incongruously with Fry's emphasis on pure artistic plasticity. In contrast to Woolf's constant photographic practice, Fry resisted the popular art of photography. In his acerbic attack on the Victorian painter Sir Lawrence Alma-Tadema, Fry rebuked him for adopting 'the plan, since exploited by the Kodak Company, "You press the button, and we do the rest". His art, therefore, demands nothing from the spectator' (Fry 1996, p. 148). Fry's selective vision encompassed only abstract photography, 'photographs of purely utilitarian structures in America, particularly vast grain elevators and storages where you get a series of immense bare cylinders supporting a flat rectangular block' (Fry 1996, p. 222). Along with photography Fry also excluded cinema, in which 'wish-fulfilment reigns supreme', from his aesthetic canon (Fry 1996, p. 359). Where Woolf's essay 'The Cinema' and her other work engage directly and positively with cinema and photography as socially constituted artefacts, Fry's legitimation of aesthetics depends on displacing popular culture.

PHOTOGRAPHY AND THE VISUAL

If one of the tenets of modernist aesthetics like Fry's is to construct artistic identity by displacing popular culture, often hypothesised as feminine, then modernist women's investment in domestic photography and cinema journalism occupies an ambivalent space. Yet photographs often embody modernity in more intense and immediate ways than non-photographic art, including the fundamental characteristic of modernity, which is its restructuring of gender relations (Marshall 1994). However, domestic photography cannot be read simply as a transgressive inscription of the feminine per se, when its products have a limited circulation. But domestic photography can contribute to shifts in aesthetic meanings in the way in which its practice allowed modernist women to blur distinctions between amateur and artist, and between art and the everyday, distinctions which some male modernists such as Fry wished to keep. For example, although the photographers Man Ray and Alexander Rodchenko, as I have pointed out above, in the 1920s regularly crossed the border between the avant-garde and mass cultures, they later downplayed their 'transgressions' (Sichel 1999, p. xix). A typically modernist approach to photography searches for the essence of the photographic medium, whereas a postmodern view, such as I am adopting in this book, sees photography 'as a conglomeration of visual signs' (Eisinger 1995, p. 5). Domestic photography necessarily betrays a predilection for associative rather than purely aesthetic determinations. Any account of domestic photography and the other marginalia of modernism, such as cinema journalism, has to shift the emphasis away from formalism to meaning processes and to the 'unconscious optics' of modernity (Benjamin 1972).

Virginia Woolf and Vanessa Bell belonged to the first generation of women to be active photographers and cinema-goers from childhood. The years from Woolf's birth in 1882 to the publication of her essay 'The Cinema' in 1926 were ones in which photography became a career option for women and more than 3,500 American women worked as professional photographers (Gover 1988). In America, as Erica Hirschler shows, photography was considered 'a proper medium for women', to whom manufacturers actively marketed cameras (Hirschler 2001, p. 56). Photography was often praised by women's magazines like *Cosmopolitan* both as an appropriate physical activity for women, an incentive to good health suitable for the feminine traits of 'cleanliness and patience', and as a possible business undertaking (Hirschler 2001, p. 56).

Many women photographers trained as painters. For example, the American Sarah Sears began photography at the same time as she was exhibiting as a water-colourist. In 1900 F. Holland Day included five of Sears' photographs in his important London exhibition 'The New School of American Photography'. Her work was displayed by Frances Benjamin Johnston in Paris, and in 1904 Sears was elected a member of Stieglitz's group the Photo-Secession (Hirschler 2001, p. 60). But many women exhibited as amateurs. Four years after Woolf's birth, Princess Fredericka opened the second amateur photographers' exhibition in London, containing over two hundred prints by women (Gover 1988). The term 'amateur' was often a compliment in photography circles, where it retained its original French definition 'to love' and amateur implied a lover of photography (Hirschler 2001, p. 56). Women were active domestic photographers, owning 'vest-pocket Kodaks', as well as actively contributing to the modernist photographic movements the Photo-Secession and the Bauhaus (Neumaier 1995).

But unlike public photography, snapshots in photo albums are, par excellence, spaces of faces and gestures not all of which are immediately readable without attention to a larger context of family history and psycho-biography. Metaphorically, photo albums and the darkroom itself could be said to be 'rooms of women's own', and modernist women's concern with the ephemera of daily life permits an exploration of the underlying psychic meanings which shape daily lives. For example, Vanessa Bell's snapshots of Clive Bell and Virginia Woolf at Studland Beach suggest the pressure of the memorial (see Chapter 3). Where Freud used the model of a photographic apparatus as a *metaphor* for the passage of psychic phenomena from invisible to visible mental images, for example in *Moses and Monotheism*, photo sequences in albums are material forms of memory (Freud 1938–9). Such sites of remembrance, as I argue in Chapter 6, recall what Pierre Nora calls *lieux de mémoire* or 'spaces, gestures, images and objects' crystallised by a body's 'unstudied reflexes' (Nora 1989, p. 12).

Virginia Woolf mounts on card, as significant frontispieces to her albums, a photograph taken at St Ives in 1892 by Vanessa Bell of Virginia together with their father and mother, as well as a photograph of their mother (figures 1 and 2). The photographs' honoured place suggests a primal scene full of familial referents, which Woolf then repeats in her own photographs of objects and settings resembling her childhood home (see Chapter 2). Significantly, the same two photographs appear in one of Vanessa Bell's albums and in the much smaller single album of their half-sister Stella Duckworth, as well as in their father Leslie Stephen's photo album (although here the family photograph is differently cropped and dated 1893: figure 3). The albums are now in the Tate Archives, in the Berg collection and at Smith College respectively. Although Violet

Dickinson was a close friend of Virginia Woolf, Dickinson does not include these photographs in her album (also in the Berg collection), suggesting the photographs were significant in terms of family rather than friends.

It is as if each member of Woolf's family needed to be in dialogue with these special photographs. The photographs have an analogical relationship with the absent parental referents, and with the much-loved and now absent childhood home in St Ives (figure 4). Such image-making needs a more expansive understanding of the Bloomsbury albums as a practice of coded resonances rather than seeing albums as a collection of fleeting snapshots or artistic artefacts. In addition, in many ways these Bloomsbury albums lack the attributes of others of the same historical period. As Grace Seiberling points out, British Victorian albums showed 'a consistency of imagery and approach' shaped by the pictorial tradition (Seiberling 1986, p. 46). In *The Politics of Focus* Lindsay Smith notes that, while albums varied in content from those displaying 'carte-de-visite portraits of family members' to those including 'drawings and water colours' (as does Violet Dickinson's album), most have a formal structure (Smith 1998, p. 57). The albums of Lewis Carroll are a good example of such formality, because they were carefully stylised and complete with a detailed and cross-referenced index of subjects and sitters (Byrne 1998). Violet Dickinson's album, unlike those of Lewis Carroll, does display an affinity with the domestic in the sense that she used a plain-leafed book originally intended for recipes, rather than a commercial photo album. However, even here, her photographs could be said to be in a careful hierarchy, since she places photographs of friends under 'vegetables' while those predominantly of herself appear under 'desserts'.

What makes the Bloomsbury albums so hauntingly different from equivalent ones is their joint encoding of psychological referents. For example, while portraits in Vanessa Bell's albums may draw on some visual vocabulary from her extensive knowledge of art history, her use of repeated themes equally reveals familial ruptures and discretions. The Bloomsbury albums also actively intervened in the construction of familial memories because the albums were displayed to friends and family, like American albums in clubs of the 1880s, which were sent around to various members for viewing and criticism (Gover 1988).

Julia Prinsep Stephen

Additionally the Bell and Woolf albums descend in a direct line from those of their great-aunt Julia Margaret Cameron, who, Smith argues, made a 'particular spatial intervention in the representation of the domestic' (Smith 1998, p. 37). One example of Bloomsbury's commitment to the domestic milieu of modernism is reflected in Woolf's choice of locale for Gisèle Freund's photo shoot (see Chapter 2). Whereas Freund's portrait of James Joyce isolates the writer sans wife and home, Virginia and Leonard are photographed together at home in Tavistock Square, with its palpable domestic texture.

So André Bazin's now classic account of modernism's 'originality in photography', where Bazin claims 'for the first time an image of the world is formed automatically, without the creative imagination', seems inapplicable to domestic photography and photo albums (Bazin 1971, p. 13). The popularity of snapshot photography fundamentally altered the ways in which people saw themselves and their worlds, not through 'automatic' formations but by encouraging a more creative, active participation in the construction of memory. From Sir John Herschel's first use of the term 'snapshot', taken from gun-shooting vocabulary in the early 1860s to describe a hurried shot, these photos have defied pictorial conventions, in the sense that snapshots are animated by the presence of the past as much as by prevailing aesthetic considerations. Where Desmond MacCarthy, in his introduction to Roger Fry's 1910 post-Impressionist exhibition, chose to attack spectators' desire for mimeticism by attacking snapshots, suggesting that post-Impressionism 'may even appear ridiculous to those who do not recall the fact that a good rocking-horse often had more of the true horse about it, than an instantaneous photograph of a Derby winner', modernist women shared a more expansive vision (MacCarthy 1943, p. 124).

For example, Virginia Woolf chooses horse-racing photography as one of the main visual references in her essay 'The Cinema', as if to comment deliberately on MacCarthy's by-then famous claim (see Chapter 5) (Woolf 1994b). Woolf includes photographic descriptions of the Grand National winner, along with other newsreel events such as 'the king shaking hands with a football team', to underscore more subtle understandings of cinematic realism (Woolf 1994b, p. 348). She shares MacCarthy's discomfort with mimeticism but argues that because cinema

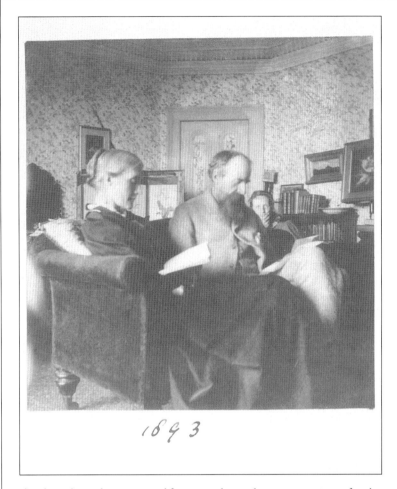

1893

'has been born the wrong end first', watching a horse-race winner for the ways in which 'movements and colours, shapes and sounds had come together' would produce a fluid aesthetic experience (Woolf 1994b, p. 352).

In any case, as Victor Burgin points out in 'Looking at Photographs', semiotics indubitably taught us that there can be no one 'language of photography, no single signifying system' (Burgin 1982, p. 37). But in spite of Burgin's more generous understanding of visual meanings, 'amateur' photography still lacks critical purchase. In John Tagg's view amateur photography can never 'carry the weight of cultural significance' (Tagg 1988, p. 8). Yet Woolf, Bell and other women photographers often rummaged differing aesthetic semantics in a search for a usable visual vocabulary. In her domestic photography, for instance,

Vanessa Bell vividly utilises a Renaissance icono-graphy of Madonna and child along with a modernist attention to significant form. Woolf's photographs similarly employ differing artistic tropes. For example, a photograph of Clive Bell presenting an apple to his mistress Mary Hutchinson seated in a garden resembles the park landscapes of eighteenth-century rococo paintings, which were impacting 'upon British painting at the turn of the

century [...] as an alternative, foreign visual code' (McConkey 2000, p. 100). Such mixtures of present experience and the pleasures of artistic pastiche suggest a more complex understanding of domestic visual cultures than the term 'snapshot' normally implies.

Snapshots in photo albums have no homogeneous view. In many ways modernist women's albums match Kaja Silverman's description of the ideal visual text as one enlisting an art of 'heteropathic recollection', or an abnormal sensitivity to the irritants of memory (Silverman 1996, p. 185). Silverman is attracted to visual mnemonics (like Bracha Lichtenberg Ettinger's matrixial gaze) which include 'what my *moi* excludes – what must be denied in order for my self to exist as such. It would, in short, introduce the "not-me" into my memory reserve' (Silverman 1996, p. 185). Silverman's description matches the quintes-sential subject of domestic photography, which always mediates the snapshot present moment through the psychic, 'a form of presence functioning as a type of protection against loss' (Smith 1998, p. 69). Aspects of this visual sensibility are picked up and repeated in much of modernist women's cinema journalism and in Virginia Woolf's visual short fictions. For instance, in her short stories Woolf frequently creates fictional images of memory in descriptions resembling snapshots in photo albums.

VIRGINIA WOOLF'S 'PORTRAITS' AND PHOTOGRAPHY

Woolf's neglected short fictions 'Portraits' provide an appropriate point at which to examine broader issues of visuality and gender in modernism (Woolf 1989, pp. 242–6). 'Portraits' did not appear in print until Susan

25

Dick's first edition of the collection was published in 1985 (Dick 1985). Although limited in length to five published pages, these experimental pieces, as much as Woolf's better-known visual fictions 'Blue and Green' and 'The Mark on the Wall', display many of the same virtues as her novels, being impressionistic collages of significant experiences. 'Portraits' figure the problem of representation in modernity as a tension between characters' memories and what they observe in fluid, feminine 'snapshots'.

As we have seen, it is now a critical commonplace that gender shapes the visible spaces of modernity in the sense that the public space of the street or the theatre is an arena for the staging of gendered gazes, as Griselda Pollock argues in *Vision and Difference* (Pollock 1988). For example, it is generally agreed that one of the key figures of modernity is the flâneur, or observing male stroller, free to move about the public space and able to direct his gaze equally at women and at goods for sale (Pollock 1988, p. 71). Although more recent work by Deborah Parsons and Elizabeth Wilson has

problematised the flâneur figure, certainly canonical modernist art, such as Manet's *Olympia*, articulates this masculine gaze at the body of woman (Parsons 2000; Wilson 2001). Charles Harrison argues, in 'Degas' *Bathers* and Other People', that this issue was central to the 'first period of the development of modernism in painting – say in the fifty years between 1860–1910' (Harrison 1999, p. 61). He suggests that by the 1870s, 'the modernity of a painting's composition would be recognized' by its representations of looking (Harrison 1999, p. 61). Griselda Pollock argues that the sexual politics of looking in modernist paintings utilises binary positions of looking/being seen and activity/passivity, in which women figures are passive, the objects of an implied or evident male voyeuristic gaze (Pollock 1988, p. 87). But if modernism's most distinctive visual feature is an implied male spectator then what role has a female spectator? Can texts by women about female (and male) spectators produce different ways of looking?

Woolf's short fictions 'Portraits' adopt a different position of viewing from this customary gender binary because she uses a specifically photographic, rather than painterly, vocabulary, like a camera negotiating vertical and horizontal frames of portrait and landscape. Although she does not divest 'Portraits' of sounds (trains, markets) and smells (urine, petrol), it is the visual surface which frames unrevealed information. This enables the urban spaces of modernity in these stories to become places of relationships rather than sites of a dominating male gaze. As I have argued, Woolf was highly familiar with photography. Even from childhood she was an inveterate photographer. In 1897, aged fifteen, she was staying in Bognor when:

> the Frend [camera] arrived from Becks, in a new box, all rubbed up and beautiful, smelling strongly of Jargonel. We tried shutting Nessa up in the cupboard to put in the films, but there were too many chinks. Then she suggested being covered by her quilt, and everything else that I could lay hands on – She was accordingly, buried in dresses and

> dressing gowns, till no light could penetrate. Soon she
> emerged almost stifled having forgotten how to put the film
> in. I hustled her back again into her burrow.
> (Woolf 1990, p. 34)

Woolf's precocious understanding of photographic processes quickly registers an interest in album-like visual narratives. By 14 February 1897, she stages photographic seriality: 'We photographed Simon [a dog] 6 times – on the chair with a coat and pipe, and lying on the ground [...] After tea, Nessa and I developed in the night nursery' (Woolf 1990, p. 35). Although seriality was a usable, heuristically productive force in much of modernist art, for example in the paintings of Cézanne, the major artist in Fry's 1910 post-Impressionist exhibition, Woolf's early interest in multiple-shot photography equally presages the later 'Portraits', in which she adopts an almost photographic seriality.

As I have argued, Virginia Woolf belonged to the first generation of women to be active photographers and cinema goers from childhood, and throughout her career as an innovative modernist writer she took, developed and mounted in albums over one thousand domestic photographs (see Chapter 2). She was also familiar with photographic challenges to representation, for example, the photography of her family, including that of her father, her brothers, her sister and her great-aunt Julia Margaret Cameron. Woolf's continuous attention to photography's visual effects must inevitably impact on all her work, including 'Portraits'. In particular, photography influences the sphere of memory, a key feature of 'Portraits' and of modernist sensibility in general.

In 'Portraits' Woolf stages a number of gendered gazes shaped by a photographic syntax. While experimental writing, per se, is neither uniquely 'feminine' nor uniquely modernist, Woolf's 'Portraits' are characteristically modernist in the way in which they subvert classic realism. At a formal level, 'Portraits' achieve an impact not simply by means of narrative elements alone but through Woolf's striking patterns. The two distinguishing features of 'Portraits' are their spatial arrangements of visual associations and a repression of chronological narrative. But the visual associations interact inside each narrator's memory pictures, so that there is a major emphasis on affect, and on pictorial mediations. This dualistic stratagem, which pitches formal arrangements against the affect of memory pictures, allows Woolf to explore the aesthetics of modernism while dramatising gender differences.

Virginia Woolf's 'Portraits' are eight miniature stories, each between one and three paragraphs in length. Although in most the sex of the narrator is not clear, in portraits 4 and 5 we follow the thoughts of female characters, portraits 2 and 3 evoke a female narrator, and three portraits view female subjects, suggesting that 'Portraits' as a whole focuses on women looking at the modern world. Each story has a different focus, takes a different photograph of what Walter Benjamin calls the 'unconscious optics of modernity' or the ways in which photographs can register moments outside immediate perception (Benjamin 1972). As Susan Dick's immaculate editorial gloss on the fictions proposes, 'Portraits' are probably part of a collaborative work called 'Faces and Voices' which Virginia Woolf and Vanessa Bell were discussing in February 1937 (Dick 1989, p. 307). Although the Monk's House Papers, University of Sussex Library Archives, number the 'Portraits' as five, Dick supplied the titles of 'Portraits' 4–8 from evidence in Woolf's manuscripts and points out that the eighth portrait derives from 'The Broad Brow', one of the 'Three Characters', another version of which is published as 'Middlebrow' in *The Death of the Moth* (Dick 1989, p. 307).

Woolf's own account of the generative moment of composition of 'Portraits', Friday 19 February 1937, reveals how such image/texts, for her, are an irresistible testimonial to epistemological novelty. In her diary she records, 'I've written this morning 3 descriptions for Nessa's pictures: they can be printed by us no doubt, & somehow put into circulation. But then theres in my drawer several I think rather good sketches; & a chapter on biography. Clearly I have here in the egg a new method of writing criticism, I rather think so' (Woolf 1984, p. 57). And she described in her diary the following day how she 'discussed a book of illustrated incidents with Nessa yesterday; we are going to produce 12 lithographs for Xmas, printed by ourselves' (Woolf 1984, p. 58). There are strong connections between lithography and photography. As Beatrice Farwell suggests in *The Cult of Images*, the early English calotype process replicated lithographic imagery, and photography and lithography existed interchangeably with each other for several decades (Farwell 1977). Lithographs can share the demotic snapshot quality of photographs, whose conventions lithographs often mimic.

Diane Gillespie, in *The Sisters' Arts*, comprehensively explores the impact of painting on Woolf's fiction and her uses of visual iconography. Gillespie touches briefly on 'Portraits' in two paragraphs, pointing out that it is a 'compendium of techniques' perhaps 'recalling Sickert's paintings of everyday life' and that the characters 'talk about paintings and people, objects and sights we cannot see' (Gillespie 1988, p. 172). Certainly Woolf argued, in *Walter Sickert: A Conversation*, 'let us hold painting by the hand a moment longer, for though they must part in the end, painting and writing have much to tell each other. They have much in common' (Woolf 1934, p. 22). But an aesthetic investment in photography is equally a significant pressure on Woolf's writing, as Gillespie expertly acknowledges elsewhere (Gillespie 1993). Recurring references to photographic activities occur in many of Woolf's novels, for example, *Jacob's Room*, as well as in her diaries and letters. There are other ways in which photography might be represented in writing. Photography arrests moments in time, capturing non-linear gestures and attitudes hitherto invisible to spectators. Photography graphically highlights personally significant details such as favourite objects, as Woolf does so often in her writing. In addition, photography's composition by field mirrors Woolf's juxtaposition of the quotidian with deep philosophical ideas.

There have been a number of critiques in the last few years of the relationship between photography and twentieth-century literature (Hirsch 1997; Rugg 1997; Davidov 1998). Nancy Armstrong's recent and important study *Fiction in the Age of Photography* describes how nineteenth-century literature (in works such as *Wuthering Heights*, *Alice's Adventures in Wonderland* and *The Picture of Dorian Gray*) often referred to 'what either was or would become a photographic commonplace', for example, representations of the picturesque or city streets (Armstrong 1999, p. 5). Armstrong's is a sophisticated argument that photography and nineteenth-century fiction shared the same tasks of miniaturising rural Britain and producing spatial classification systems, because 'realism and photography were partners in the same cultural project' of classifying the world (Armstrong 1999, p. 26).

In Armstrong's chapter on modernism she argues that 'modernism's assault on mass culture and femininity' came from a distrust of the body as an aesthetic strategy. She devotes her attention to the way modernist writers and photographers, such as D. H. Lawrence and Edward Weston, eroticise their aesthetic experiments (Armstrong 1999, p. 247). Armstrong attacks Woolf's 'Mr Bennett and Mrs Brown' specifically here for reducing realism to 'a mere caricature of itself' and argues that 'the modernist concept of authenticity was a post-photographic way of imagining one's relation to the real' (Armstrong 1999, pp. 245–6). While Armstrong's is a very nuanced account of nineteenth-century writing, her description of modernism and photography is overly focused on the pornographic at the expense of representations of visual memories, and her attack on Woolf is misplaced. Psychoanalysis teaches us that we frequently displace onto other races, classes and genders features of ourselves which we would like to disavow (Cohen 1997). The excess in Woolf's classic attack on Arnold Bennett's realism could be seen in psychoanalytic terms as exemplary of such displacement. In other words, Woolf does not caricature realism per se; her critique betrays her fascination with, but troubled view of, realism and popular culture, which would include domestic photography. She might wish to disavow realism ideologically while not rejecting tropes of realism, such as those of domestic photography, for example, in her writing.

What Woolf was calling her 'new method of writing criticism' in her concomitant diary can be glimpsed in the fresh spatial arrangements of people and objects in 'Portraits'. It resembles an album of eight synchronic moments in the lives of bourgeois women and men in modernity. The fictions are creative modernist image/texts which utilise scopic devices of looks or gazes. 'Portraits' has very different types of narrator; some stories totally lack an obvious authorial inscription, others have carefully delineated middle-class and gendered figures, and are set in differing contexts including France, London and Florence. The title of the first portrait, 'Waiting for Déjeuner', recalls Manet's *Dejeuner sur l'herbe* (1863) (Woolf 1989, p. 242). Although, in general, Roger Fry's hostility to Impressionism was consistent, he chose Manet as the forerunner of post-Impressionism, as the title of Fry's 1910 exhibition 'Manet and the Post-Impressionists' makes clear. December 1910 was, of course, a significant moment for Woolf, Fry's friend. Manet's painting acknowledges a Renaissance engraving by Marcantonio Raimondi (1520) after Raphael's *Judgement of Paris*, drawing on a detail of a late Roman sarcophagus in the Villa Medici, Rome. Woolf immediately subverts any evident indebtedness to canonical art history with a snapshot synchronicity of historical relativities. Elephants 'squelch', as the cinema announces 'the new Jungle film' (Woolf 1989, p. 242). The notion that the past is simultaneously part of the present was encouraged by a scientific Zeitgeist freighted with the idea that the external visible world cannot easily be measured and is relative to a viewer, and Woolf frequently concerns herself with issues of visible and invisible visuality, such as her use of two kinds of photography in *Three Guineas*. Persian women groom children while 'Monsieur and Madame Louvois' wait by the Seine for their lunch of tripe (Woolf 1989, p. 242).

Unlike Woolf's short fiction 'The Mark on the Wall', the focus here is less on the narrator and more on a blurring of subjective and objective. 'Monsieur and Madame Louvois stared at the mustard pot and the cruet [...] and the eyes of Monsieur and Madame Louvois lit with lustre' (Woolf 1989, p. 242). The description resembles the way in which a camera takes a literal image of a subject. But the portrait hovers between two kinds of photography. On the one hand Monsieur and Madame Louvois are described realistically, and on the other the portrait is also like a study revealing subjective personalities, which Woolf knowingly announces in her emblematic choice of name for the two principals. *Louve* is the French noun for she-wolf and *louvoyer* means to tack about or dodge. The portrait is, then, no brief *entremet* or side dish but a performative self-portrait of mocking self-deflation, as the Louvois wait for a luncheon of tripe.

The second portrait, 'The Frenchwoman in the Train', resembles Van Gogh's paintings of peasant women. Both equally exaggerate women's labouring bodies: 'Here the bull neck bears baskets of grapes' (Woolf 1989, p. 243). But unlike Van Gogh's eroticised topographic bodies, in Woolf's photographic *mise-en-scène* the woman is alternatively impressionistic, with 'undulating shoulder', and precise (Woolf 1989, p. 243). The portrait is a quite extraordinarily visual and sensual description of a parodic, peasant landscape in which a 'butting ram, men astride it', surround a monumental woman with 'wild pig eyes' (elsewhere in Woolf's work a synonym for the Duckworth brothers) (Woolf 1989, p. 243). But, just as Griselda Pollock argues in terms of Van Gogh that this production of fantastic peasant women 'brought him close to the scenes and bodies of his childhood memories', so Woolf's portrait also might register parental memories (Pollock 1999, p. 60). For example, Woolf suggests that the woman 'would be running through Clapham on her way to Highgate to renew the circle of china flowers on the grave of her husband'; and Woolf's parents and half-sister are buried in Highgate cemetery (Woolf 1989, p. 243).

Yet although the exaggeration of the portrait resembles Van Gogh's topographies the vocabulary of portrait 2 resembles the connotative and denotative quality of photographic language. Roland Barthes used these terms to characterise the meanings of different elements in a photograph (Barthes 1982, p. 195). 'Denotative' describes the literal meaning of elements, such as an object or a gesture, so that we recognise what we are seeing. In Woolf's portrait a woman is sitting in a train carrying a bag. But beyond the level of denotative meanings lie 'connotative' ones, which refer to the ways in which movements or expressions are also 'codes' reflecting underlying meanings. The woman 'at the Junction ... sits in her corner, on her knee a black bag', and simultaneously the woman 'bears on her immense and undulating shoulder the tradition; even when her mouth dribbles' (Woolf 1989, p. 243). Woolf breaks up the ordered, denotative world of a realist photograph by saturating the woman with connotative photographic signs, like intimations of an archaic fantasy of the maternal.

My argument about Woolf's photographic techniques, gender and modernism requires me to unpack this issue of how women and men look in modernity a little more. Griselda Pollock, in *Differencing the Canon*, calls for modernist criticism to read 'for *the inscriptions of the other otherness of femininity*, that is, for those traces of the unexpected articulation of what may be specific to female persons in the process of becoming subjects – subjected, subjectified and subjectivised – in the feminine through the interplay of social identities and psychic formations within histories' (Pollock 1999, p. 102). The contemporary psychoanalyst and artist Bracha Lichtenberg Ettinger, on whom Pollock has written a great deal, has created the term 'matrix' to describe more specifically Pollock's 'unexpected articulation' and what might be specific to women in the process of becoming subjects (Lichtenberg Ettinger 1995, p. 122). Lichtenberg Ettinger argues that art visualises strata of subjectivity and chronologies through objects in a field which can reveal inscriptions of the feminine, and as I have described, she herself utilises photographic fields in which repeated photographic images of family members become examples of a sub-symbolic filter, the internal/external traces of the matrixial encounter in the womb. In some ways Woolf's attention to a circulation of looks in the memory pictures in 'Portraits', across the boundaries of chronological time, suggests similar matrixial recognitions. That is to say, in Woolf's 'Portraits', narrative images often play denotative and connotative roles, as in photography, in order for the subject/narrators to appear as subjects flowing between a consciousness of everyday life and the unconscious world beyond the normally visible. I have stressed this idea of representing unconscious associations in order to specify theoretically Woolf's investment in denotative and connotative photographic vocabulary. In the case study of 'Portraits' certain recurring features of Woolf's writing can be read as a photographic means of representing strata of feminine subjectivity.

Portrait 3, a mere eleven lines, has a clearly identified narrator 'sitting in the courtyard of the French Inn', who scopically views a woman 'sitting in the sun' (Woolf 1989, p. 243). As Richard Morphet points out, Bloomsbury paintings also focused with 'unusual insistence' on the arresting gaze and on eyes (Morphet 1999, p. 29). For example, in Vanessa Bell's portrait of Mary Hutchinson, 'the look the eyes give is accentuated' as well as the eyes' shape (Morphet 1999, p. 29). But in 'Portraits' the scene is photographic more than painterly, employing shapes and light within the frame. Woolf suggests a female gaze with a narrator physically close to the woman but able to stare with non-voyeuristic attention to details of breast and skin: 'Her face was yellow and red; round too; a fruit on a body; another apple, only not on a plate. Breasts had formed apple-hard under the blouse on her body' (Woolf 1989, p. 243). The portrait lingers on the physiognomy of the woman like a camera, and the narrator's reflections touch on those aspects of mentality which can only be visible in close up photography.

The unnamed female of portrait 4 more closely resembles self-reflexive female narrators elsewhere in Woolf's fiction, for example, *Mrs Dalloway*, as the narrator floats between past and present, while enjoying a snatched day with her son before he returns to Rugby school. Like an album of snapshot pictures, the piece functions associatively. For example, the character observes that the hors d'oeuvres already lack sardines and that George, her son, has 'the eyes of a carp' (Woolf 1989, p. 244). Woolf highlights the terms of representation in the same way in which many modernist photographers exaggerated features of faces, for example, El Lissitzky the Russian constructivist photographer's *Constructor* (1904). Russian constructivist photography did not simply aim to 'reflect' the world but to make a cognitive transformation of it through an 'explicit thematisation of the art of the everyday' (Roberts 1998, p. 20). The head in Lissitzky's *Constructor* is represented by a surplus of physiognomic details, for example, Lissitzky places an eye in the constructor's adjacent hand in order to suggest a relationship between the physical and the mental (Clarke 1997, p. 191). Similarly George and the narrator's past 'sandy haired boy' are identified visually by Woolf like photographic portraits by means of physiognomy (Woolf 1989, p. 244). Like constructivist photography, Woolf defamiliarises objects through the use of an unexpected angle as a means of expanding the experience of the everyday (Roberts 1998). In narratives, memory pictures most often work by means of visual associations. Like 'screen memories' in psychoanalysis, the character's recollections have the quality of dreams in their associative displacements and repressions. Although she easily remembers a past male admirer, the character is yet unable to discuss sexuality with her son, to be 'more like his father' (Woolf 1989, p. 244). Freud's term *Nachträglichkeit* similarly refers to deferred actions where the past works on the present yet memory-traces can be retranscribed.

The constructedness of biography itself is exposed in subsequent portraits. Portrait 5 is a brief monologic pastiche of middle-class materialism and its institutionalised values. A bourgeois woman eating 'white sugared pastry' enjoys her social superiority: 'at the Hospital the men used to call me Little Mother' (Woolf 1989, p. 244). Woolf leaps into a surreal visual image of the woman's 'scent bottle which she carried in a gland in her cheek with which to sweeten the sometimes malodorous emanations of her own not sufficiently appreciated character' (Woolf 1989, p. 244). Woolf carefully portrays a state of mind by means of an exact image. In this way portrait 5 resembles the manipulation of images by modernist photographers, such as the American Alvin Langdon Coburn, whose Cubist portraits break with surface reality. To photograph *Vortograph* (1917), for example, Coburn used mirrors to create a sense of multiple perspectives, manipulating photography in order to create metaphoric images as Woolf does here with the scent bottle (Clarke 1997, p. 188). Coburn's portrait has been likened to earlier combination printing, in which a print is built up from several negatives (Clarke 1997, p. 188). Woolf similarly turns the psycho-social detail of the woman's life into object images such as the scent bottle.

Like prints in a photo album, each portrait flickers towards another. The male of portrait 6 is dislocated by contemporary life, where a 'felt hat with a dent in it' has displaced 'a topper' (Woolf 1989, p. 244).

An immediate precedent and influence on Woolf's portrait is the conclusion of Marcel Proust's *Swann's Way*, published in 1913 and immediately highly praised by Roger Fry. 'I no longer found the grey "toppers" of old [...] they passed before me in a desultory, haphazard, meaningless fashion' (Proust 1996, p. 510). There are many references to Woolf's love of Proust in her diaries and letters, particularly in those to Roger Fry: 'Oh if I could write like that! I cry. And at the moment such is the astonishing vibration and saturation and intensification that he procures – theres something sexual in it – that I feel I *can* write like that' (Woolf 1976, p. 525). Like Marcel, the male of portrait 6, 'I who should have been born in the eighties', lives in a world which is now almost entirely memorial, made up of his family's memories, of 'Oscar [Wilde] being witty' and prostitutes 'in Piccadilly' and a time with 'society, graded like one of those ices wrapped in frilled paper' (Woolf 1989, p. 245). Although the portrait is not realistic it is photographic. The male narrator thinks of his relationship to his family in photographic terms, with visual clues determining status: 'should have carried a cane, like my father' (Woolf 1989, p. 244).

The compositional structure of a photo album also shapes the subsequent, last two portraits. Portrait 7 is dedicated to Vernon Lee, the pen-name of author Violet Page, the pacifist lesbian, remembered in three momentary snapshots: at Talland House, in Florence and in the 1917 Club, places which all figure in photographs in Woolf's own family albums (see Chapter 2). The narrator, another parodic bourgeois ('No, I don't paint myself; but then one appreciates art all the better perhaps'), makes a coherent identity only by means of association with minor cultural figures (Woolf 1989, p. 245). A more extensive version of portrait 8, written as a letter to the *New Statesman*, appears as 'Middlebrow' in *The Death of the Moth* (Woolf 1961b). Unlike portrait 8, the more detailed 'Middlebrow' is a somewhat mannered essay, a linear narrative in which Woolf's persona defines herself as highbrow uniting with lowbrows against middlebrows and their love for 'Queen Anne furniture (faked, but none the less expensive)' (Woolf 1961b, p. 158). 'Middlebrow' neither creates a fictionalised reader nor revises the power relationship between author and implied reader. In contrast, portrait 8 is dialogic, spoken first by a fictive middlebrow before the speaking voice reverts to a denunciatory persona claiming that middle-brows are 'infecting the sheep' (Woolf 1989, p. 246). The fictive middlebrow is not distanced by inserted authorial devices such as physical or emotive descriptions, but parodies himself by calling Shakespeare and Wordsworth equally 'Bill' (Woolf 1989, p. 246).

Woolf utilises a modernist pictorial syntax, elements of which we can see in the penultimate paragraph of portrait 8. 'When one walks in the garden, what's that on the cabbage? Middle brow. Middle brow infecting the sheep. The moon too is under your sway. Misted. You dull tarnish' (Woolf 1989, p. 246). In some ways these lines are overtly modernist. The formal simplification is achieved by a repression of narrative and descriptive linkages in favour of Woolf's focus on images and on differing perspectives, from a close-up on the cabbage to a long-shot at the moon. The series of photographic perspectives is joined by the common theme of the imagined effect of middlebrow culture on landscape in general. Woolf's visual hyperbole in the portrait combines with an attention to detail in photographic images. Like her contemporary American modernist photographers Paul Strand and Aaron Siskind in the 1920s and 1930s, she attends to surface textures in close-up to make the commonplace into something much more than a mere object. Part of Paul Strand's assault on pictorialism was to seek the essence of photography in 'absolute unqualified objectivity' (Eisinger 1995, p. 56). Strand and Siskind photographed objects in the city and country, such as cars, shoes and windows, emphasising texture, pattern and shadow as Woolf does to make everyday detritus into something significant (Clarke 1997, p. 177).

Graham Clarke points out in *The Photograph* that 'the literal nature of so much photography would seem to place it at the opposite end of modernist aesthetics and philosophical inquiry' (Clarke 1997, p. 110). He suggests that modernist novels such as Henry James' *The Portrait of a Lady* abandoned literal forms of representation while the photograph 'insisted on the principle of representation and the depiction of space that modernism rejected' (Clarke 1997, p. 111). But the paradox remains that modernism was also a response to technological innovation, and film and photography plays a major role in modernism's symptomatic response to Western modernity. Montage was a means of bringing hidden relations into discursive view, and many modernist writers, including H. D. and James Joyce as well as Woolf, wrote about the new visual experiences of cinema, advertising and photography.

Photography's ways of looking impact on Woolf's textual structures. Associations are focused by means of each character's close-up engagement with objects, faces or food. Fragmentary elements of personal histories are remembered in single frames. Woolf includes a number of perspectives, both male and female, bourgeois and highbrow, as if capturing these in a family album. After visiting her sister Vanessa Bell's 'show' in 1928 Woolf admired Bell's elaborate optical representations in terms very similar to those of the later 'Portraits':

> I am greatly tempted to write 'Variations on a Picture by
> Vanessa Bell' for Desmonds paper – I should run the three
> women and the pot of flowers on a chair into one phantas-
> magoria. I think you are a most remarkable painter. But I
> maintain you are into the bargain, a satirist, a conveyor of
> impressions about human life: a short story writer of great
> wit and able to bring off a situation in a way that rouses my
> envy. I wonder if I could write the Three Women in prose.
> (Woolf 1977b, p. 498)

By introducing architectonic elements into her painting, Bell was free to explore the emotions of colour just as Woolf uses photographic elements to explore gendered memories. 'Portraits' fairly resonates with camera shots as Woolf turns from object to object, facial details to physiognomy. In short, 'Portraits' exhibits a fundamental tenet of modernist writing: the significance of the fragmentary and the provisional shaped by a powerful investment in the capacity of photography to provide memorial and gendered optics.

SUMMARY

'Portraits' and the photo albums and cinema journalism of Woolf and other modernist women are all concerned with issues of cultural and personal identities and memories. Photography had a profound effect on the ways in which modernist women chose to present their own identities and those of others. So that although Nancy Armstrong, as I have suggested, argues that modernism was 'a post-photographic' way of imagining a relationship with reality, I argue that modernist women's work is marked by photography, as well as by the widespread contemporary debates about visual culture and the physical sciences (Armstrong 1999, p. 246). My intent is not to argue that photo albums have some kind of hitherto unrecognised and now possible visual authority based on their marginality, but rather, by addressing modernist women's continuous attention to a continuum of visual effects, to broaden ways of thinking about the visual and the psychic in modernism. I *am* concerned with recovering such marginal forms, because I think they do offer crucial representations of gendered memories and identities.

This is not to claim that modernist men ignored the domestic or always respected generic distinctions. Often, as Armstrong points out, men's family portraits were 'somehow necessary both to their self-definition as artists and to their work' (Armstrong 1999, p. 260). But my argument is simply that modernist women seem to use such marginal spaces as imaginative structures much more frequently than do men; and they used photographic referents to explore themselves as well as aesthetics in this period. In modernist literary and aesthetic studies, *domestic* photography and prose are not usually considered together. But by doing so in *Modernist Women and Visual Cultures* I hope to make some observations about these forms and to broaden discussion of modernist aesthetics. Like her sister modernists, Virginia Woolf's imagination must have been shaped by her constant photographic activity: developing prints, watching an image emerge in a developing tray (by moving 'Irigarayan' liquids from lip to lip, making the subjective visible from objective materials). The chapters that follow examine the photographic referents of memory and gender in cinema journalism, photo albums and some examples of Woolf's non-fiction and short fiction. My underlying feeling is that modernist women's obsession with 'marginal' visual texts like snapshots hints at a crisis of gender representation in their constant turn to modes of representation outside modernism's more legitimate aesthetics.

MATRIXIAL MEMORIES: VIRGINIA WOOLF'S PHOTO ALBUMS

2

One felt a glass-like clarity, but it was not the clarity of a logician, but rather that of a kaleidoscope which throws out each time from the same set of pieces a different pattern.

Gerald Brenan, 'South from Granada'

Your films came last night [...] Two beautiful packets of superfine celluloid. Films! A thousand thanks (as the French say) my dear Herbert for this munificent gift – I shall devote not a few to your remarkable face.

Virginia Woolf, age fifteen, letter to her brother Thoby, 1897

INTRODUCTION

From the age of fifteen, photographs framed Virginia Woolf's world. She wrote about photography in her diaries, letters and essays, and used photographic terms descriptively in her fiction. Before her marriage, and then together with Leonard, she took, developed and preserved photographs in albums. Photography was a continuous part of the Woolfs' lives even if their photographic albums do not tell a coherent life story.

The Frederick Koch collection in Harvard Theatre Library houses seven albums, called the Monk's House albums, together with four boxes containing over two hundred additional loose photographs. None is catalogued. Although Woolf states in her letters that 'I keep a family album' in the singular, and many entries in the albums are in her hand, it is impossible to establish, either from their several diaries and auto-biographies, or from internal evidence in the albums, who 'authored' each album (Woolf 1980a, p. 169). Just as Leonard and Virginia often shared the taking of photographs, for example, for *Orlando*, so it seems that the albums are a joint endeavour (figure 5). They are formally constructed, with many sequential and paired matching photographs of friends sitting in armchairs, which are in close-up or medium-shot (figure 6): a striking example of the issue of finding or making 'significant form' which so intrigued Bloomsbury art critics (Bell 1914). In many ways Woolf's album-making mirrors her aesthetics. Just as in her fiction a visual image is frequently more truth-telling than a linear narrative, so the albums are composed in visual patterns rather than chronologically. Writing to her sister, the artist Vanessa Bell, in 1937, Woolf speculated 'do you think we have the same pair of eyes, only different spectacles' (Woolf 1980a, p. 158). The albums are crucial artefacts, encapsulating and emblematising Woolf's responses to the arts and to her life and friendships.

Yet, although Woolf's life and writings are the subject of voracious criticism, her photographs have been largely neglected. In the transaction between her fiction and her aesthetics (including her photographs), fiction always has the upper hand. Essays on Woolf and photography include, among others, Duffy and Davis' 'Demythologizing Facts and Photographs in *Three Guineas*', Wussow's 'Virginia Woolf and the Problematic Nature of the Photographic Image' and 'Travesties of Excellence', Flesher's 'Picturing the Truth in Fiction', Gualtieri's *Three Guineas* and the Photograph', Knowles' 'A Community of Women Looking at Men', Schaffer's 'Posing Orlando' and an insightful chapter in Dalgarno's *Virginia Woolf and the Visible World* (Duffy and Davis 1995; Wussow 1994, 1997; Flesher 1997; Gualtieri 1999; Knowles 1999; Schaffer 1994; Dalgarno 2001). Only Neverow's 'Thinking Back through Our Mothers' and Gillespie's richly detailed article '"Her Kodak Pointed at his Head": Virginia Woolf and Photography', to date, describe Woolf's photo albums, but both critics focus on her use of photographic referents in her fiction rather than judging the albums as artefacts in their own right (Neverow 1999; Gillespie 1993).

PROBLEMATICS

Photographs preserve relationships. Any album's sequencing of photographs creates meaning out of random events. In this respect albums are

vw

dw

vw

dw

memories constructed in the present but, unlike memories, photographs arranged in albums have a connectedness independent from present time. Album photographs are their own visual story. The representation of an isolated moment in time means nothing. Meaning depends on how we connect moments. As the philosopher Henri Bergson argues, a memory only becomes 'actual' by 'borrowing the body of some perception into which it slips' (Bergson 1991, p. 67).

The principles of selection, montage and tableau are the skeleton of a story, a way of making aesthetic order out of our worlds, which becomes an aesthetic narrative of that world. Psychoanalytically speaking, albums are often a testimony to our unconscious pasts rather than the pasts we consciously choose to remember. In the classic and often cited essay 'A Short History of Photography', Walter Benjamin argues that it was photography, for the first time, which displayed the optical unconscious (Benjamin 1972, pp. 5–26). The optical unconscious is Benjamin's metaphor for the way in which photographs visualise 'imperceptible moments', those outside perception. To Benjamin such a moment is historical because 'the spark of chance' that has 'seared the character in the picture' is a moment and 'in the immediacy of that long-past moment, the future so persuasively inserts itself' (Benjamin 1972, p. 7). Similarly the Monk's House albums are Woolf's unconscious testimony to her childhood past. In other words, the albums do not simply provide corroborating evidence for the role of the visual in Woolf's fiction, but, in themselves, richly reveal Woolf's subjective feelings in a visual form.

The aim of this study is therefore to shift the emphasis in discussions about Woolf from her writing to her artefacts. What is significant in the albums are not the isolated photographs per se but the conversations between the photographs and Woolf herself. Her childhood is 'off-screen' but makes the photographs resonate with meaning far beyond the historical moment of their compilation (Pollock 1994b). The weaving of photographs is crucial evidence of what Woolf unconsciously wanted to wear in her world. For these reasons my study, although primarily a piece of cultural criticism, making forays into photographic studies, is also preoccupied with the psychoanalytic in order to fix Woolf's irremediable off-screen memories.

Memories are what Jean-François Lyotard calls 'the stranger in the house' (Lyotard 1990, pp. 16–17). Where, for Freud, the stranger is 'the scene of seduction perpetrated on the child', to Lyotard the stranger represents a more general individual incapacity to 'represent and bind a certain something', a something which can 'introduce itself there without being introduced, and would exceed its powers' (Freud and Breur 1974; Lyotard 1990, p. 17). For me, it is the 1892 photograph of Woolf's seated mother and father with Woolf in the background, mounted as a significant frontispiece in Monk's House album 3, which 'exceeds its powers' and shapes Woolf's photography (figure 1 above). It is precisely for these reasons that the albums are so unusually anti-chronological, since they focus on the unrepresentable, on the immemorial; as Lyotard argues, 'the immemorial is always "present"' (Lyotard 1990, p. 20). The album photographs, in my research, seemed to be a mechanism enabling Woolf to make public repressed private configurations. In their symbolic organisation, the photographs allowed her to be in touch with the phantasmic world of her childhood. Yet, because photography, as Susan Sontag points out, 'though not an art form in itself, has the peculiar capacity to turn all its subjects into works of art', aesthetic judgements about Woolf's photographs are an inevitable corollary of the psychoanalytic (Sontag 1989, p. 149).

WOOLF AND BLOOMSBURY ON PHOTOGRAPHY

Yet Woolf's male artistic contemporaries thought photographs visually undistinguished. Although he changed his views later in life, Clive Bell, Vanessa's husband, and one of Bloomsbury's leading critics of post-Impressionism, dismissed photographs implicitly: 'we expect a work of plastic art to have more in common with a piece of music than a coloured photograph' (Bell 1914, p. 349). Indeed Simon Watney, in his landmark study of English post-Impressionism, argues that, throughout this period, photography 'served in England to define negatively what art was not' (Watney 1980, p. 20). The denigration of photography in favour of painting is

Figure 6
Lydia and J. M. Keynes, Monk's House, *c.*1931: from Virginia Woolf's Monk's House album 3
Reprinted by permission of the Harvard Theatre Collection, the Houghton Library

1931

J M Keynes

Lydia Keynes

Lydia Keynes

J M Keynes

now superseded, as Sontag argues, by the 'museum's naturalization of photography as art', yet Bloomsbury's expectations that photography was not aesthetically significant did impact on many of Woolf's written references to photography (Sontag 1989, p. 130).

Woolf frequently equates the 'snapshot' with a limited eye. Writing to Vanessa Bell in Cassis, Woolf worries that the picture of Vanessa in Woolf's biography of Roger Fry will be compromised: 'What am I to say about you?' (She eventually decided to refer to Bell and Fry's affair as 'friendship'.) 'Its rather as if you had to paint a portrait using dozens of snapshots in the paint' (Woolf 1980a, p. 285). Similarly, 'photographic' fiction is inferior. Writing about Tolstoy to her lover Vita Sackville-West in 1928, Woolf asks Vita 'what made his realism which might have been photographic, not at all; but on the contrary, moving and exciting' (Woolf 1977b, p. 529). Winifred Holtby's *South Riding*, on the other hand, is too 'obvious' precisely because 'she has a photographic mind' (Woolf 1980a, p. 382).

Yet Woolf *as* a photographer suggests a very different attitude. She skilfully transformed friends and moments into artful tableaux, and she was surrounded by female friends and family who were also energetic photographers. Lady Ottoline Morrell's photographs 'come out so much better than the professionals'; Vita Sackville-West and the artist Dora Carrington both exchanged photographs with Virginia (Woolf 1977b, p. 47). Julian Bell's girlfriend Lettice Ramsey, whose photographs are in Vanessa Bell's album 7 in the Tate Gallery archives, ran a professional photography studio, Ramsey and Muspratt. Woolf's interest in the aesthetics of photography was precocious. At fifteen she was developing her photographs, taken with a Frena camera, as her letters to Thoby Stephen and George Duckworth reveal. The Frena camera, a box-form magazine camera for forty 4-by-5-inch exposures, had just been marketed in March 1896 (Lothrop 1982, p. 122). Its fixed-focus lens and eccentric magazine handle required a dedicated camera operator. Woolf may be holding her Frena in Vanessa Bell's photograph of Virginia and Julian Bell taken at Blean in 1910, which is in the *Vanessa Bell Family Album* (Bell and Garnett 1981, p. 22).

The essence of photographs lies in the appeal of the experience or the event portrayed to a viewer. Woolf, like her sister and her great-aunt, the photographer Julia Margaret Cameron, frequently invited friends to share her reflections. The letters and diaries describe a constant exchange of photographs, in which they become a meeting-place, a conversation, aide-mémoires, and sometimes mechanisms of survival and enticement. At age sixteen, photographs were 'the best present I can think of' (Woolf 1975b, p. 18). Virginia was happy to send a photograph of herself to Emma Vaughan, even if it is 'somewhat like an ancient beast of my acquaintance' (Woolf 1975b, p. 29). Visiting the professional photographer Beresford was 'an entertainment' (Woolf 1975b, p. 78).

By the age of twenty-one, friends' photographs were like erotic emblems. 'I have Marny's [Madge Vaughan's] photograph on my shelf, like a madonna to which I pray. She makes my room refined, as lavender in my drawers – (!!)' (Woolf 1975b, p. 88). The first volume of Woolf's collected letters ends appropriately with Virginia sending her photograph to Leonard: 'D'you like this photograph? – rather too noble, I think. Here's another' (Woolf 1975b, p. 497). Photographs taken by friends were crucial to her sense of identity. In 1916, writing to Roger Fry, she acknowledged, 'The photographs certainly are masterpieces – the one of Leonard is far the best that I've ever seen of him – How does that minute camera produce such large pictures' (Woolf 1976, p. 121); although in 1938, writing to Ethel Smyth, Woolf felt about herself that her image was not 'a beauty [...] Why shd. I reflect "what a beautiful woman" I am? I'm not, and never think so. (This is true)' (Woolf 1980a, p. 235).

Woolf invited friends to share their lives with her through photographs. She liked 'very much' to have baby photographs: 'he's [Katherine Arnold-Forster's son Mark] an interesting little boy' (Woolf 1976, p. 495). Barbara Bagenal's photograph of herself and her son, 'exactly like his father', is stuck 'in my book', and an exchange is impossible because 'mine all got the foggy dew this summer' (Woolf 1976, p. 49). The Bagenal photographs are mounted on card in Monk's House album 2 (p. 16), visually replicating the way Woolf carefully conserved her friendships. After their deaths, photographs of friends were important memento mori. She wanted to send Jacques Raverat, the French painter, 'a picture of me done for a vulgar paper called *Vogue*', and after he died in 1925 she needed photographs to continue her mental conversations with him, desperately asking Gwen Raverat for 'a snapshot or any photograph of him? I go on making things up to tell him' (Woolf 1977b, pp. 130, 172–3). In the *Vogue* photograph Virginia is wearing her mother's dress.

Sharing albums with friends and family helped Woolf to under-

stand her friendships. On visits, Aunt Mary Fisher 'always gives L. [Leonard] a book of old photographs to look at, and half kisses him in the Hall' (Woolf 1976, p. 97). Woolf's own albums were more enduringly invitational. Monk's House album 5 (pp. 45–6) contains one of the Woolf's favourite 'comfy chair' paired sequences of Dorothy Bussy

sitting framed by the sharply angled attic roof, together with her daughter Janie (figure 7). Magnification revealed that Dorothy was smiling at the very album in which the Bussys would themselves appear. It is as if the album's viewers share the album's narrative construction. Woolf's frequent use of invitational or rhetorical questions in her fiction is matched here by the album's appeal to an active spectator. The album is being spectated in the act of memorialising, as if the Bussys see themselves through the photographic gaze of another. Psychoanalytically speaking, these subjects gain a sense of identity through their recognition by another.

Perhaps for this reason Woolf believed that photographs could help her to survive those identity-destroying moments of her own life – her incoherent illnesses. For example, writing to Margaret Llewelyn Davies in 1915, Woolf 'wanted to say that all through that terrible time' (a week's attack of apparent insanity) 'I thought of you, and wanted to look at a picture of you, but was afraid to ask!' (Woolf 1976, p. 60). Friends' photographs often provide solidly visible autobiographical evidence when feelings of loss of identity become overwhelming.

Mutual image-making would also create relationships. Woolf used photographs to entice Vita Sackville-West. Writing to 'Mrs Nicolson' in 1923, Woolf asked Vita to visit in order 'to look at my great aunt's photographs of Tennyson and other people' (Woolf 1977b, p. 4). By 1926, more desperately, Woolf was writing to Vita's mother, Lady Sackville, for the name of Vita's passport photographer so 'that I may write to him myself' for a copy of the photograph (Woolf 1977b, p. 246). Virginia took Vita to London to be photographed for *Orlando* and used the excuse of further illustrations to make additional visits to Knole and for more photography sessions (figure 8): 'You'll lunch here at *one sharp* on Monday wont you: bringing your curls and clothes. Nessa [Vanessa Bell] wants to photograph you at 2' (Woolf 1977b, p. 435). The photograph appears in *Orlando* as 'Orlando about the year 1840'. Angelica Bell posed for the photograph of 'Sasha' which is in Monk's House album 3, p. 14. Complimenting Vanessa, Woolf enthused that the photographs were 'most lovely [...] I'm showing them to Vita, who doesn't want to be accused of raping the under age. My God – I shall rape Angelica one of these days' (Woolf 1977b, p. 497). Perhaps it is not surprising that in her own copy of *Orlando*, Lady Sackville pasted a photograph of Virginia alongside the words 'the awful face of a mad woman whose successful mad desire is to separate people who care for each other. I loathe this woman for having changed my Vita and taken her away from me' (Woolf 1977b, p. 548).

Mutual image-making encourages reciprocity between photographer and sitter. The albums' photographs are invitational rather than voyeuristic and, together with Woolf's constant exchange of photographs with friends, influenced her ideas about representation and about herself. The scale of the Harvard collection, and the inclusion of out-of-focus images in the albums, betray her reluctance to discard photographs and the narratives about herself that photographs could tell. Writing to her friend Ethel Smyth in 1940, Woolf compared her own subjective feelings to a photographic process: 'How then do I transfer these images to my sensitive paper brain? Because I have a heart. Yes, and it is the heart that makes the paper take, as they say' (Woolf 1980a, p. 393). In 'The Cook', a fictional description of Sophie Farrell, the family servant, Woolf directly connects family identity with photography: 'Her room is hung with photographs. Her mind is like a family album. You turn up Uncle George you turn up Aunt Maria. She has a story about each of them' (Lee 1996, p. 49).

Photographs could be powerfully truth-telling. In 1905 Woolf implored her friend Violet Dickinson to buy photographs during Dickinson's American tour. Again, in 1929, Woolf realised that she depended on photographs in order to visualise friends: 'Please send me, what I'm sure there must be – a picture postcard of Hugh Walpoles house [...] I have a childish wish to consolidate my friends and embed them in their own tables and *chairs*' (Woolf 1978b, p. 84, my italics). Her positivist use of photographs as evidence here balances her subjective cherishing of friends' images. An important item of holiday luggage was a friend's photograph. For example,

Figure 8
Vita Sackville-West with Virginia Woolf, *c.*1933: from Virginia Woolf's Monk's House album 3
Reprinted by permission of the Harvard Theatre Collection, the Houghton Library

1933

V.W. Vita Nicolson

Vita Nicolson

V. Nicolson

V. Nicolson V.W.

she took Violet Dickinson's photograph on holiday to Netherhampton House, Salisbury. Woolf floods letters to friends with requests for photographs, and, equally frequently, describes the dispatching of photographs of herself, Monk's House and other friends.

Woolf needed photographs in order to write. For example, she asked Vita, in 1931, for 'a photograph of Henry' (Harold Nicolson's cocker spaniel): 'I ask for a special reason, connected with a little escapade', which became Woolf's book *Flush* (Woolf 1978b, p. 380). The ironic photographs in *Flush* and *Three Guineas*, the loving construction of Vita and Angelica's photographs in *Orlando*, parallel the multiple references to photographs in Woolf's fiction. For example, in *Night and Day* Woolf judges characters by the photographs they display in their houses (Gillespie 1993, p. 45). In short, photographs may be 'only an eye', but they enabled Woolf to see more clearly.

Still, for all her enthusiasm as an amateur photographer, in her letters Woolf consistently condemns professional photography. The *New Statesman* published Woolf's autobiographically revealing attack on the paparazzi of the 1930s: 'The click of the camera is heard behind the altar rails during the marriage service [...] private people, musicians, writers, artists of all kinds. Their homes are photographed, their families, their gardens, their studios, their bedrooms and their writing tables' (Woolf 1979, pp. 237–8). Woolf deplored the intrusive professional. She refused to be photographed by Cecil Beaton: 'I'm so furious at being in Beaton's Book – I was never asked – never sat – never saw the horrid worm and there I am seized forever' (Woolf 1978b, p. 258). Certainly Beaton's Surrealist-inspired baroque settings are remote from the Woolfs' complicit, humanist portraits.

Even being photographed by a woman photographer, Gisèle Freund, seemed to Woolf like 'being hoisted about on top of a stick for any one to stare at' (Woolf 1980a, p. 351). Yet Freund – 'la femme aux images', as she was called, following her dissertation on photography at the Sorbonne, inspired by Norbert Elias – was known for her empathy with artists and writers. Freund photographed Sylvia Beach, Walter Benjamin and James Joyce, among others, and undertook socially committed reportage of economic depression in northern England for *Life* magazine (Hanssen 1995, pp. 6–10). Yet Woolf was

Figure 9
Virginia Woolf by Gisèle Freund, Tavistock Square, 1939
Reprinted by permission of the Harvard Theatre Collection, the Houghton Library

shocked that Freund had 'filched and pilfered and gate crashed – the treacherous vermin' (Woolf 1980a, p. 351). Freund's autobiography remembers a much more invitational occasion. She describes being asked by Woolf to return the next day for further photographs and, in addition, that Woolf happily changed her clothing to suit the needs of Freund's special colour film (Freund 1974). As Nicola Luckhurst points out, Woolf wore three different shirts for the sitting (Luckhurst 2001, p. 7). Naomi Rosenblum argues that Freund's sensitivity 'to the relationship between character and facial expression' bears 'a marked similarity to Julia Margaret Cameron's', suggesting a further reason why Woolf might have found Freund's work congenial (Rosenblum 2000, pp. 124–5). Freund used a discreet Leica and Kodachrome Agfacolour film, requiring a very co-operative sitter (Freund 1974). Woolf never saw the photographs, but the Harvard Theatre Collection contains several Freund prints revealing the accuracy of her account rather than Woolf's. Presumably Freund gave the prints to Leonard herself, after Woolf's death, when she returned to photograph Leonard in his library in 1965 (box 4). Grouping the differently sized photographs of Woolf from the different boxes together (boxes 6, 2 and 3), it is clear that Woolf was a supportive sitter, and changed her clothing for Freund (figure 9).

THE MONK'S HOUSE ALBUMS

Stuart Hall accurately points out that there *can* be no simple, unitary thing 'photography', since the meanings of photographs are inflected by 'the diversity of practices, institutions and historical conjunctions in which the photographic text is produced' (Hall 1991, p. 152). In terms of historical practices, while albums range from nineteenth-century political scrapbooks to twentieth-century family pictures, most share a predictable format (Spence and Holland 1991). The Woolfs' albums, like others, do not make visible the worlds of politics and work that inhabit Virginia's letters, diaries and fiction. In this sense Woolf's albums sit comfortably within a traditional form. That is, the albums memorialise family and friends. But, unlike the typical multiple photos of immaculately happy friends and sunny days, the Woolfs' albums contain out-of-focus photographs alongside perfected takes of the same sitter. Again, Woolf avoids conventional album shots, favouring the close-up portrait and large group scene. The albums are not chronologically catalogued, nor do they crudely order friendships into cyclical events, for example weddings. The Woolfs do not construct ideal versions of their lives and friendships, and both husband and wife are equally visible. There is no absent, implied male photographer as in most albums, as many photographs are evidently taken by Virginia.

Virginia Woolf's own account of her albums is untrustworthy. In a letter to Margaret Llewelyn Davies in April 1940, Woolf states 'I stuck all your photographs' (of Virginia's childhood at St Ives) 'into a great book and called it Eminent Victorians' (Woolf 1980a, p. 392). While Monk's House albums 1 and 6 do contain a large number of Victorian photographs, they also contain many which are contemporary, and neither album is entitled 'Eminent Victorians'. Monk's House album 1 has seventy-one pages of photographs. The first eighteen contain Victorian studio portraits of Virginia's vast, extended family, for example, 1866 photographs of G. Holmes, the Fisher family, the Prinseps, and the Mackimeras. Like the opening of Vera Brittain's *Testament of Youth*, this panorama suggests, perhaps, a longing for a confirmed familial world. Yet, just as in her writing, Woolf never loses her capacity to ironise. While the Victorian photographs have no apparent patterns (similarities are not grouped, nor are there obvious themes), the insertion of the odd photograph of dog or cat into a frieze of Victorian notables teases the viewer.

The album contains the first photographs which Virginia so eagerly solicited from friends; a 6-by-4¼ photograph of Violet Dickinson (possibly taken with the 4A folding Kodak camera) as well as photographs of Julian and Quentin Bell as naked children, probably taken by Vanessa Bell since there are duplicates in the Tate Gallery Bell albums. Pages 26–45 contain Leonard's documentary photographs of his colonial service in Ceylon, from which he resigned to marry Virginia. Leonard's folkloric documentation of his personal career jarringly contrasts with Virginia's extensive family past. The marked disjunction is not the result of chance, determined simply by available photographs, but an index of the Woolfs' different notions of self-identity and family memories.

The boxes of loose photographs do contain Leonard's equivalent Victorian family photographs, among them one of Leonard's uniformed father, inscribed on the reverse 'to my darling Leonard on the 9th anniversary of his birthday from his loving father Sidney'. For Virginia, on the other hand, family photographs directly shade her personal

STERED
ETON

landscape. A studio portrait of Stella Duckworth is succeeded by further photographs of the Stephen family, including one of Virginia's half-sister Laura as a baby held by her father, Leslie Stephen (figure 10), as well as a photograph of her mother, Julia Stephen, holding the infant George Duckworth. The contingency of the photographs, the Woolfs' refusal

of conventional chronology, is confirmed by the final pages, entitled '1914 July'. Photographs of G. E. Moore, Vanessa and the Woolfs' servants Lily and Annie, taken at Asheham House (the Woolfs' first country home in Sussex), are immediately followed by photographs dated 1912 and then by one of Adrian Stephen, Virginia's brother, photographed in Fitzroy Square in 1920.

The arbitrariness of chronology, the sense that reality is fundamentally unclassifiable which so pervades Woolf's fiction, is much in evidence here. In addition the nostalgia-provoking quality of the album is reinforced by the almost childlike scrapbook appearance, with thick card covers inscribed:

PHO-

TO-

GRAPHS

and crude hand-cut slits rather than professional mounts. The Woolfs' preference for contiguity over chronology suggests a past which haunts the present rather than a past which precedes the present.

Monk's House album 2 has similar brown leaves and thick card covers, with twenty-three pages of photographs taken between 1916 and 1922. Now living at Monk's House, the Woolfs prolifically photograph each other, members of the Bell family, Marjorie and Lytton Strachey and Leonard's family. Visitors include E. M. Forster (figure 11), T. S. Eliot, Desmond MacCarthy and Noel Olivier. There are holiday photographs of Margaret Llewelyn Davies and the Woolfs in Cornwall in 1916. Out-of-focus photographs of Charleston and over exposed double negatives jostle with the careful portrait. There is no overt 'policing', no artificially perfected images of friendship. For example, hidden behind a photograph of Ka Arnold-Forster writing at her desk is a better duplicate (p. 17).

Monk's House album 3 is bound in beautiful 'tumbling-dice'

patterned paper but has the same hand-made slits, with sixty-eight pages
of carefully arranged photographs. Woolf was a knowledgeable
bookbinder who personally chose and bound the illustrations for dust-
jackets and covers for the Hogarth Press books, collaborating with
Vanessa, who designed the cross-hatched, geometric covers. Monk's
House album 3 is not only the album with most photographs but a very
rich example of the Woolfs' unusual method of photographing life
stories. The past vividly 'narrates' the present. The framing frontispiece is
a large, 6-by-7½ photograph of Julia Stephen (figure 2 above), immediately followed by the 1892 St Ives photograph of Julia, Leslie and Virginia
Stephen (figure 1 above), yet page 3 is marked 'August 1931'.

The Woolfs photograph each other in similar poses in similar
comfy chairs, and similarly photograph friends in comfy chairs in
multiple shots taken on different days, sometimes in different years, but

grouped together in the album. Some album pages have a real gravitas and impact. For example, four 4-by-3 photographs of Ethel Smyth (probably taken with a 3A vest pocket Kodak) resemble cinema stills, each with Smyth in a comfy chair but with different eye-lines (figure 12). Another powerful sequence is that of the photographs of William Plomer, Vita Nicolson and Charles Siepmann, united across time by the chair motif (figure 13).

Figure 11
E. M. Forster and Leonard Woolf, Monk's House, *c.*1922: from Virginia Woolf's Monk's House album 2
Reprinted by permission of the Harvard Theatre Collection, the Houghton Library

By 1939, the sitters' collusion with constructed poses becomes an established feature of Monk's House album 4. Adrian and Karin Stephen sit in comfy chairs in close-up with only a discontinuity of sight-line. Molly Sturgeon and E. M. Forster are photographed on separate occasions in the same chair and position. The chronology of this album, like its predecessors', is very eclectic. Dated '1939', the album's first photographs are of the Stracheys at Ottoline Morrell's in 1923 and Carrington, Ralph Partridge and Lytton at Ham Spray in 1930. Framing is consciously arty. Trees vertically frame landscape scenes. Groups are not always centred but framed by a strong vertical flower or statue. There is little 'leakage'. The thirty-seven pages of photographs contain the Woolfs' favourite bowling scenes; photographs of their newer animals, Sappho and Pluto; photographs of Brittany and Tavistock Square. Although less professional in appearance than the close-ups of friends, the Brittany scenes also exploit strong sequencing. Buildings, the preferred subject matter, are always photographed angled sequentially. For example, a castle is photographed *de haut en bas*, and again in medium-shot and close-up.

For this reason Monk's House album 5 has less allure. Of the eighty-three pages, seven contain scenic views of the Woolfs' 1937 French holiday and ten are of location photographs of their 1928 visit to Scotland. Yet, like Monk's House album 3, the album is shaped by Virginia's childhood memories. Pages 1–12 contain photographs of her favourite childhood home – Talland House, St Ives – taken in 1892, together with studio portraits of Leslie Stephen. The past is not hierarchically ordered, for example, photographs of servants are not separated from family photographs. Neither is the past past, that is to say, past photographs impact on contemporary scenes. For example, the 1892 sequential photographs of servants – Paddy the gardener, Amy the seamstress and Ellen Eldridge, which are probably photographed by Gerald Duckworth, since a subsequent, similar photograph of Pascoe the boatman is titled 'by Gerald Duckworth' – are revivified in the Woolfs' dedicated sequencing (figure 14). Gerald, however, adopts what the artist Susan Hiller would call a quasi-anthropological view, freezing each servant often full-face to camera, in isolation from colleagues, as an aestheticised subject (Hiller 1991, p. 186). Gerald's choice of 'props' and costume individualises by function, in marked contrast to the young Virginia's $2^3/_4$-by-$3^3/_4$ photograph of Vanessa laughingly helping Lisa Stillman at the cooking range (figure 15). Yet Gerald's sequencing does impact on the present by obviously underscoring for Woolf the aesthetic effectuality of sequential photography. For example, there follow sequential images of Sally Graves and Richard Chilver sitting in Virginia's favourite nook, between her featheredged wooden writing lodge and adjacent flint wall (pp. 18–20). The precise nature of these sequential montages, or, rather, the *reasons* for such an unusual form, may become clearer in a moment when I discuss the relevance of Roland Barthes's *Camera Lucida* and the ideas of Bracha Lichtenberg Ettinger and other psychoanalytic theory. For now, suffice it to say that these albums reveal what Sontag suggests, that old photographs can 'transform the present into the past and the past into pastness' (Sontag 1989, p. 77). Woolf's family past animates the albums. The past processes the present 'in *topoi* of loss and memorial' (Luckhurst 2001, p. 6).

CONTEMPORARY CAMERA TECHNOLOGY

The Woolfs' skilful intent is not constrained by the limitations of camera technology, which it might be appropriate to consider. Until the acquisition, 'with violent impetuosity', of a Zeiss camera costing £20 in July

Figure 12
Ethel Smyth, Monk's House, *c.*1931: from Virginia Woolf's Monk's House album 3
Reprinted by permission of the Harvard Theatre Collection, the Houghton Library

1931, 'and said to be unrivalled in the portrayal of the human – if mine can be said to be human – face', and assuming from the size of the album prints, the Woolfs probably relied on the popular 3A vest pocket Kodak which succeeded Virginia's Frena (Woolf 1978b, p. 361). Few options and manipulations were available with these cameras. The 3A was introduced to Britain in 1903, with 100,000 sold by

Ethel Smyth

William Plomer

Vita Nicolson

Charles Siepmann

1914 (Coe and Gates 1977). The 3A Kodak took postcard-sized photographs, and many of the album prints are on cards with pre-printed backs for posting – a standard Kodak feature. The camera was billed as 'broader in scope than anything heretofore attained in pocket photography', but the relation between aperture and shutter-speed could not be manipulated, as on contemporary cameras, to alter depths of field. For example, the standard

photograph was exterior, at five feet from the subject (Lothrop 1982, p. 118).

The inexpensive, light cameras were particularly popular with women. The *Photographic News* reported, in September 1905, that 'thousands of Birmingham girls are scattered about the holiday resorts of Britain this month, and a very large percentage of them are armed with cameras' (Coe and Gates 1977, p. 28). Queen Alexandra's favourite camera was a No. 4 Bulls-Eye Special Kodak, with a Kodak No. 2 camera for her visits abroad, and 140 of her snapshots were published and in travelling exhibitions (Williams 1994, p. 75). The Monk's House albums 3–5 also include 3-by-4 photographs, the exposure size of the newer 2A Kodak with its superior lens, suggesting that the Woolfs made use of more than one camera. Despite Susan Sontag's claim that 'a photograph loses much less of its essential quality when reproduced in a book than a painting does', implying that photographs have lower tonal quality than do paintings, that of the original Monk's House prints is often high (Sontag 1989, p. 5).

FAMILY PHOTOGRAPHS

The Woolfs' albums may be usefully compared to three other collections of family photographs or visual memories which Virginia knew well: those by her great-aunt Julia Margaret Cameron, her father Leslie Stephen's *Mausoleum Book* and photograph album, and Vanessa Bell's albums now in the Tate Gallery. Although all three collections favour portraiture, there are marked differences between the studies. Using a wet collodion process with glass plates, rather than paper, Julia Cameron took hundreds of photographs of friends and family between 1864 and her death in 1879 (Powell 1973, p. 9). There are portraits of famous men, including Tennyson, Carlyle and Darwin, as well as ones of Virginia's mother Julia and Pre-Raphaelite young girls. Woolf shared Cameron's disregard for sharp images and *Freshwater*, Woolf's play about the life of her great-aunt, describes Cameron's use of visual metaphors. Just as Vanessa's first act, on leaving the Stephen home, was to decorate 46 Gordon Square with Cameron portraits, so Virginia includes Cameron portraits in her albums.

Together with Roger Fry, Woolf edited and introduced a book collection of Cameron's photographs. Woolf's introduction makes Cameron into a convex mirror of Virginia herself. Both Cameron and Woolf knew Ceylon (Virginia through marriage and Cameron through residence); both gave generously to family and friends (Woolf gave Angelica an annual allowance); and both were 'profuse' and productive artists. Both carefully posed sitters in particular locations (Virginia's favourite comfy chairs, Cameron's garden bowers). Both utilised chiaroscuro, the play of light and shadow. Yet Woolf's devotion to sequential and associative poses differs from Cameron's singular portraits. Although, as Deborah Cherry points out, Cameron's photographs of Julia Stephen were repetitive, each of Cameron's album pages contains only one photograph and her photographic imagery is often heterogeneous (Cherry 2000, p. 169). In Lacanian terms, Woolf's continual photographic repetitions would suggest the 'return' of a visual event which took place outside her contemporary frames. As Lacan suggests, 'the real is that which always comes back to the same place' (Lacan 1978, p. 42).

The Monk's House albums also tell a different story of that family past from Leslie Stephen's *Mausoleum Book*, part of which Leslie dictated to Virginia, and from Stephen's photo album. Immediately following Julia's death, Stephen set out to write an epistolary account of his life as a record for his children of 'two or three little memory pictures' (Stephen 1977, p. 16). Linda Anderson argues that the *Mausoleum Book*'s masculine narrative 'takes precedence over the feminine' and Stephen's surprising intellectual control parallels an exaggerated, sentimental portrait of Julia as an abstract, passive madonna, as

Figure 14

Servants: Paddy and Amy, Ellen Eldridge and delivery boy, Talland House, St Ives, *c.*1892: from Virginia Woolf's Monk's House album 5

Reprinted by permission of the Harvard Theatre Collection, the Houghton Library

Paddy gardener

Amy

?

?

she had been depicted in Burne-Jones's *Annunciation* of 1879: as I remember 'the Sistine Madonna or any other presentation of superlative beauty' (Anderson 2001, p. 93; Stephen 1977, p. 31). Yet, in some senses, Stephen's frozen family images are revivified in Woolf's writing. Both translate family members into characters in similar ways. For example, Stephen's description of Anny Thackeray, his first wife's sister, who 'wrote

fragments as thoughts' and stuck these with pins 'at odd parts of her Ms', resembles Virginia's frequent descriptions of Vanessa's 'shabby, loose, easy' clothing attached with pins (Stephen 1977, p. 14; Woolf 1978c, p. 246). Both father and daughter loved 'purple sweetscented cyclamens', which Woolf transforms into purple anemones in the opening passage of 'A Sketch of the Past', and she curtained her first room of her own in Fitzroy Square with flowing purple. As I have pointed out elsewhere, the Woolfs built their library on the nucleus of books which Virginia inherited from her father, her annotations resemble Stephen's practice – both marked cant with an 'O' – and Woolf's essays focus on the same writers as Stephen chose (Humm 1986, p. 149). Both father and daughter wrote about De Quincey, George Eliot, the Brontës and Hazlitt, and they both wrote accessibly and engagingly about the same aspects of literary form – autobiography and historical narratives (Stephen 1874). Both believed that photographs of Julia were more timelessly affective than painted portraits: 'The beautiful series of portraits taken by Mrs Cameron [...] recall her like nothing else' (Stephen 1977, p. 32). Julia becomes their 'stranger in the house', since 'she lived in me, in her mother, in her children' (Stephen 1977, p. 58).

Stephen's photo album contains seventy-three photographs taken between 1856 and 1894, mounted by him on sixteen leaves (Stephen 1895). Although he mounts photographs much less formally than Woolf does in her photo albums (figures 16 and 18), yet in his *Mausoleum Book* Stephen explicitly memorialises the exact photograph which Virginia avidly highlights in the opening of Monk's House album 3 (figure 3 above): 'When I look at certain little photographs, at one in which I am reading by her side at St Ives with Virginia [...] I see as with my bodily eyes the love, the holy and tender love' (Stephen 1977, p. 58). Stephen's own photographs of Julia and the children are much more idealised with

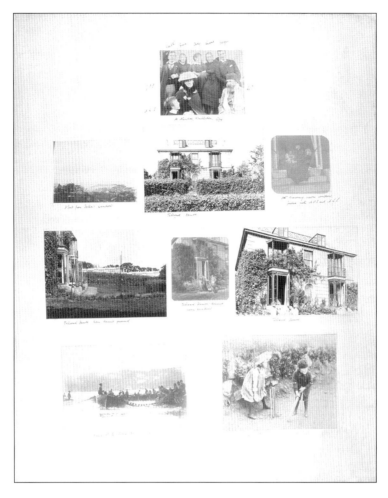

his use of averted gazes (figure 18). The connotative power of this image of Julia shapes both father and daughter's wider circles of reflection, and the photo also appears in Stella Duckworth's album (see Chapter 1). It is the visual language of this particular photograph, what we might call its trauma fragments, which determines Woolf's own photographic constructions.

Figure 16

Talland House, St Ives, *c.*1892–4: from Leslie Stephen's photograph album, Smith College

Reprinted by permission of Mortimer Rare Book Room, Smith College

There are similar quiet connections and discontinuities between the sisters' albums. Both Vanessa and Virginia are drawn to the maternal. Pregnant, Vanessa fantasises to Virginia that 'I shall see you every day and gaze at the most beautiful of Aunt Julia's photographs [that of their mother]

incessantly' (Marler 1993, p. 67). Later, in 1927, she pleads with Virginia 'to write a book about the maternal instinct. In all my wide reading I haven't yet found it properly explored' (Marler 1993, p. 315). Both shared a Bloomsbury party visit to a film

Figure 17
Talland House,
St Ives, today
By permission of
Rodger Sykes

of a Caesarean operation: Bell commented, 'Really it was quite the oddest entertainment I've ever been to [...] Leonard felt very ill' (Marler 1993, pp. 361–2). Yet although Bell and Woolf mount some of the same photographs in their albums, for example, those of the Empress Eugenie, Mrs MacNamara and the Bell children, Julia Stephen does not haunt Vanessa's albums as a shaping spirit.

The radical nature of the Monk's House albums seems all the more impressive in relation to the Bell albums (see Chapter 3 below). Although, as an artist, Vanessa took more highly skilled close-ups (particularly those of Duncan Grant and the children), in general, her albums are immaculately chronological, organised in the pattern of the Bell year: Charleston in winter and Cassis in summer, and around folkloric events: the grape harvest and Charleston theatricals. In addition Vanessa includes photographs of public events, for example, the 1897 Jubilee procession.

In marked contrast, the Woolf albums, as noted, are not chronologically ordered. For example, the cover of Monk's House album 4 bears the date '1939', yet the album begins with a *News Chronicle* cutting of Lady Baldwin dated 1938, followed by photographs taken at Ottoline

1 T·S., V·S., A.V.S., Julia, A·L·S. (lessons)

Morrell's in 1923 (figure 19). Woolf's albums share *Orlando*'s historical largesse. In addition, Virginia refuses to memorialise public events. For example, while her letters contain a vivid description of George V's funeral procession – 'we stood in the Sqr to see the hearse […] the mob was on us, and Leonard who is a democrat was squashed between 5 fat grocers' – there are no photographs of it in either the albums or the boxes (Woolf 1980a, p. 8).

Figure 18

Julia Stephen with Stephen children at lessons: Thoby, Vanessa, Virginia, Julia Duckworth and Adrian Stephen, Talland House, St Ives, *c.*1894: from Leslie Stephen's photograph album, Smith College

Reprinted by permission of Mortimer Rare Book Room, Smith College

A preoccupation with family memories informs Woolf's choices of image. Windows are centred in many photographs or are framing devices. Monk's House album 1 contains Julian spread-eagled over the Asheham House windows (figure 28 below); friends photographed through windows, for example, Gertrude Minnheimer (p. 68); sequential photographs of Leonard, Vanessa, Virginia and Roger Fry framed by the Asheham House windows in 1912 (p. 69); and a family photograph of C. E. Stephen sitting in profile lit by a garden window (p. 62). In Monk's House album 2

Leonard's sister Bella and mother are sequenced with the Asheham windows and Margaret Llewelyn Davies moves towards camera through windows (p. 5). In Monk's House albums 3 and 5 windows are visible, major light sources, for example, in the Mitz and Bussy photographs and in further sequences of Virginia and Leonard (p. 3). Photographs taken at Ham Spray in 1930 renew this theme, with Lytton Strachey in humorous mock surprise leaning out of upper windows. Windows and doorways carry more semantic currency than simply as the common trope of post-Impressionist paintings. Such images resonate with family memories. Writing to Roger Fry in 1921, Virginia has a metaphoric 'passion for taking feelings to the window and looking at them' (Woolf 1976, p. 490). Frances Spalding clarifies this foundational motif more precisely in her biography of Vanessa Bell. As Spalding points out, although windows were a common feature of modernism's picture planes, Vanessa's constant use of this motif had much greater personal significance: 'It is interesting that the photograph of her mother which she kept for many years on her desk shows Julia leaning against a closed window, her face turned to the light' (Spalding 1983, p. 153).

More surprisingly, even in Woolf's house-party photographs there are traces of family memories. These photographs of friends seated in deck chairs, on the terrace or bowling are numerous (seventy-five in total) but unorthodox (figure 20). There are no ritualistic serried rows of people simultaneously smiling at a fixed point of view, or ranked by height, age or gender, but rather expressive moments snapped from ongoing events. The implied narrative of each group – book readings, discussions, walking tours – continues outside the frame. Not all group members acknowledge the camera's presence as, for example, in the scene of Adrian and Karin Stephen and Virginia (Monk's House album 3, p. 44). In addition, groups are frequently shot from behind from a low camera position rather than with the conventional, full-fronted medium- or long-shot.

The house-party scenes closely resemble an 1892 Stephen family exterior photograph taken at St Ives (Monk's House album 5, p. 6). As in the later photographs, the family is not in a formal pose, but rather people are caught smiling and chattering in the middle of activity. Not all see the camera. At the centre of the photograph Julia Stephen pensively looks down in a reflective moment. It is as if this 1892 photograph shapes Woolf's later photographic desires, for example, the majority of Woolf's sitters adopt the three-quarter gaze, a viewpoint which avoids a confrontational relation to a spectator.

MODERNISM

The albums were being constructed during the period of Woolf's 'strongest commitment to formalism', the mid-1920s, with its anti-mimetic aesthetic (Reed 1993, p. 21). The modernity of the albums is striking and owes much to Woolf's knowledge of modernism, including Cézanne's painting series and Eisenstein and German cinema. The Woolfs' use of composite images, the recognition that the process of construction is part of the content of a constructed piece, synchronises with other modernist developments in the 1920s and 1930s. For example, John Heartfield's montages and techniques of juxtaposition featured in popular culture such as advertising as well as high art (Collecott 1987). Cézanne's still lifes, with their new spatial relation between objects, such as pitchers and fruits, and figures, were the central attraction at Roger Fry's 1910 post-Impressionist exhibition. In his preface to the catalogue for the New Movement in Art exhibition of 1917, Fry claimed that Cézanne sought to express emotion, not mimetically, but precisely through spatial relationships (Watney 1980, p. 20). Woolf's quadruple portraits of Ethel Smyth (Monk's House album 3, p. 12) form a sequential series of photographs in which overlapping eye-lines and seated positions carry an emotional charge (figure 12 above). As Woolf suggested in a letter to Smyth, 'your ambit [...] no minor agitation in the foreground will upset me. You see I like your circumference' (Woolf 1978b, p. 199). In Woolf's novels characters' memories often overlap in sequences, for example, in *Mrs Dalloway*, and both novels and photographs catch something of the prismatic quality of Vanessa Bell's modernist work.

Susan Sontag argues that 'photography is the most successful vehicle of modernist taste in its pop version' (Sontag 1989, p. 131). A modernist aesthetic does inform Woolf's landscape photographs and 'still life' animal photographs. Flat, elegiac snow scenes with black, vertical elms are

Figure 19
Lytton Strachey, Virginia Woolf and Goldsworthy Lowes ('Goldie') Dickinson; Marjorie and Lytton Strachey; Garsington c.1923, probably by Ottoline Morrell: from Virginia Woolf's Monk's House album 4
Reprinted by permission of the Harvard Theatre Collection, the Houghton Library

Lytton Strachey & Yeats at Ottoline Morrell's

Marjorie Strachey & Lytton

Adrian Stephen V.W. Karin   Adrian L. Karin

Quentin Ann Raymond Mortimer

common (such as the view from the upper windows of Monk's House of the elms they named Virginia and Leonard), as are particular textured surfaces, such as Virginia's featheredged work lodge, which appears in twelve photographs in Monk's House albums 4, 5 and 6. Yet the camera operator is not a detached observer. The repetition of particular landscapes and textures has the same emotional

intensity as Woolf's ecstatic perceptions of landscape in her novels, as in *The Waves*. The interpretation of exterior and interior in Vanessa's paintings and Woolf's novels and photographs is never a purely formal modernism. Memories, or ghosts of the past as Woolf repeatedly suggests, often occur in gardens, for example, Lily's sight of the Ramsays in *To the Lighthouse*. It is as if these scenes are both real, materially there, and discursive metaphors for hidden emotions, like transitional spaces between psyche and spectator.

CINEMA

The albums, like Vanessa's paintings, also synchronise with cinema's new range of effects in the 1920s and 1930s. Vanessa wrote to Roger Fry that Duncan Grant 'has started on a long painting which is meant to be rolled up after the manner of those Chinese paintings and seen by degrees' (Marler 1993, p. 169). Simon Watney explains that the fifteen-foot *Abstract Kinetic Collage Painting with Sound* was less a painting that moves than an analysis of movement itself, resembling the early abstract films of Hans Richter (Watney 1980, p. 98). Like other modernist writers and artists, such as James Joyce, Dorothy Richardson and the poet H. D., the Bells and Woolfs were cinema-goers fully aware of film's stylistic devices, such as montage.

In her first diary Woolf describes her 1915 birthday treat 'at a Picture Palace' as well as the attraction of regular movie going over political meetings (Woolf 1977a, p. 28): 'I went to my picture palace, & L. to his Fabians; & he thought, on the whole, that his mind & spirit & body would have profited more by the pictures than by the Webbs' (Woolf 1977a, p. 18). Like Vanessa, who equally enjoyed Tarzan films, Chaplin's *Modern Times* and Russian films, the Woolfs made eclectic cinema choices. In 1927 Woolf describes seeing a movie with 'a great seduction scene in China' (Woolf 1977b, p. 349). In 1931 she saw 'a very good French one' – *Le Million*, written and directed by René Clair – whose experiments with spatial and temporal dislocations would impact on Woolf's own techniques; as well as being 'given stalls for a night of *Wuthering Heights*' (Woolf 1978b, p. 332). Visiting the Nicolsons in Berlin in 1929, Virginia, together with Vanessa, saw Pudovkin's *Storm Over Asia*, banned in England, and admired its visual landscapes (Spalding 1983, p. 228). The fixing of phenomena, the accumulation of associations through the composition of montage sequences character-istic of Russian cinema, offered a 'new catalytic thesis' (Eisenstein 1988b, p. 23). As Eisenstein argues, in cinema 'the shot merely *interprets* the object in a setting to use it in juxtaposition to other *sequences*' (Eisenstein 1988b, p. 80). The Woolfs acknowledged the importance of cinema by publishing in the Hogarth Press a film text – Eric White's *Parnassus to Let: An Essay About Rhythm in Film* (1928).

As Lyotard claims, cinematography is the 'a priori condition of all narration' (Lyotard 1990, p. 19). Woolf's own writings about cinema, more than most, have a keen-eyed modernist vision. 'The Cinema', first published in *Arts* in New York in 1926, explores relationships between movement and repetition, emotions and spatial organisations (see Chapter 5 and Humm 1997). Woolf's account of film as a space which subverts chronology is very striking: 'The most fantastic contrasts could be flashed before us with a speed which the writer can only toil after in vain; the dream architecture of arches and battlements, of cascades falling and fountains rising, which sometimes visits us in sleep or shapes itself in half-darkened rooms, could be realized before our waking eyes' (Woolf 1994b, p. 595). Woolf uses film language. Omitting her earlier qualifying vocabulary of 'seems' and 'impressions' in the manuscript version, she used descriptive close-ups, such as seeing the 'very quivers of [Vronsky's] lips' in *War and Peace* (Woolf 1926). She avidly responds to *Dr Caligari*'s expressionist perspectives, angles and shapes, claiming that these new spatial representations offered a new visual aesthetics, 'a new art to be transfixed' (Woolf 1994b, p. 595). In some senses the Monk's House albums transfix that 'new art'. It could be argued that the Woolfs' understanding of the emotional power of spatial arrangements meshed with modernist experiments of the 1920s and 1930s such as Eisenstein's montages.

PSYCHOANALYTIC AND PHOTOGRAPHY THEORY

Yet, while the Monk's House albums, in some respects, reveal Woolf to be an enthusiastic modernist, in other respects they are too repetitious, too obsessive to be classified simply as modernist. Out of 140 photographs that are not of holidays or house parties, over 41 per cent (58) are of friends in padded armchairs. Equally crucially, in two albums photographs of Woolf's mother and father are placed out of chronology as frontispieces. The photomontages in the albums suggest that some other preoccupation, whether conscious or unconscious, informs a modernist facade. The page compositions and repeated use of particular objects – the armchairs and vertical flowers and bookcases – seem shaped as much by the psychic as by the formally aesthetic. Like a palimpsest, the album sequences offer a crucial insight into those psychic mechanisms structuring Woolf's aesthetics.

All photographs are a language and Woolf's language was maternal: 'She has haunted me' (Woolf 1977b, p. 374). As George Johnson notes, Leslie Stephen had been a member of the Society for Psychical Research before becoming an agnostic, and Woolf herself in 1918 reviewed Dorothy Scarborough's *The Supernatural in Modern English Fiction*, which introduced Woolf 'to a discussion of the spirits of dead mothers in the section on ghostly psychology' (Johnson 1997, p. 238). Woolf literally wrote 'through' the maternal: 'Here I am experimenting with the parent of all pens – the black J, *the* pen, as I used to think it, along with other objects, as a child, because mother used it' (Woolf 1977a, p. 208). Woolf's *To the Lighthouse* visually recreates her mother and father at St Ives in the figures of Mrs and Mr Ramsay. In the novel Woolf was able to translate abstract metaphysical questions about memory, such as 'what is the meaning of memory?', into epistemological processes: *how* to know the meaning of memory by constructing the present time of characters through memories of the past. The publication of *To the Lighthouse* encouraged Woolf's family to remember Julia: 'A voice on the telephone plunged me into the wildest memories – of St. Ives – Gerald [...] "I am trying to find Cameron photographs of Mama – Can you lend me any negatives?"' (Woolf 1977b, p. 380).

Woolf realised that this pictorial enthusiasm raised complex epistemological questions about the psychoanalytic. She frequently said about her mother, 'it is a psychological mystery why she should be: how a child could know about her; except that she has always haunted me' (Woolf 1977b, p. 383). Jane Marcus argues that Woolf's feminism was, 'emotionally, part of the project of the daughter's recovery of the mother' (Marcus 1987, p. 9). Julia Stephen's early death meant that, to Woolf, she became the phantasmic mother, that is, a mother who can exist only as an image, who can be seen or mirrored only in identifications and who might incite the visual imagination (of a photographer) into hallucinatory significations (Jacobus 1995, p. iii). Just as the family, as Hermione Lee suggests, was Woolf's 'political blueprint', so the death of her mother gave Woolf a visual blueprint (Lee 1996, p. 52). In 'A Sketch of the Past' Woolf describes how it was her mother's death which 'made me suddenly develop perceptions' (Woolf 1985, p. 93).

Contemporary feminism celebrates a new maternal Imaginary. Adrienne Rich's *Of Woman Born* questions the social construction of motherhood, making a mythical recreation of the psychic pleasures of mothering (Rich 1976). In 'Stabat Mater', her essay on the cult of the Virgin Mary, Julia Kristeva suggests that it is a twentieth-century decline in religious belief, rather than Rich's social constructions, which curtailed a language of maternity (Kristeva 1992). Kristeva goes on to argue that women need a specular identification with the mother in order to symbolise, that is, to mourn a lost object. In contemporary photographic studies, the phototherapy work of Jo Spence and Rosy Martin offers a vivid answer to Rich and Kristeva's questions. In phototherapy the camera operator (or phototherapist), through the camera, takes up the gaze of the 'good-enough' mother, one who can mirror back the reflection of the other without projecting her own distress. As Spence argues, 'after I had been through the pain and pleasure of enacting fragments of my mother's life [...] it finally felt safe enough for me to dredge up the traumatic image of the mother I had originally created' (Spence 1991, p. 236).

This creation of self-identity through maternal memories is the key theme of the work of Bracha Lichtenberg Ettinger. In *The Matrixial Gaze* and her many essays in *Differences* and elsewhere, Lichtenberg Ettinger challenges Freud's specular account of Oedipal identity in favour of a matrixial source of identity (see Chapter 1). The matrixial corresponds, she suggests, to a new, feminine, symbolic discourse of the co-existence of the maternal 'I' and infant 'Not-I'. Lichtenberg Ettinger argues that the Oedipal stage/structure, in which masculine development is the norm by which all individuals are measured, is culturally privileged. Hence we are all trapped in the language of the Phallus; the 'whole symbolic universe is unbalanced' (Lichtenberg Ettinger 1992, p. 191). In contrast, she describes matrixial (maternal) representations. Art, she suggests, can 'posit new symbols', a language of margins exploring 'holes in the discourse', perhaps like Woolf's palimpsest photographs (Lichtenberg Ettinger 1992, p. 194). Artists, Lichtenberg Ettinger claims, inscribe 'traces of subjectivity' in cultural objects, and by analysing these 'inscriptions' it might be possible, she hopes, to 'elaborate traces of another Real' (Lichtenberg Ettinger 1992, p. 196).

Lichtenberg Ettinger goes on to describe what this might mean in practice as matrixial '*joint* recordings of experience [...] emanating from the joint bodily contacts and joint psychic *borderspace*' of mother and infant (Lichtenberg Ettinger 1994c, p. 41). 'I have hypothesized that a certain awareness of a borderspace shared with an intimate stranger and of a joint *co-emergence in difference* is a feminine dimension in subjectivity' (Lichtenberg Ettinger 1994c, p. 41). 'Metamorphosis' is the 'becoming threshold' of this activity which 'alternates between memory and oblivion [...] between what has already been created and what has been lost' (Lichtenberg Ettinger 1994c, p. 45). The Monk's House albums could be read as a 'becoming threshold', as a 'borderspace' where Woolf metamorphosed her mother. The albums are matrixial encounters giving meaning 'to a *real* which might otherwise pass by unthinkable, unnoticed and unrecognized' (Lichtenberg Ettinger 1994c, p. 45).

To understand how these ideas might actually function in photography, the 'matrixial' theme of Roland Barthes's *Camera Lucida* offers precise motifs. There, memory and the mother are intimate in photography. Barthes's aim is 'to learn at all costs what Photography [is] "in itself"', and he sets out to find the derivation of those details in photographs which so please him in the present (Barthes 1981, p. 3). He characterises these photographic motifs as 'studium' and 'punctum'. The photograph is a field of study (studium) punctuated by odd details (punctum), for example, a person's bad teeth or incongruous shoes. Punctum will be present, above all, in 'biographies' or autobiographical moments. Following his mother's death, Barthes tells us, her photograph became his chief source of photographic memory. As he so memorably suggests, 'that is what the time when my mother was alive *before me* is –

History' (Barthes 1981, p. 65). Photographs are a mode of reproduction of the mother. 'I therefore decided to "derive" all Photography (its "nature") from the only photograph' (of his mother) 'which assuredly existed for me'; and Barthes gives himself to recreating what he calls its 'Image-Repertoire' (Barthes 1981, p. 75). The photographs which give us pleasure, according to him, are those which in some way revision, reinscribe or re-present the matrixial, maternal past.

It is also striking that these contemporary understandings of psychoanalytic representational processes were anticipated in part by Henri Bergson and were very current in modernism in the 1920s. The aesthetic context in which Woolf worked was shaped by Bergsonian theories of perception. In *Matter and Memory* Bergson points out that we inaccurately 'imagine perception to be a kind of photographic view', when in reality 'the photograph [...] is already taken' (Bergson 1991, p. 38, and Chapter 1 above). The past is always present. Every perception is already memory: 'There comes a moment when the recollection thus brought down is capable of blending so well with the present perception that we cannot say where perception ends or where memory begins' (Bergson 1991, p. 106).

Exploring the ways in which present perceptions interact with memory, Bergson finds 'chains' or relations between discrete percep-tions. Moments are in simultaneous interpenetration rather than isolated in time. Bergson argues that objects and forms feature in transitional moments of personal memory and that discrete moments, or percep-tions, only possess meaning in relational sequences. Although Woolf claimed in 1932 'I may say that I have never read Bergson', this (like her claim never to have read Freud until 1939, although the Hogarth Press published Freud and her brother Adrian studied with him) ignores her cultural context. In any case the impact of Bergson's ideas on Bloomsbury's aesthetics is incontrovertible. Simon Watney describes Duncan Grant's *Abstract Kinetic Collage Painting with Sound* as a framework of Bergsonian thought (Watney 1980, p. 20).

Bergson's ideas very much resemble key themes of Lichtenberg Ettinger and Barthes *avant la lettre*, and together their critical motifs provide vital clues to Woolf's photographic selections. It could be argued that the Woolfs' favourite sequences are a form of the matrixial, in a chain of perceptions. As I have described, Monk's House album 3 opens with an enlarged 6-by-7½ photograph of Julia Stephen, immediately followed by the photograph of Julia, Leslie Stephen and Virginia at St Ives in 1892 (figures 2 and 1 above). The treasured $2^1/_4$-by-$2^1/_4$ photograph, protectively mounted on buff card before insertion in the album, is made larger by the 4-by-2 card. Monk's House album 3 also contains the largest number of 'comfy chair' photographs (forty).

What is being constructed before the camera in 1892? At first glance the photograph seems to be a typical domestic interior. But details, as Barthes suggests, can be 'punctums'. The first punctum might be that Julia and Leslie Stephen in half-profile are encased side by side in a large, plush sofa with rounded arms, which looms between the camera's point of view and subjects. A second punctum is the door immediately behind Stephen's head, with its two panels in which erect flowers match the flowered wallpaper. A third punctum is the prominent bookcase and the Stephens' desire to continue reading books, uninterrupted, rather than acknowledge the presence of a camera.

The details, or punctums, of this childhood photograph appear again and again in the Woolfs' photo sequences. The photograph's authority stems both from its place, out of chronology, prefacing the subsequent sequences, and from the silent connections between photograph and sequences. The forty 'comfy chair' photographs in Monk's House album 3 were taken on different occasions in different years but are mounted synchronically. The chair is not always placed close to a light source but is a very dominating 'character' in each photograph. The synchronic matching of the St Ives and Monk's House furniture recalls Lichtenberg Ettinger's idea that the language of the matrixial is a symbolisation of the maternal, childhood home. That is, Woolf constantly repeats or mirrors this matrixial transitional object. Following Bergson, the photographic sequences could be a 'chain' of reflections in the present, reflecting the past. There is no chronology. It is as if every close friend – Ethel Smyth, Lydia and J. M. Keynes, Alice Ritchie, T. S. Eliot, Charles Siepmann, William Plomer, Rosamond and Wogan Phillips, Eve Younger, Peter and Prudence Lucas, E. M. Forster, Ann and Judith Stephen, Joan and Mrs Easdale, Roger Fry, and the deeply loved Angelica Bell and Vita Sackville-West – sit hieratically in chairs in harmony and co-emergence, as Lichtenberg Ettinger argues, with the Stephen photograph.

Additional punctums appear in other photographs. Thirteen contain a tall flower, usually a lily, or a tree placed immediately behind the head of the subject, mirroring the flowers behind the Stephens at St

August 1931

Ives (figure 12 above). In each photograph the object, like the door panels at St Ives, provides the vertical compositional line. In many cases the flower or tree uncomfortably dwarfs the subject, like a residue of the past. Perhaps not surprisingly, Virginia's recurring memory of Vita Sackville-West is of her 'stalking on legs like beech trees, pink glowing, grape clustered' (Woolf 1980b, p. 52).

Bookcases are prominent objects in the majority of photographs (nineteen) in Monk's House album 3, with its prefacing Stephen family photograph (figure 5 above). The bookcases are not simply an obvious and convenient background in a writer's home, since objects on them, as well as the books, are moved and regrouped for different photographs, often in the same day, for example, in the photo sequence of E. M. Forster (Monk's House album 3, p. 39).

The photo sequences focus attention on chairs, bookcases and flowers as well as on the face of each sitter. The sitters are elusive; their interior thoughts are not signified by self-chosen objects, for example, a favourite book or garment, as is usually the case. There is no fetishistic gaze at the sitters as objects (Mulvey 1975). Some adopt a full frontal gaze, the usual point of view of an amateur model; but most look left or right or are in half-profile, as in the photograph of Julia Stephen which Vanessa treasured. In a chapter on 'the Dead Mother' (which includes depressed and absent mothers) André Green, Julia Kristeva's analyst and teacher, suggests that the 'mirror identification' with the mother 'is almost oblig-atory' (Green 1993, p. 159). Green suggestively discusses the history of psychoanalytic concepts in relation to the arts. The mother is always an imago in the child's mind that the child engages in a kind of 'mimicry' (Green 1993, p. 151). The child is always 'recathecting the traces of the trauma' of loss in 'artistic creations' (Green 1993, p. 151). Green argues that 'the fantasy of the primal scene is of capital importance' because 'the subject will be confronted with memory traces in relation to the dead mother' (Green 1993, p. 159). The 1892 photograph of Virginia with her parents at St Ives is like a primal scene, as if Virginia and Vanessa collude, as Green suggests, in 'erotic and intense destabilization of the primal scene to the advantage of intense intellectual activity' (Green 1993, p. 160). The mother is a 'framing-structure' for the child, who projects its feelings back onto the mother through 'revivifying repetitions'.

Obviously it is impossible to say how conscious Woolf was of any of these themes, but all photographs are memories. It is the obsessive repetition of the maternal which brings Woolf into Lichtenberg Ettinger's matrixial encounter. Just as Woolf was 'very glad to have' photographs of dead friends – 'how exactly it brings him [Lytton] back!' – the Monk's House albums are a matrixial encounter with the dead (Woolf 1979, p. 16). Julia Stephen was herself an active memorialist. For example, as Leslie Stephen points out, the memorial erected to James Lowell in the Westminster chapter house (1893) 'was entirely due to her' (Stephen 1977, p. 81).

FICTION AND PHOTOGRAPHS

The figuration of the dead is a crucial trope in Woolf's novels, most famously in the 'Time Passes' section of *To the Lighthouse*, in which Woolf's technique of prosopopoeia, or personification of the dead, keeps Mrs Ramsay alive in the thoughts of others. In this novel, Lily solves the problem of visually representing the dead Mrs Ramsay by repeating objects and forms in space, as Woolf's photographs do. Elizabeth Abel suggests that Lily's painting challenges the Oedipal symbolic by repre- senting 'the simultaneity of maternal absence and presence' (Abel 1989, p. 66). Both Lily's picture and the album photographs utilise a synec- dochic visual process in which the linking spaces in the repetition become part of the representation – like Lichtenberg Ettinger's border- space, Barthes's punctum and Bergson's chain of perceptions. French feminist criticism offers, perhaps, the clearest critical account of the relationship between the maternal and forms of language. The psychoan- alytic critiques of Julia Kristeva, Luce Irigaray and Hélène Cixous all focus on the 'maternal function', which precedes our entry into the symbolic and hence into literature (Kristeva 1980; Irigaray 1974; Cixous 1975). The material bodies of mothers, the relationship between mother and infant, create psychic, subjective images and rhythms which are never lost from our unconscious, although they may be forgotten. Aspects of literary style reinscribe the maternal moment in literature.

Frequently this is described in terms of 'voiced breath' musical rhythms and other features of the mother–child symbiosis. In the Freudian model mothers have a specific function – to act as a 'castrated' being until birthing a son replaces the absent phallus. French feminists, on the other hand, argue that women's understanding of mothering has been symbolically, or socially, constructed away from the exciting and vibrant fantasy of maternal origin. A return to, or re-vision of, the mother and maternal rhythms and tones, of the semiotic element in language, could be a mechanism for subverting traditional literary representations.

The figure of a mother, or rather the difficulty of figuring mothers, is one theme of Woolf's *To the Lighthouse*. In part one of the novel, in which the window figures significantly, Mrs Ramsay comforts first child then husband:

> filled with her words, like a child who drops off satisfied, he
> said, at last, looking at her with humble gratitude, restored,
> renewed, that he would take a turn; he would watch the
> children playing cricket. He went. Immediately, Mrs Ramsay
> seemed to fold herself together, one petal closed in another,
> and the whole fabric fell in exhaustion upon itself, so that
> she had only strength enough to move her finger, in exquisite
> abandonment to exhaustion, across the page of Grimm's
> fairy story, while there throbbed through her, like the pulse
> in a spring which has expanded to its full width and now
> gently ceases to beat, the rapture of successful creation.
> Every throb of this pulse seemed, as he walked away, to
> enclose her and her husband, and to give to each that solace
> which two different notes, one high, one low, struck
> together, seem to give each other as they combine. (Woolf
> 1927, pp. 38–9)

Mr and Mrs Ramsay have different 'languages'. His is the world of 'universities and people wanting him, lectures and books and their being of the highest importance', and hers is in continuous process, with 'every throb of this pulse' making a 'rapture of successful creation' (Woolf 1927, pp. 40, 39). Mr and Mrs Ramsay are 'two different notes, one high, one low', which *seem* to 'give each other [solace] as they combine'. The long continuous paragraph shows the different ways in which Woolf manages to mark the strength and creativity of Mrs Ramsay's perceptions against what the novel reveals to be the aridity of masculine intellect. First Mrs Ramsay is represented figuratively with 'one petal closed in another', 'like the pulse in a spring', understanding gender identities in terms of 'waves' which when they 'fall' diminish the 'joy of the two notes' (Woolf 1927, p. 40). The continuous repetition of these images and Woolf's extended use of synaesthesia, or the mixing of sensations, from *within* Mrs Ramsay's point of view privileges the sensual over the symbolic. The syntactical structure of the passage privileges 'fluids' over 'solids', to utilise Irigaray's terms.

The lack of an assertive authorial presence, in French feminist thinking, creates room for the Other. In contrast to Mr Ramsay trying to complete his book by 'digging his heels in at Q' (p. 40), Mrs Ramsay is capable of a synthetic, non-linear vision. These moments exceed the symbolic boundaries of patriarchal discourse, as French feminists would argue. The recourse to multiple, indefinite pronouns, the use of silent graphic notations, allow Woolf to avoid an omniscient narrator. Nor are the events of the novel in chronological order. The discussion between Mr and Mrs Ramsay about the possibility of reaching the lighthouse begins the novel but it is not the beginning of the narrative in time. There are long passages, like the one just quoted, of subjective reflections which deviate from any linear plot. Textually, the continuous use of long sentences and intense figuration produces a sense of irregular time. The whole tonal quality of *To the Lighthouse*, Hermione Lee claims, is inflected by Woolf's memory of Cameron's photographs, and, I would add, Woolf's own photography. Frances Spalding suggests that Vanessa Bell's paintings similarly revive the maternal (Spalding 1983, p. 251). *The Nursery*, inspired by *To the Lighthouse*, has two groups of female figures contained within a circle, creating 'a nostalgic evocation of motherhood' (Spalding 1983, p. 251). Bell evokes the maternal with spatial arrangements of objects, strong verticals and monumental figures of women very like Virginia's photo sequences. Woolf's albums might be considered to be an artistic reflection of Vanessa's paintings, in that, very unusually, the albums are constructed, not from conventional albums with mounts, but from French artists' sketchbooks (the watermarks were visible with magnification) and with Woolf's experimental coloured endpapers.

It could be argued that both sisters 'refuse' their mother's death by constantly revivifying the maternal in art. Woolf writes in her first diary, 'I keep thinking of different ways to manage my scenes [...] seeing life as an immense block of material', and 'in the intervals I've been thinking a good deal about this melancholy state of impending age' and death (Woolf 1977a, pp. 214–15).

It is hardly surprising that all of Woolf's work is obsessed with visual memories. As Lyotard suggests, 'the time of writing does not pass. Every writing' (and we could include art) 'worthy of its name wrestles with the Angel and, at best, comes out limping' (Lyotard 1990, p. 34). Julia Stephen was Woolf's Angel in the house and becomes her 'stranger in the house' in the album photographs. Woolf continually wrestled with a chain of reflecting memories in photographs that mirror a familial past. They connected Woolf to the past, particularly to the matrixial. Their repeated sequences, spatially organising sitter, chair and flowers, are momentary memories of the past. Her sister's paintings taught Woolf that representations can resist death, and like those paintings, Woolf's albums are a palimpsest, 'this strange painters' world, in which mortality does not enter, and psychology is held at bay' (Woolf 1975a, p. 205).

MODERNISM, THE MATERNAL AND THE EROTIC: VANESSA BELL'S PHOTO ALBUMS

3

INTRODUCTION

In November 1896 Vanessa Stephen, then aged seventeen, wrote to her sister Virginia describing a trip to Amiens which Vanessa made together with Thoby Stephen, their brother: 'We took a lot of photographs, but we haven't had time to develop any yet. We had chocolate and rolls in our rooms at about 8.30, luncheon at 12 of about 6 courses and dinner at 7. On Saturday we went to a very improper French play' (Marler 1993, p. 6). Bell's desire to describe her photographs first, before mentioning the potentially more fascinating 'French play', suggests how important photography was to both herself and Virginia. This year, 1896, was also the one in which Vanessa began drawing classes, 'first with Ebenezer Cooke', then with Sir Arthur Cope. R. A. (Marler 1993, p. xxii). Bell's new attention to the combined visual spaces of canvas and view-finder suggest that, for her, photographs would have a far greater visual value than simply as documents of holiday moments. Indeed photography became a passionate part of her life. Throughout her entire career as an innovative modernist painter, Bell took, developed and mounted into family albums over one thousand photographs.

In what follows, I look first at the problematics of gender, modernism and domestic photography, then at the occlusion and misrepresentation of Bell's photography by art historians and her children, then at the impact of Roger Fry and Julia Margaret Cameron on Bell's work, and finally at Bell's photographs in detail and issues of objectification and the maternal.

Bell's albums, like most family albums, preserve family moments: at Charleston, holidays at Studland, Cassis and elsewhere, and portraits of family and friends. But the scale, range and constant repetition of these moments and portraits must also in some way preserve Bell's psychic and imaginative visual landscapes. In her art she crossed multiple genres: portraiture, still life, collage, murals, ceramics, textiles, book designs at the Omega Workshops, and decorations at her homes in Asheham, Charleston and Bloomsbury. Her photographs have an equivalent multi-generic quality. The democratisation of photography with the introduction of Kodak roll film cameras in 1888 produced a proliferation of family albums with more varied contents, including studio portraits alongside trade processed snapshots (Stokes 1992). Philip Stokes points out in 'The Family Photograph Album', his account of American amateur album-making, that the variety of albums suggests a 'public aspiration' to place 'instant' photographs into a continuum with 'traditional forms of art' (Stokes 1992, p. 194).

Similarly Bell's albums include blurred snapshots, photographic narratives, high art simulacrums, erotic photographs of her children and careful Expressionist portraits. Conventional art history tends to describe such diversity teleologically, as if Bell 'progressed' from inferior amateur photo to professional high art, abstract portrait. Descriptions of her as a modernist are often couched in these terms (Shone 1976). The art historian Richard Shone constructs Bell as a modernist in this way by privileging her paintings and leaving an account of her applied arts to feminist critics (Anscombe 1981; Gillespie 1988).

Even Val Williams' pioneering introduction to twentieth-century British women's photography, *The Other Observers*, similarly devalues Bell by calling her an 'amateur, snapshot' photographer and falsely claiming that she neither developed nor enlarged her work (Williams 1994, p. 79). Rather than being an 'amateur', Bell's constant devotion to a range of genres signals instead an attention to non-painterly experiences and viewpoints which could be artistically liberatory. In any case, as Pam Roberts points out in her introduction to the American photographer Alfred Stieglitz, Bell's contemporary, 'the words "amateur" and "artist" were synonymous. Only an amateur, unshackled by the chains of commerce such as bound professional photographers, had the freedom to produce truthful and meaningful work' (Roberts 1997, p. 9). As Alvin Coburn says of Stieglitz's 'Winter on Fifth Avenue', 'if you call it a "glorified snapshot" you must remember that life has much of this same quality. We are comets across the sky of eternity' (Coburn 1997, p. 599).

Bell's eclectic switching from banal snapshot to monumental portrait may not be a sign of amateur 'slippage' but rather a mark of differentiation, a way of representing her subjects and herself with other connotations than those of high art modernism alone. The family album format allowed her to hold together the aesthetic with the personal and alerts us to the gendered nature of modernism. But the very ordinariness of photo albums is precisely what makes them at once so potent as purveyors of gendered aesthetics, in the sense that albums are usually compiled by women, and so hard to read.

Like other modernist women, including Gertrude Stein and Dorothy Richardson, Vanessa Bell seems to share an interest in, and preference for, the everyday, repetitive moment, for serial forms, as much as singular works. While some critics argue that repetition is the antithesis of modernism's defamiliarisation of the everyday because repetition is an attempt to control time, Eysteinsson claims that women modernists such as Gertrude Stein turn 'repetition into a joyous mode of defamiliarization' (Eysteinsson 1990, p. 156). One of the aims of this chapter, therefore, is to move Vanessa Bell's photographs from the margins of modernism by seeing how domestic images might develop a different picture of modernism, against the grain of conventional histories, as a feminine, multi-generic space.

That the role of photography in Vanessa Bell's oeuvre is ignored or misrepresented by art historians is perhaps predictable, because domestic photography is non-canonical (Shone 1976). Art critics prefer to describe a painter's career as an orderly, developmental progress rather than as an eclectic, multi-generic mixture. But the particular choices of Bell's photographs by her children Angelica Garnett and Quentin Bell for their jointly compiled *Vanessa Bell's Family Album* is also hugely selective (Bell and Garnett 1981). The book is prefaced by an amusing, but very unrepresentative, photograph of Vanessa photo-graphing while wearing an immaculate and incongruous white hat and frilly pinafore. This image overemphasises Bell's femininity, domesticity and class at the expense of her professional artistic expertise. In his introduction Quentin Bell claims that the album provides 'a photographic record of Bloomsbury at home, Bloomsbury, as the French say, "in its slippers"' (Bell and Garnett 1981, p. 8). But both selection and picture layout are idiosyncratic and misrepresentative.

First, Bell and Garnett do not include a representative selection of the full range of Bell's differing subjects, genres and print sizes. Bell and Garnett overrepresent their own images, which occludes Bell's very eclectic and diverse photographic practices. Second, many photographs are badly cropped from the original sizes in the Tate Gallery Albums. The effect of the cropping is to distort Bell's careful artistic compositions, which often utilise space, framing and distance in novel ways. Third, Bell's more diverse representations of her close family members are reduced in Bell and Garnett's selection to particular family stereotypes. For example, Virginia Woolf appears only as a dour oddity, since Bell and Garnett deliberately choose photographs of her grim-faced. Bell and Garnett ignore a cluster of other available photographs which portray Virginia in smiling, relaxed poses, photographs which are frequently on the same album page in the Tate Gallery collection as those selected by Bell and Garnett.

For these reasons, it is particularly sad that Bell and Garnett's misconstrued family photographic narrative is adopted as an accurate representation of Bell's career by subsequent critics. For example, Val Williams characterises Bell's 'snapshot photography' as 'skilled and subtle family propaganda' (Williams 1994, p. 7). Williams anchors Bell as an amateur at the expense of engaging with the photographs' more complex psychic traces and multi-generic qualities.

What interests me about Vanessa Bell's photographs and album constructions is the possibility of finding a feminist modernism, or at the very least forming questions about such a possibility, and what Bell's undervalued photographic practices might tell us about modernist aesthetics. Domestic photography and album-making are often the prerogative of women and difficult to classify aesthetically (Spence and Holland 1991). For these reasons photo albums are at the margins of aesthetic discourse (Spence and Holland 1991). Yet taking photographs and making albums was a central activity in Bell's creative life. As a whole, her photographs employ various conventions and genres and are too slippery to fit easily into the modernist paradigm of a progressive careerist's 'experiments'. The narrative contexts of the albums and the kind of psychic stories which meta-texts like albums can tell often disrupt the authority of single photographs. Such images demand ways of reading which can draw on biography, psychoanalysis and cultural studies.

For this reason I want to try to avoid a notion of modernist individualism, of early or later Bell photographs, because this would restrict an account of her albums to the purely formal qualities of her work, such as lighting or surface composition. I want to address issues of modernism and gender in Bell's albums using a semiotic approach. Semiotics allows us to read photographs as a play of signs and images, as an outline of a story. I want to favour questions about the interaction between sexual politics and photographic processes when a woman artist looks through a camera.

Bell's photographs are mobile and expressive, ranging from monumental portraits and tableaux to erotic portraits of her children. Her photographs owe much to the influence of her great-aunt Julia Margaret Cameron, the famous Victorian photographer. There are also clear analogies between Bell's paintings and photographs. For example, her most significant paintings, *Studland Beach* and *The Tub*, were painted at the same time as she composed her most interesting photographs. There is no consistent style in the albums; she often switches sizing formats and point of view and repeats many images again and again. In brief, the albums are far too eclectic and repetitive to be neatly pigeonholed.

In a sense, Bell's very eclecticism, together with her devotion to seriality, provides a key to answering questions about gender and modernism. Domestic photography is a gendered process because it often naturalises the social attributes of femininity. What we witness in the writing of Gertrude Stein and the albums of Virginia Woolf and Vanessa Bell are the tensions of gendered modernism: the ways in which everyday reality is a necessarily more contingent force in the thinking of women artists and writers, and the ways in which this contingency might be represented artistically in repetitive as well as eclectic forms, particularly in photography.

Inevitably any art practice, whether a high art oil painting or a domestic photograph, is shaped by the dominant discourses from which it emerges. That is to say, art practices have to be in dialogue, consciously or unconsciously, with available artistic conventions and 'permitted' ideological representations. In addition, the very desire to produce art has its own psycho-class logic. To some extent Bell's albums must be shaped by her cultural milieu. Douglas Crimp claims that late 1920s modernism 'can be understood as a time of extreme conservative backlash in the arts', evidenced, he suggests, by Picasso's turn away from his radical Cubism to more traditional representations (Crimp 1992, p. 5). The preceding decade, 1910 to 1920 (a key one in Bell's photography), which that backlash attacked, witnessed more radical artistic experiments.

The two post-Impressionist exhibitions organised by the painter and critic Roger Fry, Vanessa's friend and one-time lover, deliberately challenged traditional aesthetic tastes and values and were described by Fry's contemporary, Desmond MacCarthy, as the Art Quake of 1910. The first post-Impressionist exhibition, attended by over 25,000 people, displayed a representative range of what are now regarded as the great modernists: Cézanne, Gauguin, Manet, Picasso, Roualt, Seurat and Van Gogh (Robins 1997, p. 15). Two years later, thirty-five key Futurist works were exhibited at the Sackville Gallery and the second post-Impressionist exhibition, with its eye-catching poster collectively designed by Bell, Grant, Fry and Etchells, drew 50,000 people (Robins 1997, p. 64). Together the exhibitions made modernism into an international and institutional movement. As Robins suggests, in her catalogue of the commemorative Barbican exhibition *Modern Art in Britain 1910–1914*, the paintings of Bell and Grant in particular utilised a new modernist vocabulary in their compositions, colours and formal values.

Roger Fry, together with the Bloomsbury group, created a new critical language to describe this new aesthetic world, which was visibly feminised (Tillyard 1988). As S. K. Tillyard points out, 'there was a large female contingent among the followers of Post-Impressionism', precisely because Fry's vocabulary of pattern and decoration allowed women 'to participate in the reception of the new art in a way they had never been before' (Tillyard 1988, pp. 102–3). In her own retrospective account of Roger Fry in 1934, Bell specifically remembers and celebrates Fry's democratic, accessible manner. She describes feeling 'very nervous' sitting next to Fry at a dinner because she associated him with other 'terrifying figures of about the same age', but 'I must have ventured some remark and found it listened to and understood and felt encouraged to continue' (Bell 1997, p. 118).

For Bell, the impact of the post-Impressionist exhibitions was professionally as well as personally dramatic:

> That autumn of 1910 is to me a time when everything
> seemed springing to new life – a time when all was a sizzle
> of excitement, new relationships, new ideas, different and
> intense emotions all seemed crowding into one's life [...]
> The world of painting – how can one possibly describe the
> effect of that first Post-Impressionist exhibition on English
> painters at that time? (Bell 1997, pp. 126–7)

Matisse's *Le Luxe II* inspired Bell's *The Tub* and her use of anti-naturalistic colour as well as featureless mask-like faces (Robins 1997). Similarly, Picasso's *Jars With Lemon* and Gauguin's paintings are acknowledged sources of her palette of colours and heavy outlines (Robins 1997). It would be likely that such a period of intense interest in European modernism would similarly impact on her photography. For example, Picasso's collages, his *papier collé*, might equally be a source of Bell's eclectic, free photographic compositions, just as Isabelle Anscombe argues that his collages are the sources of her Omega Workshops' marquetry (Anscombe 1981).

But while the modernist aesthetics of Fry and Vanessa's husband Clive Bell were a crucial artistic inspiration, they were, in some ways, in conflict with Vanessa's eclectic everyday vision. One of the central themes of Fry's modernism was an impulse to purify art. In *Vision and Design* he carefully distinguishes what he calls 'natural life' from the superior 'imaginative life' (Fry 1921, p. 24). Representations, according to him, have a self-contained, self-sufficient nature which could be understood through formal rules of perception. Clive Bell similarly created a history of art in which art is progressive and evolutionary, emerging into post-Impressionism (Bell 1914). In addition, Fry's and Clive Bell's devotion to pure form gave representative space only to those images 'useful as a means to the perception of formal relations and in no other way' (Bell 1914, p. 225). This shift in interest from the external world to the art product, to art rather than life, is problematic for a woman artist and photographer busy narrativising the domestic. Fry's disciplined aesthetic vision, seeking the pure experience of an art work, was resistant to narrative. But the problem, for Vanessa Bell, was one of reconciling formalism with intensely domestic and familial subjects and her recognition that photographs always refer to life beyond the image.

In a very general way, photographs, particularly portraits, represent social and psychic relations as much as formal expressive relations. The act of selecting photographs for a family album impacts on different issues from the formally aesthetic, including the significance of Bell's gaze as a camera operator and album compiler. Nor do family albums fit comfortably into the conventions of photographic theory, which tends to fetishise the individual photograph and the individual photographer. Albums are repetitive, feminine forms (inasmuch as they are most often constructed by women), not collections of seminal, masculine images (Spence and Holland 1991).

Indeed Pierre Bourdieu claims that photograph albums preserve fictional versions of the gendered world because they immortalise a false sense of the psychic and social significance of each family group, artificially *re*-presenting to a family 'the sense that it has both of itself and of its unity' (Bourdieu 1990, p. 19). In *Photography: A Middle-Brow Art*, he surveys the photographic practices of 692 people living in Paris and the provinces in terms of differences of class, education and identity (Bourdieu 1990). He finds that photographic practice, which he claims 'expresses and nourishes what we might roughly call a technical attitude to the world', is a masculine 'privilege' while the business of remembering photographic occasions, for example in albums, is generally incumbent on wives (Bourdieu 1990, p. 129). According to Bourdieu, photography is a public ritual of the domestic sphere, and he helpfully points to the ways in which album constructions are not merely technical processes but intensely gendered practices criss-crossing the binary of the public and the private – the publicly visible moment of photography and the private album consumption of that moment – always a very problematic binary for women. As Frances Spalding suggests in her biography of Vanessa Bell:

> In February 1956 the Adams Gallery in London gave Vanessa
> an exhibition which sold well. When Angelica praised the
> show, Vanessa was touched, admitting that it mattered more
> to her that her children should think her paintings good
> than anyone. She had no conception of the public and
> exhibitions were never her goal. (Spalding 1983, p. 354)

In addition, as Walter Benjamin suggests, the enlargement of snapshots (Bell's constant album activity) reveals 'entirely new structural formations of the subject' (Benjamin 1973, p. 238). Benjamin's aim – to examine how mechanical reproductions could assist 'the formulation of revolutionary demands in the politics of art' – is not of immediate relevance to Bell's work, but his view that photographic reproductions release subjectivities by revealing repressions in multiple forms offers a way of thinking through Bell's attachment to her albums, to seriality (Benjamin 1973, p. 236). As Benjamin argues, there is a 'tremendous difference' between pictures in photography and 'pictures in art', since photography consists of 'multiple fragments' (Benjamin 1973, p. 236). For example, Bell's photographs of her children match Benjamin's idea that a modernist perception involves the reciprocal gaze – 'the person we look at or who feels he is being looked at, looks at us in turn' – more than they match Fry or Bell's notion of a pure, modernist, disinterested spectator (Benjamin 1973, p. 190).

VANESSA BELL'S ALBUMS AND PHOTOGRAPHS

The significance of Bell's photography derives partly from the important place which photography occupies in her life, letters and art. Her first camera, the Frena, introduced into Britain in 1892, was a film-pack camera. The Frena's technology was difficult to manipulate and required a careful camera operator. Bell's early photographs, such as those of Queen Victoria's funeral, were not always successful: 'The Frena went wrong somehow and they (the photographs) were not even taken' (Marler 1993, p. 7). Not only were the Stephen sisters dedicated practitioners, but Vanessa and Virginia often wrote about photography. In a constant exchange of photographs Vanessa, Virginia and their women friends seem to be reinforcing their friendships and also their identities, particularly the maternal identity. Photographs helped Bell to act out her maternal role. Writing to Duncan Grant as 'Rodent' in 1919, Bell tried to bring Duncan and Angelica close to her with photographs: 'I've got some very good photographs of her [Angelica] and the other children which I'll bring up to show you' (Marler 1993, p. 232). Photographs were also an important artistic aide-mémoire. In 1938 Vanessa pleaded with Virginia: 'as for the Italian churches, etc., you meet with *en route*, I hope you're taking snaps of them. I find them more difficult to believe in than the patient spinsters' (Marler 1993, p. 445).

Bell's own discussion of the structure and syntax of repetitive photographs in her letters shows that, in her mind, photographs can be read as carefully as any other art. Thanking her daughter Angelica in 1914 for returning Vanessa's 'snap-shots', Bell conceptualises photographs: 'I see two of mine came out, to my surprise. It's a pity they aren't better focussed as the composition is rather lovely. Some of those of you feeding A. almost had the effect of cinema on me, one seemed to see the movement going on from one to another' (Marler 1993, p. 483). Like other modernists, for example James Joyce and H. D., Bell loved cinema going and was very knowledgeable about cinematic devices.

The Tate Gallery Archives in London house Vanessa Bell's ten family albums. These are a unique documentary record of her family and friends, as well as of her aesthetic and psychic interests and enthusiasms. The first album (1A) opens with photographs dated 1896 (Bell was born in 1879), and album 9 ends with photographs of Fitzroy Square, one of Bell's homes, dated 1939 (Bell died in 1961). The albums are marked by the domestic through Bell's use of handwritten captions. She carefully paginates her albums and identifies dates of composition, places and people. The layout is clear and quasi-chronological. Some captions resemble the narrative titles of contemporary commercial postcards. For example, album 1A depicts Adrian Stephen 'looking for beetles' at Manor House, Ringwood, in 1898 (Bell 1896, p. 28). Album 5 frames Leonard Woolf together with Clive Bell at Charleston in 1935, described as 'someone anointing Leonard with leaves' (Bell 1935, p. 280). As Naomi Rosenblum points out, in the 1910s and 1920s women photographers found 'genre themes particularly appealing', especially narrative genres (Rosenblum 2000, p. 100). However, the albums do not follow each other in exact chronological order, as Val Williams claims. For example, album 1 figures family scenes at St Ives and elsewhere dated 1890, preceding the 1896 date of the first album, 1A.

The scale of the collection is immense. Most albums contain over forty pages and several photographs are mounted on each page. Not all are by Vanessa Bell. She includes family photographs taken before her birth and also warmly 'invites' into her albums family photographs taken by Virginia and Leonard, as well as photographs of Angelica 'taken by Mrs. Curtis' (album 7, p. 14 onwards), photographs of Julian Bell taken by Lettice Ramsey (album 7, p. 22 onwards), a Charleston interior taken by Barbara Bagenal in 1936 (album 8, p. 20), Janie Bussy's family photographs, and Angelica in Italy 'taken by Mrs. Gledwyn Jebb' in 1935. It is tempting to read this generosity as a self-conscious deconstruction of the myth of artistic individualism. Not surprisingly, Vanessa's three children Angelica, Julian and Quentin, together with her lover Duncan Grant, are the subjects of the largest number of individual portraits. Again unsurprisingly, Virginia Woolf is photographed more frequently than Vanessa's husband Clive Bell. Although the albums' detailed captions as well as their volume of family portraits might seem to match Leslie Stephen's photograph album in its single-minded record of family 'time passing', Bell does not contextualise the present in a family past. Nor does she match Woolf's use of her mother's photograph as a frontispiece and shaping motif in album construction.

Vanessa Bell's photographs vary enormously in size, genre and quality. The most imposing are monumental portraits of family and friends such as those of J. M. Keynes, Roger Fry and Walter Sickert taken at Asheham, and Duncan Grant at Cassis (albums 2 and 3). Others, particularly those of family events at Charleston in albums 4 and 5, are small snapshots, no larger than $2\frac{1}{2}$-by-$3\frac{1}{4}$ inches, and some photographs are even of photo booth scale ($1\frac{1}{2}$-by-$1\frac{1}{4}$ inches). Bell seems less concerned with any progressive development of her photographic techniques than with making full and detailed first-hand studies of her world. Every intimate image has a precious quality. For example, of the six photographs of Angelica taken at Charleston in 1920, five are out of focus (album 5, p. 12). Bell's careful mounting of out-of-focus snapshot photographs is not a slippage from the modernist monumentality of her portraits of Clive Bell, Grant or Fry, but a recognition that Angelica's childhood is transitory rather than an idealised representation. The volume of Angelica's portraits reveals Vanessa Bell's close identification with her daughter and Angelica's role as the erotic object of Bell's gaze. As Carol Armstrong points out, in her essay about Julia Margaret Cameron, the repeated photographs of Cameron's servant Hillier represent Cameron's 'photographic gaze as much as she poses as its object' (Armstrong 1996, p. 37).

Vanessa Bell's inclusion of the out-of-focus photograph together with careful portraits suggests wider familial and historical influences. As I have said, Bell's first act, on leaving her father Leslie Stephen's family home for 46 Gordon Square, was to hang on her walls Julia Margaret Cameron's Victorian photographs of the Stephen family. Cameron, Vanessa's great-aunt, photographed many Victorian notables, including Tennyson, Browning, Longfellow and Herschel, together with family members between 1864 and Cameron's death in Ceylon in 1879. Her wet collodion process and long lens created a soft focus. In 'Annals of My Glass House', her unpublished autobiography, Cameron describes how her 'habit of running into the dining room with my wet pictures has stained such an immense quantity of table linen with nitrate of silver'

(Cameron 1996, p. 13). As it was later to do for Bell, the domestic arena provided not only the site of Cameron's photographs but also their representational co-ordinates. Looking at the prize-winning photograph in the first exhibition to which she submitted, Cameron noted 'that detail of table-cover, chair and crinoline skirt were essential to the judges of the art' (Cameron 1996, p. 13).

Cameron also compiled photographs in albums, like those of Bell and Woolf. From 1866 Cameron gave albums to family and close friends and sent others to Colnaghi, her London dealer. Although, unlike Bell and Woolf, Cameron used whole album pages for individual portraits, the purple and red ribbons with which she bound her albums are echoed in those interlacing Woolf's Monk House albums. Just as Bell and Woolf gave photographs to their family servant Sophie Farrell, so Cameron gave her nanny at Freshwater small-scale copies of photographs and pencil sketches for a scrapbook. Albums encourage a circulation of looks beyond the singular portrait.

Cameron imitated the Renaissance painting technique *sfumato*, in which outlines and tones seem 'smoky' (the meaning of the Italian term). Bell too was devoted to Renaissance painting. Both she and Cameron employ the vocabulary of Old Master paintings. It was Cameron's portrait of her niece Julia, later Bell's mother, which inspired Burne-Jones to paint Julia as a madonna. She was the subject of many Cameron portraits between 1865 and 1872 (figure 2 above). As the widow of Herbert Duckworth, Julia could represent 'the ideal of beauty through sublimity' without association to archetypes (Hamilton 1996, p. 39). Bell matched Cameron's subjects and topics, for example, photographing Angelica dressed as Ellen Terry for *Freshwater*, Virginia's play about Cameron in which Vanessa herself played Cameron. The portraits of Angelica as Sasha taken to illustrate Woolf's *Orlando* very much resemble Cameron's notable *A Study for the Cenci*, May 1868. Talia Schaffer suggests that Bell places Angelica in Eastern clothing against a muted background much like Cameron's photographs (Schaffer 1994, p. 43). Bell may also have shared Cameron's desire to represent women as heroines or poetic muses in response to Victorian gender constraints.

But Bell's photographs, particularly those of Studland Beach, are familial and autobiographically revealing in a wider sense than simply as imitations of Cameron's portraits. In *Modern Life and Modern Subjects* Lisa Tickner discusses Bell's several paintings of Studland Beach, painted

at the same time as the photographs were taken. Tickner notes 'a certain psychological intensity' in the work and suggests that Bell's abstractions and their 'perverse melancholy' entail some form of 'secondary revision' (Tickner 2000, p. 121). Tickner goes on to suggest, very convincingly, that *Studland Beach*'s dreamlike quality and its use of metaphor have to do with 'a psychic charge that links *Studland* with Julia', Vanessa's mother (Tickner 2000, p. 141). Tickner rightly points out, that, as a recent mother, Bell would be renewing her psychic contact with her mother. Encouraged by Tickner's turn from a formal reading of Bell's paintings, I feel that the photographs of Studland Beach also project psychological intensity, albeit in a way tangential to Tickner's discovery of maternal metaphors.

Two photographs vividly encapsulate this theme. Album 1, pages 38 and 40, contains photographs of Clive Bell together with Virginia, taken at Studland Beach in 1910 (figures 22 and 23). In both photographs Clive and Virginia collude with Vanessa's gaze, but both are passive. If we take the idea of each photograph as an image operative in terms of psychic signs, we can look at what the patterns and arrangements of signs might reveal about Bell. In each scene the figures almost exactly mirror each other in positionality. Both sitters have right arms parallel to their lower legs and both bend their right legs at the same angle. Such parallelism is reinforced by a pairing of shoes to the right of the frame as well as beach huts to the rear. In one photograph the raised seams of Virginia's gloves parallel the swollen veins of Clive's downward pointing hands. The deliberate parallelism of the gloves and hand suggest a psychic 'excess': as if there is something uncertain in both photographs which has to be constantly re-enacted.

In 'Perverse Spaces', an essay about fetishism, the 'gaze' and Helmut Newton's photograph *Self-portrait with wife June and models, Vogue Studio, Paris 1981*, the photography theorist Victor Burgin calls a similar parallelism in Newton's photograph 'a subsidiary and "combined figure" of chiasmus ("mirroring")' (Burgin 1992, p. 224). Burgin argues that we sometimes recognise this rhetorical structure in a photograph only 'intuitively', as in my reading of Bell's 'chiasmus' or 'mirroring' of Virginia and Clive. Such intuitive parallels, he claims, entail the opening up of the unconscious, and he describes Newton's body rhetoric as containing invisible psychic traces. Similarly Bell's photographs depict Clive and Virginia's bodies not only realistically but also indexically, as if Clive and Virginia's relationship is being unconsciously represented by Bell. Clive and Virginia's beach meeting is photographed by Bell with intense parallelism in which body gestures seem to act out a more dramatic and significant familial narrative. As in her paintings, bodies are the principal bearers of Bell's meanings. The snapshots of Clive and Virginia are particularly unsettling images because they are products of Bell's psychic feelings rather than simply a holiday record.

After the birth of Vanessa's first child, Julian, in February 1908, Clive and Vanessa interrupted their sex life and Clive began to flirt with Virginia. Hermione Lee suggests that 'from this time – May of 1908 – they began to play a game of intimacy and intrigue which lasted for perhaps two years', that is until the Studland photographs of 1910 (Lee 1996, p. 249). The Studland photographs carry this hidden psychic narrative. Bell grapples, consciously or unconsciously, with psychic dilemmas which emerge in the repetitions and patterning of each image, like Burgin's rhetorical structure. Bell shows how a photograph can represent repressed feelings and somehow through its visual field bring these into vision. Rudolf Carnap, the 1920s philosopher, one of the leaders of the Vienna Circle of Logical Positivists, calls this form 'perceived space', which, he suggests, is only comprehended 'through perception or imagination' (Carnap 1995, p. 78). He opposes 'perceived space' to 'formal space', in which relations are subject to certain formal conditions, as in Fry's modernism. Carnap developed a theory that all knowledge beliefs are derived from immediate experiences rather than from positivist science, and this theory may have influenced modernist photographers, particularly Moholy-Nagy (Yates 1995).

Like Carnap, Bell refuses to 'formalise' spatial perceptions. The ontology of the photographic image, its being or essence, dissents from constraining formality by testifying to something which cannot be spoken

Figure 23
Virginia Stephen and
Clive Bell, Studland,
1910: from the
Vanessa Bell photo
albums, Tate Archive
Reprinted by permission
of the Tate Archive and
the Charleston Trust

but cannot be silenced (Benjamin 1973). Bell's repetitive photographs allow psychic relations to be traced. As W. J. T. Mitchell suggests in *Picture Theory*, an account of the literary and textual aspects of picture theories, photographs can equally project a private point of view and materialise 'a memory trace embedded in the context of

personal associations' (Mitchell 1994, p. 301).

In other photographs Bell does adopt schemas consistent with art conventions. For example, some photographs forefront, in a sophisticated way, the surface opacity of the photographic image. Light creates figuration in Bell's photograph of Oliver Strachey, Lytton's brother, at Asheham with

a halo of light surrounding his head (album 2, p. 16). Bell deftly places her light source exactly at face level, creating chiaroscuro for the lower figure, and endows Strachey with a sacral significance, a technique common in Renaissance painting, which Bell much admired.

Other photographs make the surface texture more evident. As Orton and Pollock point out, modernism is often characterised 'as the gradual "victory" of *surface* over subject' (Orton and Pollock 1996, p. 96). In album 2, photographs of Leonard Woolf at Asheham and of Julian and Quentin taken at Seend are juxtaposed on the same page, not by association of date or subject but because all three photographs share a dominating motif of textured terrace flagstones, with family members spatially positioned to focus on the textured stone. As Vanessa revealingly wrote to Leonard about Asheham's terrace, 'it is the most gorgeous September day. Saxon, Clive and I are sitting on the terrace [...] I envy you very much in Italy now but I doubt if it's more beautiful than this' (Marler 1993, pp. 127–8).

Bell's portraits of Roger Fry and Duncan Grant display expressionist techniques. The monumental three-dimensional portrait of Duncan at Asheham in 1912 is shot from below with an expressionist point of view. Duncan turns his face to the light source, which partially bleaches facial details in favour of a more abstract figuration in profile. Expressionist art and photography abandoned literal forms of representation in favour of picturing internal as well as external processes, for example, Man Ray's photographs (Clarke 1997, p. 111). Bell's love for Grant injects an intensity into the image by means of her expressionist angles. A powerful dynamism shapes Grant's recumbent body. Portrait photographs always imply a contract between subject and photographer.

In the same album (no. 2) the painters Walter Sickert and Roger Fry pose formally at Newington in 1913, each alongside different garden pillars capped with a round ball, at opposite sides of the frame (figure 24). The photograph carefully places frame, volume and plane in tension

with the figures in a structural form. Bell creates a parallelism between Fry and Sickert's very different body shapes (Fry is tall and thin and Sickert short and stout) by using formal perspective projection. She suggests a visual counterpointing and association between the figures through her structural composition and figure positioning. In album 3 Fry

is photographed at Guildford in 1914 from a particularly low vantage point (figure 25). The photograph has a symbolic, architectural energy. Fry's face is a central mass contrasting with the lines of his chair and the garden wall. There is space and depth in these photographs, whose three-dimensional quality reveal Bell's sure knowledge of formal spacing and tone, more in line with Peter Wollen's characterisation of late modernist photography as a move towards 'hard-edge designs and clear delineations of detail' (Wollen 1978/9, p. 17).

A European tradition of figure painting clearly inflects the physical arrangement of friends and family in particular photographs. A group photograph of Julian and Pamela Fry with Julian Bell, taken at Studland Beach in 1911, centres the erect and taller Julian Fry with his companions on either side downcast, one engaged in digging (figure 26, album 2, p. 2). The tableau resembles the peasant figures in Van Gogh's *Two Women Digging* (1883) or Millet's three women gleaners in *Des Glaneuses* of 1857. The children are positioned for their compositional strengths rather than in terms of their family relationships. Bell's photograph seems unmediated. The camera is not positioned at a low or high angle of vision, and Bell does not narrow or widen her field of vision.

Other high art tableau effects occur in photographs of Vanessa herself with Quentin or Julian sitting on her lap, carefully positioned within a window frame (figure 27). The positioning and arrangement of Vanessa's clothing resemble the madonna iconography of Renaissance painting, with her elaborate dress spilling out over the edge of the frame. As Emily Dalgarno points out, in Woolf's *To the Lighthouse* Lily Briscoe is caught up in a similar 'archaic visualization of Mrs. Ramsay as a Madonna through a window' (Dalgarno 2001, p. 15). The use of this framing device is a constant leitmotif in Bell's paintings. Richard Shone suggests that 'the subject of a still life in front of a window runs through Vanessa Bell's work' (Shone 1976, p. 136). Bell reworked the motif of the window frame in her paintings of the 1920s and in *Charleston*

Garden (1933). A number of her dust-jacket designs repeat window motifs, as in the covers of *The Waves* and *Jacob's Room* (Gillespie 1988).

Family tableaux and window framing are common pictorial devices which show Bell's understanding of artistic codes. But her repetitions and enlargements of these particular photographs suggest the presence of other tensions than simply her facility in translating painting codes into photography. Why did she need to represent herself as a madonna so frequently? Why are window frames so deliberately evident? As Frances Spalding points out, the window motif 'may reflect on her need for domestic security and on the protected position from which, because of her sex and class, she viewed the world' (Spalding 1983, p. 153). As noted elsewhere, Bell treasured most of all the photograph of her mother, Julia Stephen, 'leaning against a closed window' (Spalding 1983, p. 153). In addition, Julia Margaret Cameron's major portraits are of women as madonnas. There is a constant synchronisation of the psychic, the pressure of the autobiographical, together with art conventions throughout Bell's photographs. To try to fit her repeated photographic motifs neatly within a formal modernism negates the pressure of the psychic which equally shapes her work. It is as if two languages often co-exist in the photographs: the uncoded familial together with conventions from art practice. As Roland Barthes argues in his analysis of photographic messages, photographs do create a 'free exchange' of messages. He suggests that photographs always contain 'denotation', that is, mythical uncoded messages, and 'connotation' or specific messages (Barthes 1977, p. 19). It could be argued that Bell's photographs problematise modernist connotations with autobiographical denotations.

Some of Bell's paintings flow out of her antecedent photographic experiments, and photographic figures and objects are often revived in successor paintings. For example, album 2 contains photographs of Julian and Quentin together with Irene Noel and Clive Bell, taken at Asheham in 1912, clustered around a large oval bath tub which is markedly in the foreground. The relations between figures and the tub in the photographs are repeated in Bell's painting *The Tub* of 1918, about which Vanessa wrote to Roger Fry, 'I've been working at my big bath picture and am rather excited about that. I've taken out the woman's chemise and in consequence she is quite nude and

Figure 26
Julian and Pamela
Fry and Julian Bell,
Studland, 1911:
from the Vanessa
Bell photo albums,
Tate Archive
Reprinted by permission
of the Tate Archive and
the Charleston Trust

much more decent' (Marler 1993, p. 209). While *The Tub* may draw on Matisse's *Le Lux II* as Robins claims, and Bell may have known Degas's *The Tub* (1886), Frances Spalding's more detailed observation of the painting, whose bath tub is 'so severely tilted up towards the picture plane that it creates an almost perfect circle', could be an exact description of the tub in Bell's photographs (Spalding 1983, p. 171). As Roger Fry argued, post-Impressionist painters 'do not seek to give what can, after all, be but a pale reflex of actual appearance but to arouse conviction of a new and definite reality', which in Bell's case is the new, reproductive reality of photography (Watney 1980, p. 5). For example, album 8 contains photographs of Angelica dressed in a toga-like garment in Rome dated 1935, presaging the religious iconography of Bell's Berwick church paintings, which she began in 1941. The improvised costumes and props in the Angelica photographs are more formally positioned in Bell's paintings.

BELL'S DECORATIVE WORK

Bell's photographs often acted as design fields. The album photographs detail figure positions, textures and costumes in much the same way as an artist collects swatches of fabric and makes tiny anatomy sketches in an art journal. While continuously a photographer, Bell designed book jackets, ceramics, textiles, interior decorations, costumes and murals. Inevitably her photography reflects features of these applied arts: a use of repeated motifs and a mixture of the formal with the expressive. Vanessa Bell's active enjoyment of both the domestic arts and the public world of modernist art is reflected in the careers of other modernist women artists. Many women, including Sonia Delaunay and Marie Laurencin, earned their living from the decorative arts (Perry 1995).

Bell helped Roger Fry found the Omega Workshops in 1913 to make and sell interior design objects. She was preoccupied with Omega designs during the period of her most distinctive photography. The combination of family scenes with more formally expressive photographs matches Omega's mixture of formal modernist themes and eclectic object-making. Bell liked making a fire screen because 'it's quicker than cross-stitch and it's more amusing to do' (Marler 1993, p. 144). Omega's lack of hierarchy between high and applied arts was noted by Dorothy Todd and Raymond Mortimer in their influential contemporary assessment *The New Interior Decoration* (Todd and Mortimer 1977). 'A painter of good pictures, since he conceives them primarily in terms of design, is likely to show more aptitude in planning textiles than a painter who conceives his pictures as representations of nature' (Todd and Mortimer 1977, p. 12). Bell's lack of concern with boundaries and hierarchies in art is evident, for example, in her use of the same colour palette for paintings as for interior decoration and textiles.

Bell designed rooms for Adrian and Karin Stephen, fireplaces for Virginia, furniture for Clive Bell, carpets for Beatrice Mayor, a complete Music Room for the Lefevre Galleries, carpets and panels for the cruise ship the *Queen Mary* and a dinner set for the art historian Kenneth Clark, as well as continuously decorating her own homes. Cyril Connolly's incisive comment about Bell's Music Room, installed at the Lefevre Galleries in 1932, 'a rare union of intellect and imagination', points to Bell's life-long attempt to reconcile formalism with expressivism (Shone 1976, p. 239). In an *Architectural Review* competition to redesign Lord Benbow's apartment, Bell's room design won third prize. The assessors thought that she showed 'contempt for the plan provided by Lord Benbow' but acknowledged her 'largeness of conception ... which puts it in a class apart' (*Architectural Review* 1930, p. 203).

Bell's dust-jacket designs for the Hogarth Press, including *Kew Gardens*, *The Waves*, *Flush* and *To the Lighthouse* among others, similarly experiment with the tension between structural forms and interior details. Bell's book designs would, Virginia claimed, 'be a tremendous draw' (Woolf 1976, p. 298). As Diane Gillespie points out, Bell's book-jacket designs at one and the same time are formally consistent with 'justified left margins' and have 'uneven right ones' and 'all sorts of variations from diagonals to curves' (Gillespie 1988, p. 125). Simon Watney claims that Bell's interior designs for her own home at 46 Gordon Square were similarly 'at once descriptive and starkly abstract' (Watney 1980, p. 40). The tension in Bell's photography between the formal and the expressive matches the mixture of the abstract and expressive in Gordon Square and in her dust-jackets and other designs. Decorative work in turn impacted on her paintings, making her formal transitions in oils much 'more fluent' (Spalding 1983, p. 260).

BELL'S PHOTOGRAPHS
OF HER CHILDREN

That tension between formalism and expressivity, between artistic convention and intimate autobiography, becomes immediately a more problematic issue in Bell's photographs of her naked children. Her albums contain over fifty photographs of her children naked and approximately ten in which the naked children appear with fully clothed adults. The first photographs taken at Asheham in 1913 frame Julian and Quentin Bell half turned to camera, stretching across Asheham's French windows. The photographs are strongly erotic in the sense that the children are positioned spectacularly. For example, Bell sometimes makes use of strong sunlight thrown onto both boys' semi-erect but necessarily small penises. The fleshy bodies of the children are key referents. Again and again the photographs erotically focus on details of skin, bodies and hair. The children collude with Bell as camera operator. Frequently Julian looks intimately and directly to camera. There is an implied exchange of looks, preventing a closure of the photograph on itself. These photographic moments are reciprocal and intersubjective. Bell's photographs were unusual for the 1920s, a time when most photographs of children were taken in studios.

A fresh and powerful engagement with issues of childhood in literature, the arts and education marks Bell's moment of modernity. As Fineberg points out, there were many exhibitions of child art at the turn of the century, and artists looked at how children draw 'as a stimulus to their own work' (Fineberg 1997, p. 5). The American photographer Alfred Stieglitz promoted an exhibition of children's drawings in 1912 at his Little Galleries, Fifth Avenue, which, a contemporary claimed, 'was like a commentary on modern art ideas, it recalled some elemental qualities that art has lost and which might do much, if attainable at all, to imbue it with a fresh and exquisite virility' (Hartmann 1997, p. 644). In 1917 Roger Fry wrote articles and exhibition catalogues promoting children's drawings collected by their tutor Marion Richardson, and noted the similarities between children's art and modernist ideals of individual creativity (Fry 1921). Almost all the modernist movements, including 'expressionists, cubists, futurists and the artists of the avant-garde Russian movements[,] all hung the art of children alongside their own pioneering exhibitions in the early years of the century' (Fineberg

1997, p. 5). Modernist photography shared this enthusiasm. For example, Edward Weston made nude studies of his children, most notably *Torso of Neil* in 1925. Although, unlike Bell, Weston makes a studio portrait, it too documents the 'bodily existence of a much loved son' (Dimock 2000, p. 71). Both Weston and Bell detail the sensuality of torsos, 'the soft delicacy of skin stretched tautly over belly' in close framing (Dimock 2000, p. 71). Clarence White placed naked boys in classical settings in his *Boys Wrestling* (1908) and Alice Boughton made nude compositions of children in *Nude* (1909). White, like Bell, was considered to be an amateur: 'His early environment [...] a clerkship in a store offered neither encouragement nor impediment to his artistic development', but led him in 'directions opposed to the current traditions of photography. Thus he levelled his camera directly toward the light [...] there is never a suggestion of exploiting the sitter' (Caffin 1997, pp. 425–6). In the 1890s Sarah Sears, the American photographer and artist, also influenced by Cameron, frequently photographed her daughter Helen nude as well as in elaborate costumes (Hirschler 2001). But, as Erica Hirschler points out, although women artists were encouraged to portray their children, this was 'both a trap and an opportunity. Children were seldom the subject of important public commissions' (Hirschler 2001, p. 110).

The physical and mental wellbeing of children were key issues of concern to educationists at the beginning of the twentieth century. 'Mothercraft' was introduced into the English language in 1907 by Dr John Sykes, founder of the St Pancras School for Mothers, in his concern for infant mortality (Rose 1994, p. 132). An increase in state aid to schools in the first decades of the century underpinned a new state educational policy on language. J. M. Barrie's *Peter and Wendy* was published in 1911, by which time *Peter Pan* had become 'a universally acclaimed cultural phenomenon', and itself had an authorised school edition in 1915 (Rose 1994, p. 67). Women writers shared this ongoing interest in child psychology and development. Five of Alice Meynell's twelve books of essays, in particular *The Children* (1897) and *Childhood* (1913), 'invoke a behavioural rhetoric' close to contemporary child psychology (Frawley 1997, p. 35): 'But even the naughty child is an individual, and must not be treated in the mass' (Meynell 1930, p. 235). Vanessa Bell shared Alice Meynell's unsentimental view of childhood, just as Meynell shared Bell's interest in Julia Margaret

Cameron's photographs; Meynell wrote an introduction to the 1904 exhibition of Cameron's work (Howard 1990).

Bell was herself interested in early childhood development and education and attempted to set up and teach a nursery school at Charleston. Together with Clive Bell, Vanessa painted a nursery at 33 Fitzroy Square, exhibited in December 1913, which incorporated large, Matisse-like animal reliefs flowing across ceiling and walls. Bell's letters reveal her deep understanding of modern theories about child rearing and the value of play. Writing to Virginia in 1918 with instructions for the care of Julian and Quentin while Vanessa was to give birth to Angelica, Vanessa pressed Virginia to cook 'plain' food and to allow the children their own natural state of being:

> They'll be quite contented alone all the morning if they may have pencil and paper and a book or two. You needn't bother about them at all. Any small objects they can pretend are armies, such as peas or beans, or cards, will keep them happy for hours, too. Everything will be new to them and it's good for them to be left to themselves a good deal. [...] They're really very independent and have lots of games of their own. (Marler 1993, p. 224)

Bell's description of her children mimicking the adult world of armies with peas and beans with unspoilt innocence matches the tension in her photographs between eroticism and innocence. But the first and most important thing to say about Bell's photographs of the naked Julian, as well as those of Quentin and Angelica, is that Bell only begins to photograph her son naked not, conventionally, as an infant but as a young male child. It might be argued that the absence of naked baby photographs in her albums could be simply a result of historical circumstance. For example, very young children were at that time fully dressed for outdoor play on the beach or in the garden, the most likely places for a photography technically dependent on strong light sources. Yet the eroticism of these photographs is pronounced. In album 2, page 37, there are photographs, taken from the rear, of the naked Julian alone spread-eagled across the French windows at Asheham (figure 28). Julian's face is obscured, emphasising the specular quality of his to-be-looked-at, young, firm body. These photographs disturb the viewer perhaps because Julian

is clearly posing artificially while the camera details his unblemished skin. The use of natural light emphasises the nuanced physicality.

Other powerful photographs dated 1913, again taken at Asheham, place Julian in chiaroscuro, half-hidden under a shadow of dappled leaves just touching his penis (figure 29, album 3, p. 24). Sunlight falls on Julian's belly and his face is partly in shadow. The photograph does forefront what Abigail Solomon-Godeau calls a typical erotics of the fragmentary. That is to say, the photograph isolates parts of Julian's body in a sexually coded way – a common convention in pornographic photography (Solomon-Godeau 1991). Two slightly later photographs continue to utilise these devices. In one Julian stands, legs apart, pensively looking downwards away from camera, while sunlight falls fully on his naked figure (figure 30). The Tate catalogue dates this as 1913, but it is dated 1914 in album 3, page 11. In the other Julian and Quentin are rolling naked together on the lawn with Julian poised over Quentin, lips distended as if to kiss (figure 31, album 3, p. 12). The whiteness of both boys' bodies gives each child a further to-be-looked-at, specular quality.

Such photographs evoke what Jacqueline Rose describes as 'the necessary presence of the one who is watching' (Rose 1994, p. 3). In a later photograph of Angelica's friend Judith Bagenal (album 5, p. 5, Cassis, 1928), the naked Judith is photographed lying stretched out on her side on top of a short wall, her arm obscuring her face (figure 32). She is objectified, 'available' as it were to a spectator's gaze as an erotic nude form. The combination of chiaroscuro in the photograph and Bagnell's hidden face distances her. She is not contextualised in any way as a social being, since Bell obliterates any specificity of objects or clothes.

Quentin Bell remembers the chemist Boots' refusal to print Bell's photographs: 'would Mrs Bell please mark those rolls of film which contained images unsuitable for the eyes of the young ladies' (Bell and Garnett 1981, p. 10). But the sequencing of photographs suggests a more complex mixture of personal, ideological and artistic pressures. For example, Julia Margaret Cameron's view was that 'children play the roles of erotic boys', and her photographs 'My Grandchild Archie' (1865), with the infant's bare bottom, and 'The Return After Three Days' (July 1865) have children in poses similar to those chosen by Bell (Armstrong 1996, p. 119).

The album contexts of Bell's photographs provide a term of reference different from voyeurism. By placing different shots of her children taken at different moments onto the same page, she makes sequence and narrativity an important feature of her albums. She does not necessarily select the most compelling, singular

image of each naked child, although, as an artist, she could be thought to have a vested interest in careful selections, but constantly juxtaposes the erotic portrait with out-of-focus snapshots or with photographs of herself posing together with her children. Such album juxtapositions and constant repetitions problematise the issue of spectatorship and, to some extent, recuperate the erotic or at least place it in a more conventional context. Like other modernist women, Bell turns away from the unique, 'pure' image to repetition, as if to make her art part of a natural, everyday, non-hierarchical world.

The 1990s dramatically highlighted issues about representations of children's naked bodies and how we should spectate or not spectate such bodies. The problematic issue of spectating naked children currently occupies many disciplines, including psychoanalysis and legal studies as well as art history. The publicity given to cases of child sexual abuse, to film censorship and media representations, for example, the association between the killing of the child Jamie Bulger in Britain and horror video viewing, occurs in a context of a right-wing backlash against aesthetic libertarianism. In this context any photograph of a naked child taken in intimacy becomes a fantasy of violation, while at the same time sexualised bodies are increasingly on public display in advertising.

Many contemporary women photographers also frequently use their own and friends' children as naked models, such as Sally Mann and Alice Sims (against whom obscenity charges were lodged in 1988) (Rosenblum 2000, p. 264). Sally Mann photographs the daily lives of her three children in intimate poses and scenes, such as a wet bed or her girls' mimicry of women's make-up and appearance. The children's naked presences are substantial and full of vitality. They are self-possessed, caught with an 'utterly characteristic thought' in collusion with the mother as camera operator (Price 1992, p. 79). Marianne Hirsch notes how the 'fictions Mann creates with her children's collabo-ration, enhanced by the archaic-looking quality of her prints and the old-fashioned large-format camera she uses, evoke profound cultural fantasies of an innocent, "natural" childhood' (Hirsch 1997, p. 152). Hirsch acknowledges the paradoxical way in which children can be represented as self-absorbed in childhood fantasy and also mediators of unsettling and sensational cultural representations, a paradox which, I have argued, similarly informs Bell's photographs (Hirsch 1997, p. 152). Hirsch agrees that photographing one's own children must entail, as I have suggested, the photographer's self-representation and the family's unconscious optics. Pursuing Daniel Stern's notion of a familial intersubjectivity in his *The Interpersonal World of the Infant*, Hirsch argues that Mann's children reflect Mann's own maternal subjectivity. Yet although Hirsch appreciates the intersubjective qualities of Mann's images, Hirsch is daunted by Mann's unwillingness to 'include herself or her husband in any of her images', and suggests that what we see in the photographs are Mann's own transgressive emotions, the 'fears of her own exposure' (Hirsch 1997, pp. 164–5).

However, Sally Mann also produces tableau effects in which, as Naomi Rosenblum points out, 'the management of collodion and albumen materials mimics the sometimes clumsy handling of the same processes by Julia Margaret Cameron' (Rosenblum 2000, p. 281). In addition, Mann's photographs, like Bell's, 'explore the nature of family love, *maternal* love and child response' precisely through sequencing. The images are edited in books which reveal the developmental processes of childhood (Price 1992, p. 80). The images are corporeal, but their sequencing and development produce scripted narratives of childhood rather than voyeuristic distancing. Similarly, Bell's children are clearly comfortable in her world. Bell documents the ever-changing days of her children at play: on the beach, in Charleston pond, acting with sticks as swords (figure 33, album 4, Charleston 1919). She also photographs the children absorbed in their own activities, in their own self-absorbed lives. The juxtaposition of sometimes out-of-focus snapshot with erotic portrait unsettles the erotic gaze. It was Freud who argued that childhood narcissism is at first an innocent Imaginary. Laurence Rickels suggests that, for Freud, narcissism only becomes 'a logic of inversion' through the interventions of 'internal institutions or courts...for example, dream censor' (Rickels 1988, p. 361). Bell's photographs of childhood narcissism

Figure 30
Julian Bell, Asheham, 1914: from the Vanessa Bell photo albums, Tate Archive
Reprinted by permission of the Tate Archive and the Charleston Trust

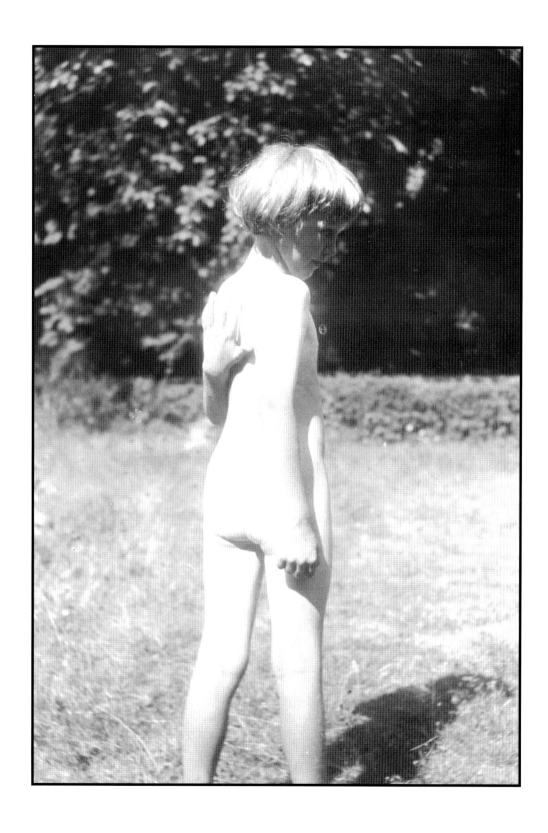

could as easily be read as reflecting back to the child the narcissism he or she so earnestly desires and needs to perform. As Jacqueline Rose argues in the context of writing, 'it is a way of "knowing" the child. Loving the child and knowing the child – the idea is one of an innocent attachment' (Rose 1994, p. 20). Bell photographs reciprocal moments, interconnections between her children and between herself and her children, what

anthropologists would call the intersubjective moment. Where Sally Mann often represents her children as 'white trash', with trailer-park and Lolita-like codes, Bell is present with her children in a number of images. Victor Burgin notes a similar device at play in Helmut Newton's photograph and argues that Newton's lack of a 'framing edge' and jumble of visual elements is 'counterproductive to fetishism' (Burgin 1992, p. 238). Where fetishism demands coherence, Burgin argues, Newton's image is a '*mise-en-scène*, a staging, of the fundamental incoherence of sexuality' (Burgin 1992, p. 238).

As I read them, Bell's photographs are innocently erotic because she portrays the children *as* children, complete with their dirtiness, their awkward gestures and pretences at adulthood, even if the sheer saturation of their bodies moves in another direction. There is no soft focus, no glycerine, no muslin obscuring their world. Bodies are not isolated in tight spaces, subjected to harsh illumination or to an unreturnable gaze. In addition, Bell firmly believed in a child's artistic vision: 'If we could see our end clearly at the beginning as children do – and state it, and leave it – our pictures would no doubt be as lovely in technique as are those of the old painters in fresco' (Bell 1997, p. 165). And in her photographs it is children, not adults, who have an active gaze, for example, in the photograph of a naked Angelica standing next to the fully clothed Roger Fry (figure 34, album 4, p. 57, Charleston 1926). Angelica looks actively at Fry while Fry is carefully *not* observing the naked girl. The photograph does not centre any implied relation between clothed adult male and naked girl, since Fry avoids the gaze. Kaja Silverman describes how, psychoanalytically, the mother–daughter relationship is one of identification and desire and the endless interchangeability of their positions (Silverman 1988). Reading Bell's photograph from within Silverman's framework, it could be said that the photograph shows the possibility of interchangeable subject–object viewing

123

positions, with Angelica *substituting* for Bell, rather than Bell's voyeurism. Vanessa might be describing Angelica as an erotic stand-in for herself in a letter to Roger Fry in 1923: 'I send you a photograph of myself and Angelica to remind you at any rate that there is *one* very lovely *and* witty *and* brilliant *and* charming creature to be seen in Gordon Square' (Marler 1993, p. 273).

There is a harmony of counterpoint in the photograph, achieved by Bell's careful spatial composition, which brings the two figures into a visual dialogue. The photograph is frontal. Bell brings Angelica and Fry visually towards the foreground into an area of potential intimacy, but keeps each sufficiently apart. The contrapuntal difference of the naked Angelica and fully clothed Fry is balanced by their opposite relation to Bell's point of view. Modernism offered Bell aesthetic co-ordinates, and by aestheticising the potential voyeurism of camera/spectator she is able to handle the potentially erotic scene safely.

CONCLUSION: GENDER AND MODERNISM

Vanessa Bell's photographs seem to function simultaneously as creative prequels to paintings, as formal artistic representations in themselves, and as autobiographical and emotive expressions of her psychic and family concerns. These functions are not necessarily antinomic to each other, but they reveal the tensions of a woman modernist. Bell's albums are marginal to conventional art history but a particularly pertinent site of the struggles between the public and the private, between the formally expressive and the everyday moment, which occur in other modernist women's work.

Vanessa Bell's photography brings into modernism's formalism the autobiographically repetitive and other identifications. As Luce Irigaray suggests, identification 'is never simply active or passive, but rather frustrates that opposition by the economy of repetition that it puts "into play"' (Irigaray 1974, p. 77). Bell's everyday, 'playful' world with her children at Charleston interacts with modernist aesthetics in her work, not only in terms of subject matter (the albums' mixture of formal monumental portraits with expressive snapshots) but in each album's

125

composition in itself. She weaves together her public and private aesthetics through repetition. She frequently doubles photographs in serial layouts as much as she 'fixes' the formal portrait. For example, album 3 contains repeated photographs of Lytton Strachey taken at Asheham in 1913. Differently dated photographs of Adrian Stephen are juxtaposed with those of Lytton on the page, not because the photographs are compositionally similar but as if Vanessa is consciously constructing a relationship between family and friends by means of repetition. By the 1930s, she experiments with David Hockney-like cut-ups in her albums, superimposing a photograph of Eve Younger on one of Adrian and Karin boating at Thorpe-le-Soken to suggest a similar viewpoint. As Moholy-Nagy, the prolific theorist and practitioner of modern art in the 1920s, argues, the superimposition of photographs can be utilised to personalise the formal as a 'visual representational form of dreams' (Moholy-Nagy 1995, p. 155). 'Space', first published in *Von Material Zu Architektur* in 1929, describes these freer forms of space articulation (Moholy-Nagy 1995). The power of assemblage is a distinctive feature of modernist art but assemblage in photo albums also allows, as Moholy-Nagy suggests, the 'simultaneous penetration of inside and outside' to integrate 'everybody's daily routine', concomitant with modernist women's views of art and life (Moholy-Nagy 1995, p. 155).

Bloomsbury modernism did go some way to try to accommodate both the notion of pure form and expressive discontinuities. For example, Roger Fry's 'An Essay in Aesthetics' describes both 'the unity in a picture which results from a balance of a number of attractions presented to the eye simultaneously' and 'successive elements' which can also have a 'fundamental and harmonious relation' (Fry 1921, p. 22). Yet Bell's photographs illustrate a further tension that is also present in the work of other women modernists: the tension between the artist and the amateur when the everyday feminine forces its way into conventions of artistic formalism. There was, Bridget Elliott and Jo-Ann Wallace claim, a similar, if differently focused, tension in Bell's paintings:

Figure 33
Quentin and Julian Bell, Charleston, 1919: from the Vanessa Bell photo albums, Tate Archive
Reprinted by permission of the Tate Archive and the Charleston Trust

> This sense of what we are calling a double marginality – Englishness in a modernist art world which looked to Paris, and femininity in a patriarchal avant-garde – operated throughout

Bell's painting, particularly in her self-representations as an artist during the period from 1910 to 1920, the period in which Bell was engaged in her most experimentally avant-garde work.
(Elliott and Wallace 1994, pp. 81–2)

The years 1910–20 were also the period of Bell's most eclectic yet powerfully creative photographs and album-making. From a feminist perspective, it could be argued that Bell perhaps turned so frequently to photography because it allowed her the freedom of duality. While paintings also contain multiple meanings, albums in particular are by definition intensely personal; at the same time, Bell's albums contain experimental portraits offering a testing site for her to judge the 'significant form' of her subsequent paintings. Her combination of the repetitive personal with the avant-garde makes her albums a representative site of gendered modernism. As Roger Fry argued in his 1922 review of Bell's Independent Gallery exhibition, 'She follows her own vision unhesitatingly and confidently, without troubling at all where it may lead her. If the result is not very legible, so much the worse [...] she realises it is only the unconscious charm of the gesture which counts in the end' (Fry 1922, p. 237).

MODERNISM, CINEMA, GENDER AND *BORDERLINE*

4

INTRODUCTION

'Modernity realized itself in and through the cinema' (Hansen 1995, p. 363). As Miriam Hansen argues, the industrialisation of art, most notably the invention of cinema, is a quintessential modern development. Equally, the main features of modernity, its mass urban subjectivities and new modes of perception, mark modernism's artistic strategies and new technologies of perception and representation. In *Modern Life and Modern Subjects*, Lisa Tickner suggests that modernism in the arts was very heterogeneous in its response to modernity, embracing artists such as the Futurists who engaged 'with urban subject matter' and others, including Kandinsky and Vanessa Bell, 'who appeared, at least indifferent' (Tickner 2000, p. 184). But the *modernisation* of art, such as the development of avant-garde international audiences, did create distinctive communities of artists, film-makers and critics.

The pivotal decades of twentieth-century modernist art, from Roger Fry's 1910 Post-Impressionist Exhibition to the end of the Harlem Renaissance in the 1930s, are also the decades of the founding of the influential London Film Society, the major avant-garde film journal *Close Up*, and the flourishing European cinema of Sergei Eisenstein, G. W. Pabst and Carl Dreyer. Just as the invention of cinema is part of other technological and cultural changes that characterise modernity, so too cinema encouraged changes in modernist aesthetics (Friedberg 1993, p. 163). Although early, like later, cinema could be often drama-led, shaped by literary narratives and mimetic conventions, such as *The Pickwick Papers* (1913), modernism's fluid points of view and decentring of subjectivities match cinema's more innovative disruption of chronology and fascination with new subjectivities (Rado 1994). While modernity comprises both material and cultural experiences and modernism is usually characterised as aesthetic practices expressive of modernity, writing about cinema, in particular, enabled intellectuals to 'come to terms with the traumatic impact of modernization' (Hansen 1995, p. 366). For example, Walter Benjamin began his revelatory project on the Paris Arcades in the same year as *Close Up*'s first edition.

The Little Magazine is an overview of the contribution made by small journals to the development of modernist writing (Hoffman, Allen and Ulrich 1946). Although the book focuses on male modernists, notably Ezra Pound, it does point out that in the first half of the twentieth century more than six hundred little magazines focusing on the arts and cinema were published (Hoffman, Allen and Ulrich 1946). In France, the influential film journal *Le Film* was founded in 1914, and by 1925 there were six French periodicals devoted to cinema. By 1929 forty-eight Parisian and twenty provincial periodicals had regular film columns (Friedberg 1983). In Britain, Ivor Montagu and Iris Barry mirrored the ciné-clubs of France by founding the London Film Society in 1925. Societies offered not only exhibition spaces for independent films but also practical advice such as lectures on film techniques. Ken Macpherson's journal *Close Up*, which began publishing during the early years of the London Film Society, quickly gained a pre-eminent place in European avant-garde circles. Although the numbers of individual subscribers remained low, the international range of its correspondents included Eisenstein as well as the women writers H. D., Bryher, Dorothy Richardson and Gertrude Stein. Just as the technical term 'close-up' means enlarging the subject at the expense of long-shot, so the journal broadened the subjects of film analysis. Alongside critiques of national cinemas and new cinematic techniques, the journal attacked censorship and promoted alternative networks of ciné-clubs as well as developing film theory.

In the 1920s and 1930s serious cinema debates appeared in the popular media. The *Daily Mail*, *Vanity Fair*, the *Adelphi* and *Vogue* all contained regular film reviews. These decades also witnessed an intense involvement in cinema and film theory by European and American émigré avant-garde writers and artists, including James Joyce and Picasso, as well as British and European left-wing critics. H. D. and Bryher, Macpherson's co-editors and owners of *Close Up*, together with the British critics Herbert Read, Oswell Blakeston and Paul Rotha, shared an enthusiasm for international film as well as a distrust of Hollywood commercialism. All were busily creating a new, modernist cinema aesthetic informed by the Soviet film experiments of Eisenstein and Pudovkin in order to short circuit the commercial allure of Hollywood. All addressed a wider, democratic world which included film clubs, avant-garde publications and cinema's most avid audiences – women and children.

Matching the ever-increasing numbers of female participants in the commercial venues of department stores and cinemas in the 1920s, women writers enjoyed a new visibility in the intellectual world of cinema journals. Modernist women founded several small journals: Bryher financed *Close Up*, and women writers, including Colette, Dorothy Richardson and H. D., were regular contributors to film journals as well as to film practice. H. D. helped to script and act in Ken Macpherson's film *Borderline*. Colette acted in and scripted several films. Nor did women writers such as Colette isolate film from other artistic experiments. For example, in her catalogue of an exhibition by the French artist Emilie Charmy, Colette noted parallels between her own film style and Charmy's democratic, painterly sensuality (Perry 1995).

The convergence of experimental film, the new institutional freedoms of small journals and ciné-clubs shaped by a radical anti-establishment aesthetic, created an intellectual space apparently welcoming to women. But although these new cross-fertilisations of modernism crossed the boundaries of nations and media, men and women did not equally share such a culture. Just as going to the cinema was a more quotidian experience for women than for men, so women's cinema writing focuses on the everyday world of women's spectatorship and has a very different, autobiographical quality from the authoritative distancing of popular audiences by male writers. If literary modernism, as Andreas Huyssen argues, was veined by masculinity in the 1920s, so too masculinity shaped cinema modernism (Huyssen 1986). Just as it is often argued that the poets Ezra Pound and T. S. Eliot sometimes share a hard, objective polemics, so too the articles of film critics Oswell Blakeston and Ken Macpherson project a tough, anti-sentimental rhetoric (Vanacker 1997).

Before looking in more detail at modernist women's criticism and women's place in the complex cultures of cinema modernism, this chapter will examine the context of cinema modernism in general, including issues of commercialism and censorship, as well as the cinema writing of the male modernists Ken Macpherson, Herbert Read and others. Rather than constructing an essentialist binary between masculine and feminine textual practices I hope, by examining the problematic relation between aesthetic text and cultural constraints, to see how cinema modernisms might be differently inflected for women and for men. All representations are gender-inflected by institutional and historical practices, albeit in sometimes subtle ways.

FILM CULTURES, ART AND PHILOSOPHY

The film criticism of the 1920s, like any other representation, had a particular location. Contributors to cinema journals were very aware of, even obsessed by, issues of cultural location and sometimes contributors' self-chosen marginality. For example, Ken Macpherson's monthly editorial 'As Is' in *Close Up* consistently 'Othered' the commercial spaces of Hollywood and London from his cosmopolitan, avant-garde eyrie in Switzerland, demanding an alternative cinema exhibition system and avant-garde culture. The term 'avant-garde' rather than 'modernism' (a more retrospective, literary term) is usually given to the key historical formations between the early years of Cubism and the collapse of Soviet experimentation in the 1930s (when *Close Up* ceased publication) (O'Pray 1996). Peter Bürger's classic account, *The Theory of the Avant-garde*, characterises avant-garde as including any experimental film, art, photography and theatre which claims artistic autonomy from bourgeois nationalisms, censorship and commercialism (Bürger 1984). However, Bürger draws his conclusions from a study of artistic content and skirts discursive issues. Nor does he pay attention to institutional issues such as the role of small, independent journals like *Close Up*, or to the cultural impact of technology (Giles 1993; Eysteinssen 1990). But to characterise avant-garde as experimental art and modernism as a literary form is less than helpful for understanding gender discourses, as well as the larger historical and perceptive realities impacting on language.

There is an argument for making avant-garde and modernism more permeable as a shared structure of feeling. During these formative decades cinema writing crossed the disciplinary boundaries of psycho-analysis, film theory, a pubescent sociology of the mass media and aesthetics. Although it could be argued that such interdisciplinarity functioned largely within a traditional European modernist geography of

London, Paris and Berlin, cities with well-established artistic milieux, film writers were hugely antagonistic to such Eurocentric fixities. For example, *Close Up* devoted several articles to Indian and Japanese cinema and crossed other borderlines, addressing the mixture of music and fine art in the work of Hans Richter and Salvador Dali as well as modernist theatre. It is true that Strindberg's *Dream Play* displays filmic images and technical processes such as dissolves just as in the novel, Dorothy Richardson, James Joyce and Virginia Woolf created shifting viewpoints and stream of consciousness to represent time and subjectivity fluidly, in processes more akin to cinema than naturalistic narrative (Corrigan 1983). In turn, Eisenstein's theories of cinematic montage and dialectical narrative were a 'means of keeping faith with avant-garde ideas' while Eisenstein was actively making revolutionary subjects for a new Soviet world (Roberts 1998, p. 19).

In some ways, film writing was immediately more responsive to these new interdisciplinary perceptions than some strands of modernist art. For example, the British modernist group Unit One, which included the artists Ben Nicholson, Paul Nash and sculptor Barbara Hepworth, forswore involvement in film. Film criticism, on the other hand, was in intensive dialogue with the arts and with philosophy. *Close Up* discussed French surrealism as well as Man Ray's cinema experiments. Film writing attracted critics from other specialisms who were eagerly examining representations of subjectivity, for example, the psychoanalysts Barbara Low and Hanns Sachs regularly contributed to *Close Up*.

Film theory took up a range of issues in these decades: the significance of new distribution systems such as ciné-clubs, Hollywood's increasingly hegemonic control of film economies, psychoanalytic ideas of subjectivity; the new perspectives of science and science films, issues of censorship, and national cinemas and race identity. But by far the most frequently debated issue was how film could approximate art and the potential interrelation between avant-garde art and film. For example, Picasso was an avid film goer who toyed with the idea of representing movement cinematically as early as 1912 (Lawder 1975). Avant-garde film was also seen as emblematic of new modernist psychological perceptions. Art films' dissolution of narrative cause and effect resembled Freud's psychology of dreams rather than narrative literature's more naturalistic representations of character. The artist Hans Richter recalled: 'we seemed to have a new problem on our hands, that of continuity, and the more we looked, the more we realized that this new problem had to be dealt with' (Lawder 1975, p. 43). Richter's solution were the art works *Preludium* and, with his collaborator Viking Eggeling, *Horizontal-Vertical Mass*. In these pioneering drawings Richter and Eggeling created connective relationships between images analogous to cinema's montage techniques. Richter's subsequent film *Rhythmus 21* used the cinema screen as a direct substitute for the painter's canvas in order to organise kinetic plastic forms better. Although, as Lawder suggests, these works reveal the limitations of Cubism as an organising structure for film, Richter, Eggeling and Léger, among others, were radically transforming film–spectator relationships with technological effects such as kinetic speed and simultaneity (Lawder 1975).

Several experiments were made in the 1920s to create films without sequential narrative. The Surrealists and Dadaists subverted temporal representation by mirroring dreams and the absurd. For example, the surrealist film *La Coqueille et le Clergyman* (1927) by Germaine Dulac uses quick editing to project a sense of inner consciousness. As early as 1919, Man Ray's painting *Admiration of the Orchestrelle for Cinematograph* anticipated his films *Emak Bakia* (1926) and *L'Etoile de Mer* (1928). Ray uses film in a painterly way to develop aspects of art, particularly light, which could not be fully represented two-dimensionally. Although, as Deke Dusinberre argues, Man Ray elevated the status of avant-garde film by associating film with his art, Man Ray was not specifically interested in film techniques in themselves but only in how they could extend his painterly repertoire (Dusinberre 1996). The nexus of film and art was institutionally recognised in the Exposition de l'art dans le cinéma Français at the Musée Galliere in Paris in 1925. By the second half of the 1920s (the moment of *Close Up*), experimental independent art films were regularly screened by the international cinéaste movement throughout Russia, France, Germany and Britain.

Yet, as Laura Mulvey points out, the number of women filmmakers can be 'counted on the fingers of very few hands' (Mulvey 1996, p. 202). Although women had more impact in avant-garde spheres than elsewhere, the significant achievements of modernist cinema are all largely by men. For example, Germaine Dulac's poetic cinema impacted much more on 1970s women's art than on the art of her contemporaries (Mulvey 1996).

Film culture also stood in a specific, if not always explicit, relationship to the new cultural modernities of early twentieth-century philosophy. Cinema and philosophy were both self-consciously asking how perception is experienced and known. The elastic, decentred, multi-dimensional sense of time and subjectivity shared by art and film drew on the influential ideas of the philosopher Henri Bergson. In *Time and Free Will* (1889) and *Matter and Memory* (1896), he argues that memory 'spreads out its recollection over a wider surface' to give the remembrance 'a proper place' in an image resembling cinematography (Bergson 1991, p. 171). Bergson strove to comprehend life processes as 'holistic complex and dynamic continuities rather than as data collection' (Burnwick and Douglas 1992, p. 224). He described a new way of spatialising time, in which time became a continuous spatial process (see Chapter 2), and his impact on modernist thought was substantial. In just two years, from 1909 to 1911, over '200 articles on Bergson appeared in the British press alone' (Burnwick and Douglas 1992, p. 3).

Bergson's theories of perception and experience matched film's new representations, particularly avant-garde film's address to a more active spectator. He often couched his theories about the relationship between memory and present time in intensely visual images. He describes the perception of memory and knowledge as a process analogous to modernist film and art. For example, the way in which we use memory to recall the past, according to Bergson, is by means of a series of 'snapshot' views (Bergson 1991, p. 107). 'Perception is a circuit', he claims, and in a circuit 'we put the right detail and the right coloring by projecting onto its memories' (Bergson 1991, p. 107). His ideas about memory, perception and the Imaginary exactly capture the epistemological possibilities of modernist cinema. In short, both modernist art and philosophy shared cinema's ambitious project to refashion representations of subjectivity and time.

Aesthetic change also meshes in complicated ways with economic and social change. Independent film and film writing might share a new philosophical epistemology, but the period was also witnessing the growth of an intensively capitalised motion picture industry. During the 1920s American film companies began to dominate international film production, distribution and exhibition so that, by the 1930s, only five British studios continued in production (Low 1971). Cinema distribution was an essential plank in the industrial structures of 1920s capitalism. By the time of *Close Up*'s first issue (1927) there were approximately 3,500 cinemas in Britain, with twenty million annual viewers spending thirty to thirty-five million pounds each year at the box office (Low 1971, p. 47). Britain was forced into America's cinema domain, although Germany, Russia and Japan were better able to retain their domestic film markets due to government support. Not surprisingly, groups of cultural activists, frustrated by Hollywood's economic colonisation, began to critique American production and distribution systems at international congresses and in journals such as *Close Up*. In 1926, over five hundred delegates and leading film-makers attended the first International Film Congress, 'one of the most potentially progressive undertakings in the history of cinema' (Thompson 1985, p. 115).

THE LONDON FILM SOCIETY

One compelling alternative to American hegemony was the London Film Society, founded in 1925. Together with its founders Ivor Montagu and Iris Barry, members included the Bloomsbury figures Roger Fry, J. Maynard Keynes and Clive Bell, the leading film director Anthony Asquith, and the writers George Bernard Shaw and H. G. Wells. Each month the society exhibited an ambitiously comprehensive selection of films. For example, the first programme, on 25 October 1925, included Ruttmann's *Absolute Opera 2, 3 and 4* (1923–5); a 1912 Western short, *How Broncho Billy Left Bear County*; the British director Adrien Brunel's *Typical Budget*; a short comedy burlesque; a key European film – Janning's *Waxworks*; and a Charlie Chaplin short, *Champion Charlie* (Film Society Programmes 1925).

All subsequent Film Society programmes shared this innovative mixture of avant-garde and popular film. Ivor Montagu vividly describes the exciting and often dramatic confrontations inspired by such radical exhibitions: 'I shall never forget that first show. From the moment the curtain drew apart punctually (in itself a triumph) and in silence (in itself an experiment) to disclose Ruttmann's *Absolute Opera 2, 3 and 4*, the Society was made' (Montagu 1980a, p. 106). In later programmes Léger and Murphy's *Ballet Mécanique*, 'when there was nearly a riot', brought 'fights and quarrels a-plenty, and I do not think it is conceit to claim that, in the midst certainly of plenty of dull drivel, we did introduce to England new techniques, new workmen, and new films' (Montagu 1980a, p. 107).

The London Film Society was the premier London venue to screen the major avant-garde Russian films, including *Battleship Potemkin*; German films including *The Cabinet of Dr Caligari*; French films by Renoir (*Nana*); Dreyer's *The Passion of Joan of Arc*; and Lotte Reiniger's animation and the films of the American director Dorothy Arzner. The Society also screened short science films with each programme. For example, on 17 January 1926 *X Ray Cinematography* was screened with Ernst Lubitsch's *The Marriage Circle*. These detailed studies of anatomy and animal and plant behaviour had a major impact on modernist art. The slow-motion photography of science films made visible the sequential nature of passing time, paralleling Cubist and Futurist attempts to capture sequential motion in painting, for example, Marcel Duchamp's *Nude Descending a Staircase* (Lawder 1975). This simultaneous development of science, artistic modernisms and the intermingling of modernist cultures appealed to modernist women. Vanessa Bell describes seeing a film of a Caesarean operation (see Chapter 2) and both H. D. and Dorothy Richardson in their writing drew on science's detailed observations and fresh ideas of time and space.

CLOSE UP

Yet although the London Film Society was an influential source of modernist aesthetic cross-fertilisations, with the introduction of sound, Hollywood's domination of the European film industry became more complete. By 1930 in Britain 'out of some 717 films trade shown 524 were sound films' (Low 1971, p. 206). Sound inevitably subverted cinema's international appeal and *Close Up* shared the hostility of other journals to the commercial 'talkies' (Dusinberre 1996). Indeed *Close Up* became a focal point for avant-garde opposition to sound film. Each issue ends with the section 'Comment and Review' including 'Hollywood Notes', a vivid microcosm of avant-garde concerns. 'Hollywood Notes' addressed the significance of key Hollywood production practices, for example, the change to Klieg lighting. The section also publicised Movietone's burning of its newsreels of left-wing demonstrations against Sacco and Vanzetti's execution in 1927. With critical dexterity, *Close Up* did not dismiss the possibility of good commercial art, for example, praising the work of the American Dorothy Arzner. In any case, the massive migration of avant-garde European directors and film technicians to Hollywood during the rise of European fascism prevents any glib critical apartheid of avant-garde from mainstream cinema.

Close Up's most intelligent and comprehensive attacks on the talkies were in columns by women writers, particularly Dorothy Richardson's sophisticated and now classic critique 'The Film Gone Male' and H. D.'s 'The Cinema and the Classics' (see next chapter). In April 1929, *Close Up* published Ernest Betts' 'Why Talkies are Unsound', which, together with other articles in that issue, are all self-deprecatingly summarised by Ken Macpherson in his 'As Is' editorial: 'Yes *Close Up* is full – as one young lady nicely explained – of quarrelsome, chip-on-the-shoulder articles' (Macpherson 1929c, p. 7). Later that year, in July 1929, L. Saalschutz feared that 'the sound element will rob the film of much of its fantasy. Its mechanism will be rendered almost meaningless and therefore its psychological appeal will dwindle' (Saalschutz 1929, p. 37). In January of the following year, Hugh Castle was more dogmatically dismissive: 'I remember, I remember, the house where sound was born, how little Jolson's lesser son made movie men forlorn. But chiefly I remember how I wanted to kick his pants. Hard' (Castle 1930, p. 20).

By July, contributors to *Close Up* began to recognise the futility of total opposition to sound films. Robert Herring in 'The Whiteman Front' less facetiously argues that film criticism would need to make a more intelligent response to sound film: 'Sound only means we have got to understand cinema more than ever' (Herring 1930, p. 52). Herring's article marks a shift in *Close Up*'s position which was supported by more insightful articles, such as Ralph Bond's 'Dovjenko on the Sound Film', which describes Dovjenko's break with his painterly past and his move into sound films as a positive development (Bond 1930). But, as Laura Mulvey points out, Hollywood's attempt to regulate the film industry had far more sinister outcomes than merely its domination of distribution circuits and sound film (Mulvey 1996).

The climate of the 1920s and 1930s became a chilly one as Hollywood panicked at what the studios considered was a sophisticated amorality spawned by the film industry (Mulvey 1996, p. 43). Reactionary regulations and censorship legislation had as wide an international reach as the film industries themselves. Ivor Montagu's essay 'Film Censorship' situates Britain's local pattern of censorship and legal controls within this international nexus (Montagu 1980b). The exigencies of the British 1909 Cinematograph Act, which empowered local authorities to safeguard audiences from inflammable 35-mm nitrate film, was applied also to later, non-inflammable stock introduced in 1923. As Montagu points out, 'councils did not confine themselves to regulations about fire protection but [...] started to control a hundred and one things, like *no Sunday performances*, *no German to be a cinema owner*, and *censorship*' (Montagu 1980b, p. 113). Although mainly non-commercial films such as *Battleship Potemkin* and Pudovkin's *Mother* were shown at the London Film Society, even its restricted exhibition venue also suffered local authority intrusions.

Hollywood's economic power and technological advances combined with national censorships to produce not only economic and legislative barriers to creative film practice and writing, but, more importantly, a general, inhibiting anti-intellectualism. In effect, everyday audiences were being denied access to a modern radical cinema. Huntly Carter's *New Spirit in the Cinema* describes how the Federation of Workers' Film Societies, the London Film Society, the Masses, Stage and Film Guild and *Close Up* sought a common ground in their progressive battles with industrial and state controls (Carter 1930). Although each group of intellectuals and workers came with differing agendas and influences, all were committed to a progressive cultural politics.

In March 1929 Dorothy Richardson organised *Close Up*'s petition to revise British censorship legislation. The specific attack was on the way in which the Cinematograph Act of 1909 granted local authorities licensing powers for safety concerns which authorities frequently used to withhold film licences as a means of censorship, as Montagu suggested. Censorship topics took up several successive issues of *Close Up* as the journal strove to defend independent film. A copy of the petition together with a signature form had been enclosed in the January 1929 issue, and several articles focusing on censorship appeared in February 1929. Contributors characterised this political activism as an aesthetic as well as a political battle. Censorship was akin to allowing 'Landseer and Kate Greenaway controlling the art of an era of Picasso and Gertrude Stein' (Dobb 1929, p. 72). Dorothy Richardson's petition called for the film classification categories (U – Universal and A – adult) to be broadened, for censors to be more representative of average audiences, and for duties on foreign films to be revised (Richardson 1930). Colonel

Wedgewood supported Richardson's petition in the House of Commons, arguing the case that what was needed was a special category 'on behalf of films of artistic, scientific and educative value' (Richardson 1930, p. 10).

The petition failed to change the exhibition situation, even for avant-garde film, and censorship controls remained in the jurisdiction of local authorities. The prominence given in *Close Up* to Richardson's activism could be a sign that modernist women did speak beyond the margins of the feminine. Censorship is not simply a legislative practice but raises issues about democracy and about gendered agencies. The question of what kinds of citizenship and what kinds of imaginations are possible in a time of censorship is a question of knowledge made explicit in the battle between modernist aesthetics and the state. Fundamental to this issue is the concept of a full, expressive subjectivity, masculine or feminine, and how subjectivity impacts on film viewing. Whether *Close Up* and other cinema journals offered an adequately progressive *gendered* criticism to match their more radical political campaigns is an important question.

Certainly women film critics contributed to international modernism. For example, Iris Barry, the co-founder of the London Film Society, was head-hunted by the Museum of Modern Art, New York. Journals also addressed the needs of a broader audience. *Sight and Sound*, for instance, interviewed Miss M. Locket, the education manager of British Instructional Film Ltd., who avidly describes the subversive pleasures enjoyed by children's Saturday mornings clubs (visited by 60,000 children weekly): 'Grown up escort is rare […] it is *their* show, inside the theatre the children see that they get their money's worth. Shouts of laughter greet Buster Keaton' (Locket 1932, p. 27). I will turn to discursive issues of gender later in the chapter, but I need to contextualise these issues first in a general account of the work of small journals and *Close Up* in particular, as well as the film praxis of *Close Up*'s editor Ken Macpherson.

FILM JOURNALS

The major critical themes of *Close Up* – the significance of Soviet cinema, the relation of cinema to other arts, and the future of national and international cinema – were the joint concerns of the overlapping British journals *Sight and Sound* (1932), *Cinema Quarterly* (1933) and *Film Art* (1933) as well as the film society movement. All shared *Close Up*'s belief in the significance of cinema in an avant-garde milieu. What is dramatically visible in the activity of journals, ciné-clubs and the work and writings of film-makers themselves, particularly Eisenstein, is a strong internationalism and interest in multimedia, including literature, art and film.

Film (1933), becoming in its next issue *Film Art*, shared *Close Up*'s commitment to both the praxis and theory of avant-garde film, juxtaposing analysis of abstract films such as $X + X = 0$ by Robert Fairthorne and Brian Salt alongside a cinema art course containing practical advice about cinema exhibition (*Film Art* 1933–7). *Cinema Quarterly* (1932), whose contributors included the art historian Herbert Read and graphic designer McKnight Kauffer, also addressed independent film practice outside the commercial mainstream, in particular, documentary film. In the first issue of *Cinema Quarterly* the directors Paul Rotha and Basil Wright as well as the critic Ivor Montagu praised the work of independent, regional film societies that exhibited and studied experimental films alongside commercial films. 'Perhaps for the first time in cinema journalism', claimed *Cinema Quarterly*, the journal would 'present in an adequate manner the spectator's point of view' (Wilson 1932, p. 4). A film society audience 'is no small body of intellectuals but a large and steadily growing section of the general public' (Wilson 1932, p. 3).

Cinema Quarterly became the official journal of the Independent Film-Makers' Association, founded in 1933, and it encouraged regular dialogue between British directors and critics, including the key directors Paul Rotha, John Grierson and Anthony Asquith. *Cinema Quarterly* also mirrored the international reach of *Close Up*, moving easily from a discussion of the mass commercialism of Disney to analysis of Soviet film. Other types of cinema journals also contributed to this avant-garde visual milieu. There was a convergence of interest in cinema across British intellectual life. For example, the 'Mercurius' column in the *Architectural Review* in 1930 reviewed Dovjhenko's *Arsenal*, praising his experimental techniques: 'The stills shown here can convey no idea of Dovjhenko's development of this contribution to cinematic art' (Mercurius 1930a, p. 29). In October 1930 'Mercurius' admired the 'propaganda' montage techniques of Russian films 'and their uncommonly high level of technical achievement', as well as Ken Macpherson's film *Borderline*, as 'abstract cinematic art' (Mercurius 1930b, p. 258). But the *Architectural Review* concluded that, while Soviet films are sincere, 'a critical analysis will show them to have the defects of their virtues' (Mercurius 1930a, p. 29). Only *Close Up* offered a coherent analysis of Eisenstein's significance and Soviet film.

SERGEI EISENSTEIN

Eisenstein's photograph was a frontispiece in the January 1929 issue of *Close Up* and he dedicated his portrait to Ken Macpherson, 'editor of the Closest Up to what cinema should be with heartiest wishes. S. Eisenstein' (Eisenstein 1929, p. 4). Several critics made detailed analyses of Eisenstein's work. In 'Film Imagery: Eisenstein' Robert Herring describes Eisenstein's use of global images in the Odessa steps sequence of *Battleship Potemkin* (Herring 1928). Eisenstein's own essay 'The New Language of Cinematography' appeared in May 1929; in it he grandly but convincingly declares cinema to be the emblematic modernist movement (Eisenstein 1929, p. 11). Cinema must have *'its own language, its own speech, its own vocabulary, its own imagery'* (Eisenstein 1929, p. 11).

Close Up dedicated two special issues (6: 3 and 6:4, March/April 1930) to Eisenstein's key essay 'The Fourth Dimension in the Kino', which, as Ken Macpherson argues, describes Eisenstein's belief in the inseparability of the physiological and the psychical (Macpherson 1930, p. 179). The essay focuses more precisely on cinematic meanings and on what exact cinematic features, according to Eisenstein, create meaning in montage. 'The hieroglyph', he claims, is a montage 'indicator' which baptises a whole sequence of film moments in what he called intellectual cinema (Eisenstein 1930a, p. 187). His discussion of the way in which montage reorders and distorts the pre-filmic events parallels Freud's ideas about psychic distortions, and Eisenstein suggests that, like Freud's therapy, intellectual cinema 'resolves the conflict – conjunctions of the physiological and intellectual overtones' occur in a form of overall montage (Eisenstein 1930b, p. 268). In 'Principles of Film Form' Eisenstein further develops this theme, comparing the hieroglyph to Japanese script, in which 'two independent ideological signs ("shots") placed in juxtaposition explode it to a new concept' (Eisenstein 1931b, p. 174). For both Eisenstein and H. D. (see next chapter) the hieroglyph was a vital image, encapsulating both the process of composition and the concept of plurality. Virginia Woolf, too, depicts 'images of the future as an indecipherable hieroglyph' (Gilbert and Gubar 1994, p. 28). The hieroglyph opens up film to an active viewer by refusing prescriptive singular readings. What was needed in addition, Eisenstein suggests, was an orchestrated counterpoint of sight images and sound images (Eisenstein 1931a, p. 3).

Eisenstein was more flexible about sound experiments than other *Close Up* contributors. This is because, like Bergson, he is particularly interested in parallel visual and mental discursive systems of meaning, which sound could amplify. Montage fragments, like Bergson's snapshot memories, only have reality through associations, and sound adds further associations. Indeed, for Eisenstein, montage was inseparable from processes of thinking and creativity as a whole. Montage had 'the same vitalizing human qualities and determining factors that are inherent in every human and every vital art' (Eisenstein 1943, p. 59). Because montage breaks with linear time and traditional space, it matched ideas about fragmented reality present elsewhere in modernist art and philosophy. As Charles Barr concludes, 'indeed montage becomes the defining characteristic of cinema as art, in Russia (at least in the late 20s) in Britain, and internationally' (Barr 1986, p. 78).

Eisenstein's films influenced a whole raft of independent and documentary film-making. The British director John Grierson drew productively on Eisenstein in wanting spectators to identify with political arguments rather than with characters' feelings. Grierson, like Eisenstein, was both a theoretician and a practitioner, and his film *Drifters* shared a London Film Society programme with Eisenstein's *Battleship Potemkin*. Eisenstein's influence on the modernist women writers H. D. and Bryher was similarly significant. As I shall suggest in the next chapter, what his films offered modernist women was the recognition that cinema, through montage, could open up characterisations to more flexible representations of subjectivity. To question how identifications are visually constructed and can be deconstructed is an essential feminist enquiry.

The intellectual formations involved in cinema in the 1920s and 1930s seemed to comprise a broad range of interests potentially congenial to women modernists, including Dulac and H. D.'s experimental films and the contributions made by many women modernists to small journals. As Douwe Fokkema argues, groups of writers in a generation do share a semiotic community, although Fokkema ignores the impact of gender on significations (Fokkema 1984). In addition to the ideas of Bergson and Eisenstein, critics drew in particular on the ontological categories of psychoanalysis. Articles in *Close Up* by the practising psychoanalysts Barbara Low and Hanns Sachs described the psychic mechanisms of film viewing experience.

PSYCHOANALYSIS AND *CLOSE UP*

One of H. D.'s favourite directors, G. W. Pabst, consulted Hanns Sachs and Freud when filming *Secrets of the Soul* (1926), and Hollywood itself turned directly to Freud when, in 1925, the producer Sam Goldwyn 'offered Freud $100,000 to consult on a film about the great love stories of history, beginning with Antony and Cleopatra' (Friedberg 1983, p. 372). Freud refused. Freud's concept of 'projection', which he defines in *Beyond the Pleasure Principle* as a desire for union with the mother evident in signifiers of the maternal, was a concept freighted with obvious attraction for *Close Up*'s women contributors (Freud 1961). H. D.'s poem 'Projector', published in the first issue of *Close Up*, anticipates Freud's ideas, and she eventually undertook psychoanalytic therapy with him in Vienna in the 1930s. Psychic mechanisms of the specular were a key issue in both psychoanalytic and film theory of the 1920s and 1930s. *Close Up* became a focus for debates about Freudian theories of perception. In 'Film Psychology', describing Russian film-makers' use of psychic moments, Hanns Sachs argues that film is only effective in so far as it is able to make 'the psychological coherencies visible' (Sachs 1928, p. 8). How this might be achieved filmically, Sachs suggests, is by attention to Freud's concept of 'symptomatic action', the small, trivial gestures which might betray character and plot and which are an indispensable means of expression. The year previously, Sachs met Bryher and Macpherson at Pabst's house, and Sachs became Bryher's psychoanalyst.

Also in *Close Up* the psychoanalyst Barbara Low set out her complex theory about the relationship between children's perceptions of cinema and childhood development. A friend of Dorothy Richardson, Low, like Richardson, focuses not only on spectator identifications in a theoretical way but also on cinema's everyday audiences of women and children. Low realised that, although cinema might reinforce early childhood feelings of omnipotence in a regressive way, yet more radically it could be a 'therapeutic vehicle', precisely because it allowed children *not* to repress their 'magically fulfilled desires' (Low 1927, p. 49). One radical political outcome of Low's argument would be to deny the value of film censorship altogether, because childhood development might be hindered by censorship. Low's arguments match Dorothy Richardson's campaign against British censorship controls. The new linkages between screen perceptions and spectator identities being made by psychoanalytic and film theorists offered more progressive representations of subjectivity conducive to gender concerns.

BLACK IDENTITIES, *BORDERLINE* AND *CLOSE UP*

Progressive representations of Black identities were also a key concern of *Close Up*, matching other white modernists' Black figurations, which included Roger Fry's focus on Negro sculpture in his post-Impressionism exhibitions; Picasso's use of Negro masks, and Nancy Cunard's immense *Negro* anthology. A special issue of *Close Up*, 'Negro Film', was dedicated to Black film, politics and aesthetics, publishing essays by Geraldyn Dismond, 'a well known American Negro writer' and Elmer Carter, editor of *Opportunity Magazine: A Journal of Negro Life*, as well as essays on Black issues by *Close Up*'s regular contributors Ken Macpherson, Robert Herring and Oswell Blakeston (*Close Up*, 5:2, August 1929). Macpherson's editorial 'As Is' posed dramatic questions about issues of appropriation and authenticity. Attacking a conventional sentimentalising of the Negro, Macpherson daringly called for a form of separatist cinema with Black directors directing Black films: 'Let the Negro, then, film himself, be free to give something equal to his music, his dance, his sculpture', which would, Macpherson claims, be 'as trenchant in its way

Figure 35
H. D. and Bryher in *Borderline*: from *Close Up*, 7:4, October 1930
BFI National Library

as the first "shock" of Russian cinema' (Macpherson 1929b, p. 90).

Macpherson matched his critical interest in Black issues with film practice by scripting and directing *Borderline*, starring the major Black

From *Berdaha*

American actor and singer Paul Robeson together with Robeson's wife Eslanda, H. D. and Bryher (figure 35). As *Film Weekly* pointed out, Paul Robeson 'needed' a movie and was 'in trouble' without a new film. 'In a little Hampstead flat I discussed these things with Paul and Mrs Paul and a tiny chocolate-coloured person [Robeson's son] who ran about and blew kisses at his elders' (Shute 1929, p. 11). In *Borderline*, the cross-race relationships between Robeson (Pete), H. D. (Astrid), her alcoholic husband Thorne and other characters are also borderline in a psychic sense. In psychoanalysis the concept 'borderline' refers to the imprecise state between neurosis and psychosis.

Borderline melodramatically portrays cross-race love between Pete and Astrid and between Adah (Robeson's wife Eslanda) and Thorne, and Thorne's consequent jealous murder of Astrid, for which Pete is expelled from the film's Swiss village setting. As Jean Walton summarises in her account of *Borderline*'s psychoanalytic portraits, 'critical attention to *Borderline* has been diverse, characterising the film as feminist, modernist, a psychoanalytic experiment, a lesbian or queer text, a white representation of blackness, and as a significant moment in Paul Robeson's film career' (Walton 1997, p. 90). While there are clearly critical disagreements about *Borderline*, and H. D.'s contribution to the film's editing introduces a further diversity, for the purposes of this chapter I want to focus on aspects of race, modernism and inflections of masculinity in the film. Thomas Cripps argues that, throughout it, whites 'serve as images of sordid calculation and unbridled jealousy' while Robeson and his wife 'stand for all that is pure and natural' (Cripps 1970, p. 475). As Eslanda noted in her diary, 'Kenneth and H. D. used to make us shriek with laughter with their naïve ideas of Negroes that Paul and I often completely ruined our make-up with tears of laughter, had to make up all over again. We never once felt we were coloured with them' (Duberman 1989, p. 131).

Filming of the Robesons took a brief ten days in March 1930. Macpherson had already completed over 900 careful sketches of camera angles and moves, and the swift intercutting of shots was speeded by H. D. and Bryher's complex montage. While there are moments of poor continuity – for example, Thorne's cigarette randomly appears and disappears in one scene – *Borderline*'s association of inner feelings with exterior behaviours is well constructed. In addition to the borders of race and psyche, the diegesis highlighted another border: that between the inside hotel world of bars, drinking and dancing and the exterior, idyllic Swiss countryside. *Borderline*'s careful montage associates inside and outside through specific images, for example, river waves in the exterior world mirror the wave-like quality of the hotel's dancers. Similarly the deliberately artificial quality of the dancing in the bar below underscores the melodramatic, murderous tensions between Thorne and Astrid in the hotel rooms above. The frenetic camera-work and cutting in these scenes, which H. D. refers to as 'clatter montage', resembles Hans Richter's film techniques, while Macpherson's exterior long-shots of Robeson resemble the Russian director Dziga Vertov's camera angles. But Macpherson's use of even, clear lighting, with relatively few scenes in deep shadow, helps to prevent spectator unease with such complex camera movements. Just as modernist fiction frequently disrupts, but does not completely displace nineteenth-century naturalism, similarly there is an unstable gap between *Borderline*'s melodramatic plot and picture surface. Particular shots encourage the spectator to focus on the surface quality of an image, for example, in the shots of Eslanda posing against a carefully framed, textured wall. But at other points the film also offers a comforting naturalism, for example, Bryher's reflective, naturalistic acting, particularly at the film's close.

Filming was a dramatic event. Robeson attracted children 'as honey does bees' (Duberman 1989, p. 131). As the townspeople filled the streets and hung out of their windows to catch sight of '"Monsieur le Nègre", the café did unprecedented business' (Duberman 1989, p. 131). Macpherson clearly tries to create spectator identification with a positive Black hero by developing a scenario built up of small details such as Robeson's tender care for a cat, which reappears in subsequent scenes as a linking image. The camera lingers on Robeson's expressive, reflective face as he remembers a happier past before his wife's affair with the white Thorne. Robeson's expressive performance is matched by Eslanda's sensitive and intelligent portrait. Macpherson also clearly portrays Thorne as a white racist when Thorne accuses Astrid of being a 'Nigger lover' in her affection for Pete.

Yet in many ways Macpherson's anti-racist aims are undercut not so much by his choice of subject material as by the film's implicit assumptions about white and Black mentalities, which are caught up in the masculinity of Macpherson's direction. White characters in *Borderline* have complex psychological desires evident in their mobile

Borderline, the first film made by Paul Robeson. Direction : K. Macpherson. These two stills suggest the wages of virtue and the wages of sin. Paul Robeson enjoying his self-ordained canonization above, and Helga Doorn below gives her interpretation of those little deaths we die.

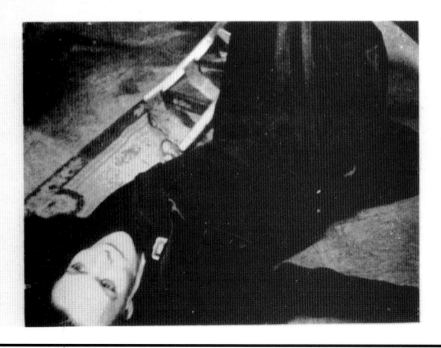

facial expressions, while Pete remains a simple, grieving lover whose Black body is constantly observed by Macpherson's camera gaze. Robeson is visually exoticised by wearing a rose behind his ear in one scene (just as Sidney Poitier similarly wears

Figure 36
Paul Robeson and
H. D. in *Borderline*:
from *Close Up*, 7:2,
August 1930
BFI National Library

a daisy in the later film *Guess Who's Coming to Dinner*), and Pete is finally rejected by the townsfolk (figure 36). The ultimate paucity of a progressive subversion of Black stereotypes is perhaps due to Macpherson's masculine inflections, evident in camera framing. For example, intense close-ups fragment Robeson in a libidinal manner and fetishise his skin at the expense of his character development. Macpherson objectifies Robeson by focusing on skin surface, revealing Macpherson's white male desire for the Black subject. In addition, Robeson is frequently shot out of doors, walking with Adah on a hillside, so that Robeson's profile can be isolated against the texture of clouds and hill. Placing a Black male figure with an idealised classical profile in naturalised settings is a common stereotype. Indoors Robeson is frequently alone, for example, when he reads Adah's written plea for forgiveness. The isolation of Robeson's figure in the field of vision forecloses any social development of his character and highlights Macpherson's masculine voyeurism. Finally, Robeson's character, Pete, leaves the village on his own.

KEN MACPHERSON, HERBERT READ AND CINEMA MASCULINITIES

Macpherson's preoccupation in *Borderline* with artistic masculinity is matched by his criticism and by other cinema writing of male critics in this period. So that while women modernists were able to contribute significantly theorised essays to *Close Up* as well as orchestrate progressive activism – for example, Dorothy Richardson's anti-censorship campaign – at the enunciative level many modernist projects such as *Borderline* and *Close Up* were gender blind. Many cinema essays and texts by key male critics, including those by Ken Macpherson and Herbert Read, are inflected with tropes of masculinity at a discursive level and therefore inevitably circumscribe progressive aims. Whether or not writers were conscious of such inflections, the generous numerical space of journal pages given to women writers is not matched by a generosity of rhetoric. This is not to say that male critics were creating a homogeneous cinema culture. For example, Paul Rotha's *The Film till Now* contains detailed accounts of cinema practices and is diametrically different from Huntly Carter's *New Spirit in the Cinema* and Carter's articles in *Close Up*, which contain somewhat lightweight mysticism (Rotha 1949; Carter 1930). Yet, without proposing an essentialist binary between masculine and feminine film writing, it does seem that male writers' choice of forms of address, metaphor and syntactical organisation shapes a style which has a characteristic masculine assertiveness, one which is both ironic and casually dismissive of popular audiences, particularly women. For example, both Ken Macpherson in *Close Up* and Herbert Read in *Cinema Quarterly* assertively dictate to readers, rather than engendering a participative welcome to audience experiences as do women contributors in their writing.

As editor of *Close Up* Ken Macpherson placed his 'As Is' columns in the first pages of each issue, which became a discursive avenue to successive contributions. In *Close Up*'s first issue he arrogantly categorises international cinema: 'We filed Germany for future reference and peeped at Vienna. Here again was tripe. Hollywood was better. Italy a shade worse: France tied up in knots on problems of continuity. While England trundled deplorably in their wake' (Macpherson 1927a, p. 7). In subsequent issues of *Close Up*, he is drawn to further absolutist pronouncements, attacking in particular the 80 per cent of cinema audiences (largely women) which has learnt only to 'want its Lya de Putti, its Tom Mix, its May McAvoy, regardless of the film in which they happen to appear' (Macpherson 1927b, p. 7).

While Macpherson did support amateur distribution networks, as well as anti-racist and anti-censorship campaigns, what he shares with other male critics is a deeply antagonistic response to commercial cinema, which is often gendered as female. Cinema audiences, the majority women, flocked to see stars, and Macpherson is deeply troubled by this feminised allure of contemporary mass culture. As Andreas Huyssen has argued, the feminisation of mass culture is a standard masculine modernist trope (Huyssen 1986). In many ways, Ken Macpherson's championing of trained and discriminating spectators, who would be sustained by his modernist cinema aesthetic, resembles Roger Fry's description of the attentive art observer intent on the harmonies of 'subtle, pure, crystalline colour rather than mimetic descriptions' (Fry 1996, p. 137).

The same concern with the notion of a film spectator's individualistic, unique artistic experience shapes Macpherson's colleague Eric Elliott's contributions to *Close Up* and Elliott's book-length account of cinema, *Anatomy of a Motion Picture Art* (Elliott 1928). The only question, according to him, 'is to what extent can the camera render the sublime expression of drawing or painting' (Elliott 1928, p. 73). The book reviews cinematic processes including pictorial composition, titling and continuity. Elliott wants spectators to become aesthetically aware individuals rather than a collective audience, 'otherwise criticism will become anybody's game these days' (Elliott 1928, p. 73). By analysing 'technical principles which will involve x-raying the framework', because 'scientific tests have shown that not more than sixty per cent of a film is seen by the spectator', he claims to offer a rigorous, 'scientific' criticism to a general public 'in need of some attention. It needs enlightening and it needs weaning of its prejudices' (Elliott 1928, p. 142).

Elliott's 'scientific' criticism and hostility to popular audiences draw on tropes of a self-conscious virility visible in other areas of modernism, such as the Vorticists' struggle against the feminisation of social life (Tickner 2000). His combative masculine stance is shared by other male critics. In 'The Revival of Naturalism', Paul Rotha argues that cinema had learnt a 'scientific method', and in 'Approach to a New Cinema' he claims that a film director should apply such a method to generate 'the excitement of the English football crowd' (Rotha 1930, p. 31, 1932, p. 18). The appropriation of a masculine working-class image, 'the football crowd', into cinema aesthetics is characteristic of male critical rhetoric. One vivid example of the opposition between a masculine modernism and modernist women's very different filmic responses is the contrast between Eric Walter White's account of the animator Lotte Reiniger and that by Bryher. In *Walking Shadows* White argues that Reiniger's work has value primarily as abstract art (White 1931). In her autobiography *The Heart to Artemis* Bryher prefers to describe Reiniger's contribution to the social and political milieu of modernism as a woman who saved Perdita, H. D.'s daughter, from the 'turmoil' of 'savage faces and clenched fists' in Nazi Berlin (Bryher 1963, p. 262). The title of White's *Walking Shadows*, published by the Woolfs' Hogarth Press, stakes a position in elite culture, with its implied references to *Macbeth*'s walking shadows as well as to the experimental film-maker Arthur Robertson's film *Warning Shadows* (Hankins 2001). Although Lotte Reiniger designed the hard-cover frontispiece especially for the book, White prefers to distance her from what Bryher later characterises as a textual politicised art, by discussing only Reiniger's expressive formal vocabulary.

The main champion of an abstract art cinema was the art historian Herbert Read, whose articles in *Cinema Quarterly* parallel Macpherson's attempt in *Close Up* to celebrate a polemically aggressive aesthetics. In 'Towards a Film Aesthetic', in the first issue of *Cinema Quarterly*, Read set out his vision of cinema and cinema art. Critics need, Read claims, to discover the 'universal laws of art' in cinema, whose primary law is 'the exercise of sensibility in the interests of a standard' (Read 1932, p. 7). Like Roger Fry, Read celebrates the individual artist at the expense of cultural context, and argues that cinema can create a truly contemporary art only if cinema expresses the artist's mind. Film is limited by its engagement with the 'lumbering material of the actual visible world', but a 'poetic master' will control reality if he has the 'visual sensibility of the painter, the vision of the poet and the time-sense of the musician' (Read 1932, p. 11). Read draws on traditional tropes of artistic self-expression, polarising an individually created cinema art against the everyday world. His ideal cinema is intensely masculinist, exemplified in his phallic image of the camera as 'a chisel of light, cutting into the reality of objects' (Read 1932, p. 8). In his view the art of cinema derives largely from an autonomous male artist remote from the lures of emotional identifications or audiences.

Not surprisingly, Virginia Woolf came to dislike Herbert Read. Although the Hogarth Press published his poems *Mutations of the Phoenix* in 1923 and his collection *In Retreat* in 1925, Woolf, writing to Stephen Spender, felt that she did not 'exactly fathom the silent and inscrutable Prof. Read' (Woolf 1979, p. 341). In his literary criticism Read had chosen Woolf along with Joyce as examples of good prose writers, but dining with the Reads and Henry Moore and his wife Woolf felt 'none of the charm of Bohemia mitigated the hard chairs, the skimpy wine, & very nice sensible conversation [...] Read devitalised' (Woolf 1982, pp. 280–1). Following Read's attack on Roger Fry for allowing a liberal outlook to distort Fry's sensibility, Woolf noted at length in her diary Read's similarity to other examples of masculine modernity:

I was finishing Herbert Read's autobiography this morning at breakfast. Little boys making sand castles. This refers to H. Read; Tom Eliot, Santayana, Wells [...] I think I can follow Read's building; so far as one can follow what one cannot build. But I am the sea which demolishes these castles. I use this image; meaning that owing to Read's article on Roger, his self that built the castle is to me destructive of its architecture. A mean, spiteful Read dwells outside. What is the value of a philosophy which has no power over life? I have the double vision. [...] I am carrying on, while I read, the idea of women discovering, like the 19th century rationalists, agnostics, that man is no longer God. My position, ceasing to accept the religion, is quite unlike Read's, Wells', Tom's or Santayana's. It is essential to remain outside; & realise my own beliefs: or rather not to accept theirs. (Woolf 1984, p. 340)

In rejecting her masculine peers, Woolf rejects a powerful discourse of the symbolic, ideal qualities of artistic masculinity. Her use of a metaphorically feminine image, 'the sea', and her positioning of women's 'double vision' on a beach, a quintessentially 'modern' place and subject matter for modern art, bring into vivid visibility the difference between masculine and feminine modernism. To Woolf, and Vanessa Bell, artistic expression was 'intimately bound up with the distillation – rather than the rejection or transcendence – of social experience' (Tickner 2000, p. 121).

SUMMARY

Although Clive Bell, by 1929, had shifted to a more tolerant understanding of cinematographic art, reading Eric Elliott, Eric Walter White, Ken Macpherson, Paul Rotha, Herbert Read and other male critics in *Close Up* and elsewhere and viewing *Borderline*, it is tempting to conclude that cinema writing by male critics pitched avant-garde cinema against the feminisation of popular cinema. For example, the arrival of sound films was accommodated in this masculine arena precisely by gendering sound as female. Sound was like 'the woman you love [who] comes out one day wearing a new dress [...] you love her in it as before' (Lenauer 1929, p. 18). Male critics came from dissimilar backgrounds and disciplines, yet seem often to share both a hostility to popular audiences and the use of generalising, aggressive declarations, combined with a belief in an autonomous artist free of cultural contexts. These features are tropes commonly characterised as masculine.

The epistemological issues involved in appeals to artistic individuality bear directly on the gendered politics of modernism. While I do not want to claim an essentialist opposition between writing by modernist men and writing by modernist women, there are obvious signs in cinema cultures of a discursive masculinity in critical practices and themes constitutive of a traditional binary of sexual difference. What it was to be a woman writer with an invested interest in women cinema goers, in cinema praxis and theory, and caught up in this space of modernism, is the topic of the next chapter.

MODERNIST
WOMEN AND CINEMA

INTRODUCTION

What makes any discussion of modernism problematic for feminist critics is that modernist aesthetics, while not directly reflecting modernity, are inevitably put under pressure by modernity's machine technologies and dynamism. Erroneously or not, such features are often characterised as masculinist. Increasingly feminists analyse modernist women's aesthetics within this wider context. Abjuring a critical tradition which addressed an exclusionary canon of key male writers (James Joyce, T. S. Eliot, Ezra Pound and D. H. Lawrence), feminists focus on the complicated tensions between modernity's gendered subjectivities and modernism's gendered stylistics. As I outlined in Chapter 1, there are now diverse feminist critiques but, in brief, feminists are revivifying modernist women's writing while simultaneously reading women's writing as a disruptive and emancipatory discourse of personal and cultural empowerment (see Chapter 1; DuPlessis 1985; Gilbert and Gubar 1988a). Yet, for the most part, feminist critiques focus on modernist women's fiction and poetry, ignoring journalism such as cinema reviews, which remain on the margins of criticism.

So that while decades of feminist contestations have transformed our knowledge and understanding of modernist women's texts, this major work of re-evaluation has not refigured the terrain of modernism itself quite so radically. For example, Virginia Woolf and H. D. are seen mainly as literary figures and in the case of Woolf as an essayist, rather than figured in a *composite* continuum of *domestic* visual practices and journalism. Analysing the interweaving of visual stylistics and the stylistics of journalism in women's cinema writing, which is the topic of this chapter, reveals how modernity's technologies did not necessarily force women into a mechanical, masculine critical rhetoric.

Although more recently Laura Marcus has brought about a significant revision of the cinema writing of H. D. and Richardson, mainstream film histories often ignore the work of women modernists both as film theorists and as practitioners (Marcus 1998). For example, three major texts about cinema of this period – Don Macpherson's *Traditions of Independence*, Jay Leyda's *Kino* and Rachael Low's *The History of the British Film 1918–1929* – make little mention of women (Macpherson 1980; Leyda 1960; Low 1971). Yet women writers in the 1920s and 1930s were forging novel, 'feminine' critiques to describe the new cinema-going experiences of women and children. Film's novelty was a major theme for commentators, and film writings address film's new models of the specular. H. D., Bryher, Richardson, Colette and Woolf wrote in an accessible, autobiographical, often experimental idiom attentive to issues of gendered spectatorship. Modernist women explore the cinema worlds of women and children and simultaneously give detailed accounts of cinema's aesthetic and technological processes. In addition, by addressing Hollywood's economic power and issues of national censorships, modernist women's journalism reveals a real material understanding of the social and economic contexts of 1920s and 1930s cinema.

Without rashly claiming essentialist differences between men's and women's film criticism, I think there are marked differences in the ways in which women modernists, more frequently than men, understand film experiences to be gendered as well as scopic processes. Unlike their male counterparts, particularly Ken Macpherson and Herbert Read, women writers refuse to engage in patronising dismissals of popular audiences, but rather create what could be termed a psycho-social aesthetics with gendered representations at its core. In many ways this aesthetic is a composite, reflecting modernist women's multimedia sweep across different orders of knowledge including literature, psychoanalysis and the sciences. One good example is the way in which Dorothy Richardson's first article in *Close Up* describes the new audience of Monday morning women viewers tired of washdays, but also utilises the image of a wave, drawing on the new physics of relativity, to describe cinema's dynamic qualities (Richardson 1927).

In addition, modernist women's journalism is not merely some kind of apprenticeship, or experimental prequel, for the more significant work of fiction and poetry, because modernist women wrote frequently about cinema throughout their careers. In the pages of *Close Up* and other journals, modernist women constructed themselves as modern women of letters making sense of cinema for a modern and gendered public. For this reason Bryher, Richardson and others were particularly hostile to any critical conception of audiences as passive consumers of mass culture, as merely star gazers. The cinema writing of modernist women makes an important intervention in the public sphere of cultural modernity, not only by exposing the ideological power of the visual but also by addressing women's ways of looking.

COLETTE AND FRENCH CINEMA WRITING

Both before and after the First World War France's avant-garde was eager to learn from cinema (Abel 1975). The writers and artists Guillaume Apollinaire, Max Jacob, Ricciota Canudo, Fernand Léger, Marc Chagall and Blaise Cendrars, were intrigued by the ways in which cinema's speed of vision could bring modernist aesthetics close to the experience of modern life. In 'Manifesto of the Seven Arts' (1911) Canudo chose cinema as the seventh art, and the film director Abel Gance predicted that cinema would unite civilisations (Abel 1975, p. 20). Colette's film writing contributed to this independent aesthetic world. From 1914 onwards, Colette indefatigably wrote film reviews and film scripts; she subtitled the key German film *Mädchen in Uniform*; and many of her novels were adapted for the screen (Virmaux and Virmaux 1980).

Like her sister critics in *Close Up* later, Colette initially preferred silent films because 'I still find, "human, all too human", the sound of the colourless voice in darkened hall', as well as favouring black-and-white film over colour for its 'gripping contrast of shadow and light' (Colette 1980, pp. 39, 64). Similarly *Close Up*'s contributors initially refused to be swayed by the attractions of colour film, unlike modernist photographers, who responded much more enthusiastically. For example, the American photographers Alfred Stieglitz and Edward Steichen rushed to Paris in 1907 to see the new Lumière autochrome plates, amazed that 'the pictures themselves are so startlingly true that they surpass anyone's keenest expectations' (Stieglitz 1997a, p. 377). But if initially hostile to cinema's newer technologies, Colette warmly welcomed cinema's new audiences of women and children. Her vision of cinema in her vivacious, anecdotal reviews is one in which women and children are active viewers enjoying the performances of powerful women stars like Mae West.

Colette was intensely interested in the impact of film on audiences and in how spectators choose and experience particular films. Rather than crafting a universalising criticism, her reviews dramatise her own reactions to film, together with those of fellow viewers and actresses. In her first article, 'Le Ciné', published in *Le Matin*, she refuses the stance of a distancing critic by ethnographically recording the gossip of women extras waiting to perform: 'Say something! We look as if we're waiting for the Metro' (Colette 1980, p. 13). While watching a film of Scott's 1910 expedition to the Antarctic, Colette realises that film can powerfully transform spectators into 'seated travellers', and she celebrates working-class women's filmic identifications: 'A female observer – age eighteen with needle-pricked fingers and dewy eyelids [...] "No, no" begged the young woman "don't tell me! Don't tell me! I don't want to know how it ends!"' (Colette 1980, p. 29).

As if presaging the 'ethnographic' film writing of the Black American critic bell hooks in the 1990s, Colette in the 1920s here deliberately 'stages' dialogue sketches of women sharing a viewing of *The Cheat* and *L'Outre* (see Humm 1997). She also loves to recreate the mother–child dialogues of active, knowledgeable viewers. In 'Bel Gazou and the Cinema', a daughter's apparently innocent eye enables Colette to make an ironic attack on inadequately intertitled silent films:

> "'The trapper, is that the man that trapper birds?"
> "The world is 'traps'".
> "Then did the movie make a mistake?'"
> (Colette 1980, p. 57)

She shows how children can be intensely knowledgeable about film techniques and technical failings:

> 'The other day an actress on the screen looked at her wrist
> and remarked, "five o'clock already!" "Listen to her!" cried
> a disillusioned child from a seat near mine. "Five o'clock!
> Look at the shadows the trees cast"'. (Colette 1980, p. 78)

Colette's close observations of children and women spectators and her view of cinema as an educational tool is mirrored in Bryher and

Richardson's writings in *Close Up*. Colette was also very aware of the historical context and the material nature of cinema. For example, as early as 1910, she warned that American cinema's commercial domination of European markets would come from the American institution of 'conservatories solely for cinema' (Colette 1980, p. 20).

Colette's film reviews describe cinema as if it were women's public space in modernity, and she created a specifically feminine style for this audience. For example, her work abounds in domestic metaphors. In a 1917 review of *Maciste Alpin*, soldiers carry captured men back to camp 'a little like a housewife bringing home the leeks' (Colette 1980, p. 28). Yet she was equally interested in avant-garde and science films and she was very sensitive to cinema's *mise-en-scène*, including in her reviews details of lighting, sets, clothing and the activities of women cinema workers:

> This young woman, the star, has been cooking under the
> glass roof, since nine in the morning. She made eleven
> changes of clothes, stockings, shoes, hats, hairstyle. The day
> before, half-naked in the gardens, she shivered under lilacs
> dripping with rain, tomorrow at 7am an automobile will
> carry her to the still snowy mountains. (Colette 1980, p. 68)

A newly heroic feminine subject emerges in Colette's reviews. Her celebration of Mae West's acting, in the essay 'Les Cinéacteurs', is exemplary here. Colette praises West as an auteur like Balzac, 'the principal interpreter of her films' (Colette 1980, p. 62). Colette also admired the way in which West escapes women's stereotypical roles, 'does not get married at the end of the film, does not die, does not take the road to exile' (Colette 1980, p. 62). Colette's construction of herself as a specifically female viewer in her writing, identifying with West as a woman, is also a key feature of other modernist women's film criticism. Colette engagingly comments on her own writing shortcomings – 'I thought I wasn't ever going to get free of that sentence!' – and encourages reader involvement by performing an apparent lack of expertise (Colette 1980, p. 23). Like H. D., she appears to attend films sometimes accidentally and often returns for more detailed viewing in very much the same way as, much later, women viewers made multiple visits to *Gone With the Wind* and *Titanic*. An American film 'I encountered by accident in the

Maillot quarter one day of torrential rain […] the next day, in fine weather, I returned to the same movie house' (Colette 1980, p. 40). Even Colette's expert, witty 'A Short Manual for the Aspiring Scenario Writer' takes the form of a dialogue question and answer, overturning the usual critical convention of a monologic, prescriptive argument. Her film writing is a lively feminine modernism of non-judgemental dialogues with women stars, women viewers and her own self-reflexive spectatorship.

Perhaps not surprisingly, Virginia Woolf was deeply moved by Colette's writings. In a rapturous letter to Ethel Smyth, describing Woolf's first encounter with Colette's work, Woolf claims:

> I'm almost floored by the extreme dexterity, insight and beauty of Colette. How does she do it? No one in all England could do a thing like that. If a copy is ever going I should like to have one – to read it again and see how its done: or guess. And to think I scarcely know her books! Are they all novels? Is it the great French tradition that lifts her so serenely, and yet with such a flare down, down to what she's saying? I'm green with envy. (Woolf 1980a, p. 49)

Jane Marcus notes parallels between Woolf's *The Pargiters* and Colette's *My Mother's House* and *Sido* (1922), which Woolf read in Una Troubridge's translation, particularly Colette's 'devastatingly ironic description of male history and literature' and her account of her brother's habit of creating a world of imaginary dead people in a miniature cemetery of tombstones and mausoleums (Marcus 1987, p. 3). Colette's attack on her brother's love of mausoleums must have resonated with Woolf's feelings about her father Leslie Stephen's *Mausoleum Book* (see Chapter 2).

JANET FLANNER
AND ADRIENNE MONNIER

Paris was also the home of other French and émigré modernist women, actively involved in small journals and film writing, whose journalism, like Colette's, is written in a specifically feminine style. Starting in September 1925, the American émigré journalist Janet Flanner (Genêt) contributed a bi-weekly column 'Letter from Paris' to *The New Yorker*. Flanner's topics include the aviator Charles Lindberg, Monet and gourmet cooking as well as cinema. Like a camera, she observes Paris and cultural life, its women artists and visual events, in particular the Paris Exhibition (Parsons 2000).

As Shari Benstock argues, Flanner consistently championed those whose work was undervalued, including the film actor and singer Paul Robeson (Benstock 1986). In her columns, Flanner describes cinema's institutional power. For example, in a review of René Clair's *The Italian Straw Hat*, she celebrates the 'French cinematographers' threat' to 'the importation of Hollywood reels' as well as Clair's appeal to women viewers: 'all these important French films show a definite new, and perhaps unconscious, quality – a Gallic romanticism' (Flanner 1972, p. 170). Like Colette and other women modernists, Flanner adopts a personalised, feminine voice, a style initially deplored by her editor Harold Ross: 'criticism to be valid, in my opinion, demanded a certain personal aspect or slant of the writer's mind' (Flanner 1972, p. xix).

Similarly Adrienne Monnier, the bookshop owner, writer and lover of Sylvia Beach, shares Flanner's engaging, autobiographical style of writing. Monnier's vivid, anecdotal essays range from sketches of the occupation of Paris, when on the day of Pétain's declaration she 'sold only one book: *Gone With the Wind*', to literature, art and film, as well as attacks on women's lack of status in Parisian culture (Monnier 1976, p. 397). *The Very Rich Hours of Adrienne Monnier* describes the adjacent bookstores run by Sylvia Beach and herself (Shakespeare and Company and La Maison des Amis des Livres), their publishing collaborations and Monnier's involvement in modernist women's media. For example, Monnier exhibited the work of the leading French photographer Gisèle Freund in 1939. Bryher, with her 'small, slender body. You grasp only certain aspects of it', was a close friend of Monnier, who specifically highlights the important way in which Bryher's 'writings are autobiographical most of the time' (Monnier 1976, p. 205).

Monnier argues that cinema is a key modernist practice, and praises Cesare Zavattini's scenarios as 'an act of intense modernism [...] facts and feelings appear in them as in the state of gestures, movements without ever taking on a solid body' (Monnier 1976, p. 284). Zavattini, the script writer of Vittorio De Sica's *Bicycle Thieves* and *Umberto D*, was noted for his 'humanist and reformist impulse' and 'honest portrayal of ordinary life' (Johnston 1999, p. 77). Monnier also notes the intimate relationship between avant-garde photography and avant-garde cinema in her comparison of Atget's photographs with the film *The Medium*. Most significantly, Monnier always writes with a feminine signature. For example, in order to draw in a common reader, she, like other modernist women critics, engagingly disclaims expertise: 'I am not in a position to judge the technical qualities of the film' (Monnier 1976, p. 268). Yet her writings reveal her to be a vivid and gifted critic. Like her sister critics, she gives her private feelings public expression in a rhetoric at once accessible and inviting to everyday women viewers.

CLOSE UP AND H. D. (HILDA DOOLITTLE)

A leading Imagist poet by 1914, the turning point of H. D.'s career was the birth of her daughter Perdita in 1919 and the beginning of H. D.'s relationship with Bryher (Boebel 1997). H. D.'s work includes Imagist poems like 'Sea Garden' as well as the modernist long poems 'Trilogy' and 'Helen in Egypt'. Critics note her innovative techniques. Susan Stanford Friedman describes H. D.'s 'Notes on Thought and Vision' as a new aesthetic of 'uterine moments of psychic suspension' (Friedman 1990, p. 88; H. D. 1990a). In *Out of Line*, Susan Edmunds cautions against characterising H. D.'s new aesthetic as marginal in relation to the work of other modernist writers. Edmunds refuses to position centre and margins as strict oppositions, because H. D. 'portrays the experience of looking in both directions across the inside/outside divide' (Edmunds 1994, p. 151). It was H. D.'s revisionary myth-making combined with her autobiographical focus in the poems 'Trilogy' and 'Helen in Egypt' which, Rachel Blau DuPlessis contends, enabled H. D. to escape patriarchal poetic perspectives (DuPlessis 1985). For example, her textual strategies have been described as utilising the rhythms of the pre-Oedipal, with early memories resembling daguerreotype photographs (Kloepfer 1989). As well as photographic devices, her fiction also makes use of filmic devices. Her 1926 novel *Palimpsest* repeatedly uses a filmic vocabulary to represent memory and history by means of flashbacks and flashforwards.

Similar themes inform H. D.'s cinema writing. One major feature of her cinema essays is the way in which she deploys autobiographical viewing experiences, which she often describes filmically. Another significant feature is her attempt to democratise cinema culture by describing everyday audiences as knowledgeable viewers. The first issue of *Close Up* in July 1927 contains H. D.'s first essay, inaugurating her series of twelve substantial pieces grouped as 'The Cinema and the Classics'. The essays bring together her ideas about cinema montage and Imagism, in critiques of Carl Dreyer, G. W. Pabst and Russian cinema, with interviews with film-makers and actresses. Working with Bryher and Ken Macpherson, H. D. helped to script, edit and possibly co-direct the film *Borderline* as well as the now vanished film *Wing Beat*. In H. D.'s essay 'The Borderline Pamphlet', issued to support the film, she describes the 'unrelenting' work of cinematography in which 'the cinema-camera is a renaissance miracle or a Greek incarnation' (H. D. 1990b, p. 114). Her interest in optical devices is thought to be inspired by her astronomer father.

H. D.'s film essays are much the longest and most carefully struc-tured of any contribution to *Close Up*. The scale of the series enabled her to combine the detailed analysis of films with discussions about cinema as an institution, including her own spectating experiences and observa-tions of cinema audiences. Whereas her poems and fiction, for example, *Nights*, were often first published in limited editions for a specialist readership – 'this edition, of 100 copies, has been printed by friends of the author for private circulation' – H. D.'s cinema writing aims at a much broader audience (Bornstein 1991, p. 105). 'The Cinema and the Classics' set out her vision for cinema under subheadings including 'Beauty' and 'The Mask and the Movietone'. 'Beauty' compares the American film *The Torrent* with Pabst's *Joyless Street*, and registers H. D.'s concern that Hollywood had 'devitalized' the actress Greta Garbo (H. D. 1927a). She begins hesitatingly, with typically Woolfian interrogatives, by gently ironising the role of criticism: 'I suppose we might begin rhetor-ically by asking, what is the cinema, what are the classics [...] For I don't believe one out of ten of us high-brow intellectual Golders Greenites [...] knows the least little bit about either' (H. D. 1927a, pp. 22–3).

H. D. locates cinema firmly as popular culture by describing cinema's world of 'pink lemonade, saw-dust' (H. D. 1927a, p. 23). She describes early cinema's debt to a vaudeville musical tradition whose direct gaze solicited the spectator. But from an attack on intellectual prejudice against cinema – 'prejudice has sprouted a rank weed' – she goes on to the prejudices of that 'gigantic Cyclops, the American Censor' (H. D. 1927a, p. 24). The degradation and devitalisation of European film stars by Hollywood, such as Greta Garbo, 'a Nordic flower', troubles

165

H. D., as does the American domination of the film industry (H. D. 1927a, p. 27). In Pabst's film *Joyless Street* Garbo is more appropriately a 'classic ancient beauty', a symbol of pre-Periclean Athens like 'the greatest master-pieces of the Renaissance' (H. D. 1927a, p. 29). H. D. contrasts those Greek and Renaissance images, the classics, with the paper flowers and paste-jewel exterior of Garbo's American incarnation (H. D. 1927a, p. 27). By staging self-reflexive memory scenes combined with descriptions of popular stars, H. D. interpellates an everyday reader/viewer into her more complex cinema theory. As she optimistically envisages in her essay 'Conrad Veidt', cinema could be 'a universal language, a universal art open alike to the pleb and the initiate' (H. D. 1927c, p. 44).

In 'The Mask and the Movietone' (November 1927), H. D. attacks sound films, preferring the imagistic silent screen because silent film resembles Greek theatre masks. The problem with sound is that it is too revelatory: 'nothing can remain hidden' (H. D. 1927d, p. 24). Silent film, on the other hand, allows us to believe in the possibility of something 'more divine' by means of metaphorical 'silent' masks through which stars can project feelings and ideas (H. D. 1927d, p. 30). H. D. highlights the 'mechanical and artificial' quality of sound with an everyday image of welding. Sound welded to image negates an active spectator: 'I want to help to add imagination to a mask, a half finished image, not have everything done for me' (H. D. 1927d, p. 22).

The paradigmatic audience for H. D. is 'pre-fifth Athenians waiting for our Aeschylus, our Sophocles, our Euripides' (H. D. 1927d, p. 24). Sound films, lacking an Aeschylus, cannot access our psyches or social worlds. Sound film literally 'records' rather than represents the true social world, which H. D. visualises as a Bakhtinian democracy of 'I and Tom Jones and the shopgirl' enjoying 'the old goat-herd and his ribald painted chorus' in a universal culture (H. D. 1927d, p. 31).

H. D.'s essay 'Restraint' makes a powerful case for directors' 'restraint' in choices of décor, lighting and *mise-en-scène* (H. D. 1927b). Watching *The Last Days of Pompeii* was 'excruciating' because a Greek interior should have 'one single fountain jet not an elaboration of Jean Bologniaesque detail' (H. D. 1927b, pp. 30–1). Films should not so unrelentingly detail a false décor of past cultures but enact our fantasies as part of films' performative processes: 'we should be

Figure 37
Greta Garbo: from
Close Up, 8:3,
September 1931
BFI National Library

somewhere with our minds' (H. D. 1927b, p. 32). An exemplary model of successful cinema, to her, is a classical Greek model using single gestures or fragments. Her deep knowledge of cinema processes informs her attack on the theatrical mimeticism of *mise-en-scène*. Instead, she prefers the ways in which cinema's own technology creates identifications: 'light is our friend and our god' (H. D. 1927b, p. 35). Films should favour 'one gesture' and imagistic symbols. H. D.'s focus on single gestures reflects two important developments in European cinema: the repeated use of tableaux in Weimar melodramas, and the disruptive image of *photogénie* in French film criticism. In *photogénie*, as in French Impressionism, single images hint at larger realities for spectators. This concept of attention, of a focus on gesture, a central theme of cinema modernism, H. D. describes as a hieroglyph, a feature of Russian films which she relished (see Chapter 4 above).

H. D. immediately responded to the shock-like attraction of Russian cinema. Her essay 'Russian Films', which appeared in *Close Up* in September 1928, grandiloquently associates Russian films with the Bible because ideas in both, according to H. D., were 'carved in lightning on the rock of Sinai' (H. D. 1928c, p. 18). She praises Russian films' depiction of women, and is particularly drawn to Eisenstein's films because they demonstrate how film can directly impact on the psyche of a viewer. As Kaja Silverman suggests, Eisenstein creates cinematic identifications 'not through rational persuasion, but through heteropathic identification'; in other words, by creating spectator sensitivity to small irritants (Silverman 1996, p. 91). H. D. found the intuitive, deep, unconscious connections between women spectators and screen stars, which so fascinated her, theorised in Russian praxis and writings, although Eisenstein's own essay 'The Cinematographic Principle and Japanese Culture', describing how film interpellates a spectator with hieroglyph montage, was not published until 1930 in *transition* (Edmunds 1994). The mixing of hieroglyphs in a dialectical montage of different times and places is a key trope in modernist cinema and literature (see Chapter 4).

Describing herself as a paradigmatic female viewer is a crucial theme in H. D.'s cinema essays. In 'Conrad Veidt', for example, she first carefully describes her own experiences before describing the film itself (H. D. 1927c). As if panning past her physical location in the cinema, she cinematically recreates her moment of arrival: 'I have got a front seat on the little balcony at the room's rear. Languages filter into my consciousness' (H. D. 1927c, p. 43). Her scene of looking does not resemble Laura Mulvey's description of spectators being sutured into film as 'male' voyeurs by film's masculine structures of looking, but is experiential and socially located (Mulvey 1975). H. D. creates a gendered film spectator because she is looking at her own image. In 'Conrad Veidt' she refuses to paraphrase the film's plot in a straightforward way, but instead records her own impressionistic responses in very short sentences, encouraging the reader to share her intellectual and emotional experiences. Similarly in 'Expiation', she restages her cinema-going experience as a quotidian event (H. D. 1928a). As any ordinary spectator might do, H. D. arrives late at the cinema, 'plunged down this little street' in Lausanne like 'an intellectual accordion', and she determinedly records the appearance of women on and off screen in a running commentary on gendered issues of spectatorship (H. D. 1928a, p. 39).

H. D.'s weaving of autobiographical narrative into critical narrative is at its most potent and persuasive in those essays directly about women stars like Garbo (figure 37) and in essays about films with female main characters, like Carl Dreyer's *Joan of Arc*. To H. D. Garbo signifies beauty, a Helen of Troy, a silver goddess whose photographs H. D. mounted in a special scrapbook. 'Greta Garbo, as I first saw her, gave me a clue, a new angle and a new sense of elation' (H. D. 1927a, p. 28). Garbo, H. D. believes, offers a new, feminine language, an intensity of representation too powerful to be dominated by a male gaze (Laity 1996). As Cassandra Laity points out, H. D. performed her character Astrid in the film *Borderline* in 'heavy, Garbo-like make-up', with 'dark intensity' (Laity 1996, p. 145). H. D.'s deep desire to locate the feminine within any cinematic diegesis shapes her interview with Pabst in 'a warm corner of an exclusive Berlin restaurant just before Christmas' (H. D. 1929, p. 56). She believes that Pabst depicts all his actresses, including Garbo and Louise Brooks, with unconscious realism. H. D. identified so mimetically with Louise Brooks' performance in *Pandora's Box* (figure 38) that she felt 'a personal right to *Pandora*, that it personally was partly of my making' (H. D. 1929, p. 56). She positions herself as a woman, not just as a general spectator. Pabst is a 'magician' precisely because he 'creates women' and 'brings out the vital and vivid forces in women as the sun in flowers' (H. D. 1929, pp. 64–5). Louise Brooks portrayed Lulu as a multiple persona, both a skilled performer and a prostitute, and in general the Lulu figure, as Rita Felski argues, exemplifies 'the quintes-

sential manifestation of a feminized modernity' (Felski 1995, p. 4). This is because Lulu combines both an erotics and an aesthetics of the feminine.

Other female representations interested H. D. Carl Dreyer's *Joan of Arc* (1928) 'is too perfect […] a series of pictures, portraits burned on copper' (H. D. 1928b, p. 15). Dreyer's film depicts Joan's trial by a fanatical church, and the face of actress Maria Falconetti (figure 39), playing Joan, became an icon of silent cinema. H. D. graphically describes the physical sensations of her film viewing. A 'nervous' reaction to the film causes her hands 'to feel that they are numb and raw and bleeding' (H. D. 1928b, p. 16). Because she distrusts Dreyer's masculinity, H. D. here does anticipate Laura Mulvey's theory of the male gaze: the idea that in classic Hollywood cinema, films create structures of looking in which spectators, the cinema and actors share a masculine gaze (Mulvey 1975). H. D. particularly dislikes the way in which Dreyer forces the spectator to adopt a male gaze, for example, by employing high camera angles from the point of view of Joan's male tormentors. H. D. progresses from this technical analysis to a social critique of cinema spectatorship, sitting with 'the baker's boy beside me and Mrs. Captain Jones-Smith's second maid', and describing differing responses to film. She is attentive both to the likely cultural expectations of a general audience and to the power of cinema to expose that audience's unconscious: 'We all have our Jeanne, each one of us in the secret, great cavernous interior of the cathedral (if I may be fantastic) of the subconscious' (H. D. 1928b, pp. 16–18). While it is possible to read Dreyer's film more positively than H. D. – for example, by noting Dreyer's powerful closure, which focuses on the faces of strong peasant women – it is true that his insistent close-ups always image Joan as a beautiful but tortured self-victim.

H. D. continues to personalise film experiences in her major essay 'The Borderline Pamphlet', published to promote the film *Borderline* (1939) (see Chapter 4). Although she characterises *Borderline* as Ken Macpherson's 'master narrative', her critical micro-narrative addresses issues of autobiography and the common viewer, topics largely neglected by her male contemporaries. Both her pamphlet and the film itself, as Susan Stanford Friedman argues, could be characterised as a modernism of the margins, particularly *Borderline*'s use of experimental techniques to represent race relations (Friedman 1990). While *Borderline*'s avant-

garde techniques suffered a hostile reception at its British exhibition, H. D.'s pamphlet avoids an avant-garde prose style in favour of an intensely personal voice. Although she does celebrate Macpherson as

auteur – 'the artist par excellence [...] it is a privilege, in no small way, to stand beside just such rare type of advanced young creative intellectual' – she also celebrates the amateur who can 'emote' with film in uncanny sympathy (H. D. 1990b, pp. 112–13). In any case, as Jean Walton argues in 'White Neurotics', H. D.'s construction of Macpherson as a modern Leonardo da Vinci recalls Freud's portrait of da Vinci's subversion of heterosexual masculinity (Walton 1999).

H. D. describes technical processes very vividly in order to place the reader in each scene of experimental film practice. She presents the filmic experience as both intensely personal and aesthetic at the same moment. On the one hand she argues that contemporary avant-garde film is an exemplary new artistic Renaissance, by associating Macpherson with Leonardo da Vinci; on the other hand, she argues that even such exemplary art can easily be understood and enjoyed by a common viewer: 'My images and my explanations must be of necessity obvious. I only want to get across something of this musical affinity. I am sure that every one of us, however, has had this [...] we all know what Miss Dorothy Richardson means when she speaks of the "parish" cinema' (H. D. 1990b, p. 119). Rather than insisting on a distancing and analytic critical style, H. D.'s gaze is social and collective. Her cinema writing contains fascinating phenomenological accounts of her film-viewing experiences, which somewhat resemble the tableau passages in her fiction; these she often arranges like film stills, with characters 'performing' events and emotions. H. D., like other modernist women, addresses a popular audience, speaking in an engaging personal voice which is always gendered. This blurring of boundaries between the psychic and the social and between the critic and the common viewer is a major theme of feminist modernism.

BRYHER

As well as co-founding *Close Up*, together with H. D. and Ken Macpherson, Bryher took on many of the journal's editorial functions, co-ordinating articles, correspondence and printing. In Bryher's twenty-three *Close Up* articles, her autobiography *The Heart to Artemis* and two film books, *Film Problems of Soviet Russia* (1929) and *Cinema Survey* (1937), she negotiates cinematic issues of gender, politics, education and avant-garde aesthetics in an always accessible style. Born Annie Ellerman, Bryher took her pseudonym from a favourite Scilly island and, with her father's wealth, could found and support *Close Up*. After its demise in 1933, she worked assiduously for refugees from Nazism throughout the 1930s and 1940s, arranging documentation and money and helping a total of 105 refugees to escape, including the writer Walter Benjamin (Bryher 1963, p. 278).

Bryher's acute political sense of her historic moment informs her powerful and polemical last essay for *Close Up*, 'What Shall You Do in the War?' (Bryher 1933). Her autobiographical narrative focuses on the horrors of Nazism with intense immediacy: 'I came from a city where police cars and machine guns raced about the streets [...] Jews. Six hundred thousand [...] are to be eliminated from the community' (Bryher 1933, p. 188). Reflecting on this momentous scene, she stresses the oppositional political role which popular culture such as cinema can play, citing Pabst's pioneering portrayal of common French and German women fraternising in *Kameradschaft* (Bryher 1933, p. 189).

Although in *The Heart to Artemis*, Bryher claimed 'it never occurred to me that I should ever take movies seriously', and 'my own interest, however, was in education rather than film', her film writing shares other modernist women's exuberant, self-reflexive attention to popular audiences and gender issues (Bryher 1963, pp. 202, 261). That openness informs the aim of her autobiography, which, as she suggests, was not to be 'mere autobiography' or period piece but 'an attempt to show how external events and unconscious drives help or hinder development' (Bryher 1963, p. 206). Her description of her autobiography matches her critical interest in psychoanalysis and understanding that modernist culture is continually in flux.

The Heart to Artemis describes Bryher's percipient interest in psychoanalysis (she was one of the first subscribers to the *British Journal of Psychoanalysis*), her friendships with women, and her understanding of modernism. In addition to her lifelong relationship with H. D., Bryher's friends included Colette, Adrienne Monnier, Sylvia Beach and the community of Paris-based modernist women writers. The rue de l'odéon is 'one of the most beautiful streets in the world. It meant naturally Sylvia and Adrienne and the happy hours that I spent in their libraries' (Bryher 1963, p. 211). These collaborations with key modernist women inform Bryher's film concerns, for example, she shares H. D.'s admiration for Pabst's portrayal of women, his character psychology and *Joyless Street*, in which Greta Garbo 'expressed our generation' (Bryher 1963, p. 251).

In one of Bryher's early contributions to *Close Up* she surveys Pabst's career. 'G. W. Pabst' begins with her understanding that film writing will need to attract a wider, non-specialist audience, which she attempts to do herself by using more conventionally literary analogies: 'What intelligent reader would buy books haphazardly because of the way they were piled in a window [...] the book buyer knows his authors' (Bryher 1927, p. 56). She modestly reveals to the reader that she came 'late' to cinema, seeing *Joyless Street* 'one wet dismal afternoon in Switzerland' (Bryher 1927, p. 58). She praises *Joyless Street* for its pacifist and psychological portrayal of war and war's 'sub-conscious impulse' (Bryher 1927, p. 60).

In 'Films for Children', Bryher moves on to address the issue of children's spectatorship (Bryher 1928d). She progressively argues that most children are able to understand avant-garde film as much as popular film. Her tone is never *de haut en bas* but often hesitant. She frequently adopts a Woolfian intimacy with the reader. For example, in 'What Can I Do?' she imagines a hypothetical film viewer immured in a tiny country town, to whom Bryher suggests that, under the aegis of a film society, the film viewer could share catholic and eclectic film experiences (Bryher 1928b). She suggests seeing 'bad films' which teach 'how not to light a set' as well as international films to keep in touch 'with the progress of cinema all over the world' (Bryher 1928b, p. 22). Bryher's strong sense of contemporary culture shapes her multi-generic approach to film writing and her movement across national, artistic and sexual boundaries. For example, her response to American film is much more discriminating than the knee-jerking chauvinism of *Close Up*'s male contributors. Hollywood, she argues in 'West and East of the Atlantic', should show the real America, 'sections where only Swedish is spoken', otherwise standardisation 'will drive people to desire violence in their cinema as a form of psychological escape' (Bryher 1932, p. 132).

Bryher underpins her international vision with a solid psycho-social critique. For example, unlike Ken Macpherson, she does not privilege Eisenstein's montage techniques over other film features, because her concern is as much with social as with technical achievements. Although she very adequately analyses Eisenstein's concept of intellectual cinema in her book *Film Problems of Soviet Russia*, issues of gender are more prominently in focus. For example, the film *Bed and Sofa* is a more significant film than *Battleship Potemkin*, Bryher claims, because *Bed and Sofa* directly addresses the sexual politics of Russian women. Following H. D.'s plea that critics should translate for, but not dictate to, audiences, *Film Problems of Soviet Russia* combines an accessible introduction to Russian films, which were not distributed commercially in Britain at that date, with detailed technical expositions (Bryher 1929a).

Women are at the centre of Bryher's work. In 'Defence of Hollywood', for example, she makes the intriguing suggestion that the 'excellent' actress Clara Bow should be directed by Dorothy Arzner so that Bow could 'be herself' (Bryher 1928a, p. 47). Like H. D., Bryher saturates her accounts of women film stars with her own identifications. She describes meeting the actress Anita Loos in the hotel hall and performs her encounter like a simulacrum of a typical woman cinema goer's dream moment, like 'the ceaseless shooting of movie scenes' (Bryher 1928c, p. 12). Bryher's invocation of the cinema-going experiences of women and children grounds her writing in the accessibly quotidian. For example, in 'Films for Children', she would 'run the risk of their seeing any film I know of to date', because censorship is only ever a political not an educational determinant (Bryher 1928d, p. 18). Facetiously exposing the absurdity of having to see the banned film *Cosmos* behind 'closed doors' in Berlin, she claims to 'have collected all the cinema enthusiasts we know and one child for the good of its education' for the screening (Bryher 1929b, p. 43).

Bryher continually focuses on the needs of everyday audiences by drawing on two resources: reflections about her own cinema-going experiences, and her psychoanalytic training. She believes that, like psychoanalysis, cinema can be a form of therapy able to free individuals from inhibiting social constructions. She refuses to adopt the customary elite tone of the avant-garde cinema writing of Ken Macpherson, for example, and this strengthens her vision of cinema as an educational force in the development of modern identities.

DOROTHY RICHARDSON

Throughout her twenty-three film essays in *Close Up*, Dorothy Richardson shares her sister modernists' concern with an autobiographical, feminine standpoint. Her themes are visibly 'feminine': refusing to discount women's need to identify with stars; refusing to separate life from art; frequently addressing an everyday woman spectator; and thinking through what a feminine language of film might involve. Under the rubric title 'Continuous Performance', Richardson's essays contain extensive reviews of cinema practices, cinema architecture and the roles of music and sound, as well as critiques of particular films. The essays also continually evoke the experiences of ordinary cinema-goers. Richardson grouped her essays under the title 'Continuous Performance' in order to highlight film's key feature: its continual process of exhibition and spectatorship.

In her first contribution to *Close Up*, Richardson immediately personalises the essay form. She describes how she gave up theatre going – 'all too high pitched' – in favour of cinema because her first sight of the screen, 'the balm of that tide', and 'the shining eyes and rested faces' of women viewers had such an impact on her (Richardson 1927, p. 36). She now prefers film's continuous performance to individual theatre plays. She democratically positions herself as an ordinary cinema-goer sharing the experience of other women in the cinema, on 'a washingday' Monday, with 'tired women, their faces sheened with toil and small children' (Richardson 1927, p. 35). Drawing this portrait of a female audience encourages Richardson to reflect on the issue of how art should be experienced, because cinema is '*with* the audience' whereas in plays, actors are 'acting *at*' the audience (Richardson 1927, p. 36). She persuasively engages the reader in her critical reflections by means of an openness to typical women cinema-goers. The essay has no obvious starting point; she begins with ellipses – '… So I gave up going to the theatre' – as if she herself is experiencing cinema-going as a weekly Monday 'continuous performance' (Richardson 1927, p. 34). The style of this first essay signals what became a key theme in Richardson's film aesthetic: the idea that good cinema must not be reserved for an elite avant-garde audience and that popular cinema can be of value and as educative as art cinema.

Richardson uses this technique of reader engagement to attack sound film. For example, in 'Dialogue in Dixie' she execrates sound film by positioning herself in an audience of assumed first-time talkie spectators (Richardson 1929a). She attacks those 'who attempt to teach us how to appreciate music, and the Royal Academy and Selfridges', and film actors, 'all of whom suffer from cleft-palate' (Richardson 1929a, p. 212). The essay reviews *Hearts in Dixie*, a recreation of the Black music and cotton-picking world of the southern states of America. Can film successfully incorporate sound, Richardson wonders? Her answer is negative, because she feels that dialogue prevents spectators engaging with a film's diegesis. Music was permissible in film, because music could cut 'through the adenoidal obstruction and because the sound was distributed rather than localised upon a single form, kept the medium intact' (Richardson 1929a, p. 214). Music and song enhanced the portrait of 'Negro life' because music emerges organically, 'as naturally as a flower', unlike speech which comes from 'ventriloquists' dummies' (Richardson 1929a, p. 213).

In Richardson's major essay 'The Film Gone Male', she genders silent film as feminine and the talkies as masculine:

> And the film, regarded as a medium of communication, in
> the day of its innocence, in its quality of being nowhere and
> everywhere, nowhere in the sense of having more intention
> than direction and more purpose than plan, everywhere by
> reason of its power to evoke, suggest, reflect, express from
> within its moving parts, and in their totality of movement,
> something of the changeless being at the heart of all
> becoming was essentially feminine. (Richardson 1932,
> p. 37)

It is impossible to say whether she regards this construction of masculine and feminine film form as a fundamental opposition. But certainly by adding speech to film, she argues, film becomes 'a medium of propaganda [...] it is a masculine destiny' (Richardson 1932, p. 38). Sound brings cinema into the masculine symbolic, that is to say, into a masculine social agenda (Radford 1991). In 'The Film Gone Male', Richardson reverses a gendered binary opposition in which the symbolic is privileged, and instead praises silent film as feminine because it is anti-linear, not directive, continually 'becoming' (Richardson 1932, p. 37).

The feminine is primarily affective rather than logically connotative because, she argues, the feminine can 'suggest, reflect, express' (Richardson 1932, p. 37). The French feminist writer Hélène Cixous' account of the female Imaginary is helpful here in understanding both Richardson's attack on male logocentricity and her innovative linguistic strategies. A feminine Imaginary, Cixous argues, will be an 'effort of the unconscious [...] which is unanalysable, uncharacterisable'; in other words, very like Richardson's feminine. The feminine Imaginary is part of the unconscious, playful and endless (Cixous 1974, p. 387). In many ways Richardson's essays resemble Cixous's writings both in content and in style, particularly in the way in which both writers do not structure arguments in a linear fashion but use associations and metaphors.

In the social world female speech is often a 'façade', Richardson suggests; and she argues that although women's 'outpouring torrents of speech' are frequently dismissed as mere gossip, such 'torrents' suggest a performance in which women deliberately 'snatch at words to cover' their 'palpitating spiritual nakedness' (Richardson 1932, pp. 36–7). This description of women's speech as a gendered performance, in which gossip and trivia create a behavioural façade, matches Judith Butler's concept of gender performance and Sheila Rowbotham's claim that women's gossip is often a feminine, behavioural defence strategy (Butler 1993; Rowbotham 1983). In *Bodies that Matter*, Judith Butler makes a powerful analysis of the discursive dimensions of bodies and of how language is performed: 'Sexual difference also operates in the formulation, the staging, of what will occupy the site of inscriptional space' (Butler 1993, p. 52). According to her, the reiterative character of performativity opens up the possibility of women's agency. Sheila Rowbotham groups gossip together with giggling and old wives' tales as features of women's thought, suggesting that gossip provides women with important ways of perceiving and describing the world (Rowbotham 1983).

These contemporary feminisms match Richardson's pioneering ideas about women's 'continuous performance' and her own performances of her experiences in reviews as well as those of a quotidian female audience. She describes women's spectatorship as active agency not passive, and as rapidly feminising the cultural space of cinema. Women's memory is not a masculine 'mere glance over the shoulder' but made of 'universal, unchanging, unevolving verities' (Richardson 1932, p. 36).

Her concept of women's universal verities presages the description by another contemporary French thinker, Julia Kristeva, in 'Women's Time', of women's 'monumental' time (Kristeva 1982). Like Richardson, Kristeva represents sexual difference in terms of memory and time. The symbolic, according to Kristeva, is the masculine time of history, which is linear, opposed to feminine time, which she calls cyclical and monumental: 'As for time, female subjectivity would seem to provide a specific measure that essentially retains *repetition* and *eternity*' (Kristeva 1982, p. 34).

Richardson's 'The Film Gone Male' is a remarkable, prescient condensation of these current feminist themes. It is silent cinema, according to her, which captures the feminine: our memories, our time, our fluidity and our language. She argues that spectators are not passive consumers and cinema itself is not a social narcotic. Women spectators who identify with women stars are not simply identifying with total artifice, with impossible fantasy, but are engaging in a form of cultural appropriation, investing their own lives with some glamour. For example, in '[*Animal Impudens* …]', she claims that women stars place 'the frail edifice of my faith in woman at last upon a secure foundation' (Richardson 1928a, p. 52). Spectators, especially 'life-educated people of the coast villages', she suggests, would become 'world citizens' by means of cinema (Richardson 1928b, p. 55). This is because 'the film is a social art, a show, something for collective seeing' (Richardson 1929b, p. 34). Richardson's fluid syntax and her continual use of the plural first person 'we' and the present tense make her essays open and collectively inclusive. Audiences might be 'life-educated' but their artistic judgements are not inferior to those of film critics. For example, women audiences do enjoy happy endings, but this desire Richardson celebrates as 'a tribute to their unconscious certainty that life is ultimately good' (Richardson 1928c, p. 50).

Women's reflexive spectatorship, Richardson finds, is duplicated in the experience of children, who are equally active spectators. When visiting the cinema one Saturday afternoon, she notices that children are not harmed by film; there is no 'feeling of glare or of eye strain' (Richardson 1928d, p. 60). Rather, the ways in which children watch cinema, 'their growth in critical grace', prepares them to see films judged by others as suitable only for adults. Children are 'the front rowers, a vast audience born and made in the last few years, initiated, disciplined and waiting' (Richardson 1928d, p. 64). In 'Films for Children', a more substantial analysis of children's cinema-going experiences and issues of child development, Richardson argues that children should have access to adult films because 'every man [...] is born adult and more than adult. And it is to this free persistent inner man that art in all its forms is addressed, that the art of children's cinema will address itself' (Richardson 1928e, p. 23).

Richardson's insights in her essays into cinema processes, the gendering of cinema and children's spectatorship match themes in her fiction. In her novels, visual processes are often metaphors of consciousness. In *Pilgrimage*, the activities of Hypo, a character based on H. G. Wells, resemble those of the fixing agent in photography, and characters' conscious and unconscious thoughts frequently resemble film montages of actors' inner thoughts and external behaviours (Richardson 1979).

Richardson's catholic breadth of expertise also includes a love of popular films. Watching 'a thoroughly popular' cinema 'show' will not 'dull discrimination', she claims, because people always prefer 'the family album of snap-shots' (Richardson 1929c, p. 56). But her attention to the marginalia of family cultures and popular cinema is not at the expense of her political activism, just as it was not for Virginia Woolf, since it was Richardson who co-ordinated *Close Up*'s censorship petition to Parliament. Her cinema essays make a major contribution to modern visual theory by focusing on the ways in which film, as well as the experience of watching film, is fundamentally gendered, and on how cinema can encourage a feminine standpoint. Richardson's celebration of the dialogic nature of women's cinema experiences, women's identifi-cation with stars and desire for happy endings (which are the experi-ences specifically devalued by male contributors to *Close Up*), opens up the possibility of assessing film by means of women's situated and subju-gated knowledges rather than only by means of a high art aesthetic.

GERTRUDE STEIN

The émigré American writer Gertrude Stein's salon at 27 rue de Fleurus, Paris, was visited by a number of modernist artists and writers, including Picasso and Ernest Hemingway. A student of William James and a fiercely experimental writer, Stein's interest in new representations of consciousness and experience attracted the attention of *Close Up*'s editor Ken Macpherson. In 1927 he sent her his novel *Poolreflection* together with an issue of *Close Up*, asking her to contribute to the journal. Stein's interest in visual modernism had surfaced as early as 1912, when Alfred Stieglitz published her fictional portraits of Matisse and Picasso in *Camera Work*, his avant-garde New York photography magazine (Stein 1997, pp. 662–7). In his introduction to the portraits, Stieglitz carefully contextualises Stein's writing within a post-Impressionist, early modernist frame, as a 'Rosetta Stone of comparison; a decipherable clew to that intellectual and aesthetic attitude which underlines and inspires the movement' (Stieglitz 1997b, p. 661). As Marianne DeKoven summarises, 'Stein uses a flattened, reduced, simplified vocabulary, much the way Picasso and the Cubists, here collaborators in the production of Modernism, use a palette reduced to a few tones of grey and brown, in order to intensify the nuance and effect of slight variation of colour' (DeKoven 1999, p. 184). While Stein's portraits of Matisse and Picasso draw on a Cubist visual language, what is also a significant feature is the way in which Stein captures in them a cinematic rhythm of successive observations.

Close Up published two essays by Stein, 'Mrs Emerson' in October 1927 and 'Three Sitting Here' in two parts in the November and December issues of that year (Stein 1927a, 1927b, 1927c). The essays do not directly describe film processes. Like all Stein's work, they are not directly referential, but some passages indicate her interest in cinema and are highly visual and abstract, drawing on her knowledge of the paintings of Matisse and Picasso. As a brief portrait, 'Mrs Emerson' belongs to a marginal genre within literature, although, as Wendy Steiner argues in 'Postmodern Portraits', Stein thought that the literary portrait could become a genre 'central to the enterprise of modernism' (Steiner 1987, p. 173):

> I will repeat. I will not play windows. In the new houses
> there are not windows for ventilation or any other use. They
> say that this is their use. They say that kindly amazing lights
> they say that kindly amazing lights and they say no that is not
> the use of a word, they say that unkindly certain lights,
> anyhow when I am pronounced that certain cheerful shapes

are fainter; they say that they have pronounced exceptionally.
(Stein 1927a, p. 24)

Stein's 'houses without windows' might refer to the new cinema palaces and 'kindly amazing lights' to the recently introduced Klieg lighting. Like contributions from other modernist women, the essays are not organised in a linear narrative nor are they critically judgemental. Incantatory repetitions are rendered in a dynamic continuous present tense and Stein's 'narrator', as elsewhere in her writing, continually notes perceptions without valuing one over another (DeKoven 1999). Stein's use of repeated single moments placed in sequence resembles film stills, and she herself later compares her use of the continuous present to the sequential nature of film (Steiner 1987). The narrator's hesitancy, giving more space to the views of others – 'they say' – than her own views, matches other modernist women's attention to the views of spectators.

In 'Three Sitting Here' Stein chooses to focus on surface detail, and the essay is more visibly modernist: 'Exhibition of peonies and petunias also with it as if ardently in difficulty rendering it as their stain. Stems and stains make orchids soon if there are strings hanging' (Stein 1927c, p. 23). While, as Catharine Stimpson rightly points out, Stein's 'literary language was neither "female" nor an unmediated return to signifiers freely wheeling in maternal space', it is also true that, like other modernist women, Stein is fascinated by the commonplace and by the details of daily life around her (Stimpson 1986, p. 194). Although Stein in her later writings, particularly in *Everybody's Autobiography*, famously constructs herself as a genius, here in the *Close Up* essays her language is anti-hierarchical, subverting linear linguistic form (Stein 1937). 'Exhibition' could refer to the pictures hanging in Stein's Paris salon in rue de Fleurus, but equally could refer to cinema exhibition, and the sketch is written in a continuous but fragmentary form like a series of close-up stills or film shots.

In *Lectures in America* Stein utilised cinematic processes more precisely by creating a continuous present from slowly building 'shot' descriptions, stimulated perhaps by her earlier contributions to *Close Up* (Stein 1935). In her later writing she describes her enthusiasm for cinema more directly; for example, a key scene in *Everybody's Autobiography* dramatises her meeting with Charlie Chaplin at a party in Beverly Hills (Stein 1937). In 'Portraits and Repetition' she conceptualises cinematic principles and processes and describes her use of these in writing: 'I continued to do what I was doing in *The Making of Americans* I was doing what the cinema was doing' (Stein 1967, p. 104). She clarifies what she means by this analogy: 'in a cinema picture no two pictures are exactly alike each one is just that much different from the one before, and so in those early portraits there was as I am sure you will realize as I read them to you also as there was in *The Making of Americans* no repetition' (Stein 1967, p. 105). Not only had cinema offered Stein 'a solution of this thing' but, she believed, cinema was the defining feature of her moment of modernity: 'our period was undoubtedly the period of the cinema' (Stein 1967, p. 105).

THE CLOSE OF *CLOSE UP*

Ironically, just as *Close Up* was devoting more space to modernist women's writing it ceased publication, in 1933. In that last year the American poet Marianne Moore contributed two reviews; Marie Seton and Trude Weiss reviewed Turkish films and those of other national cinemas; and Nancy Cunard dramatically publicised the Scottsboro case, in which Black hobos were wrongfully sentenced for the rape of a white girl. It was Bryher who had helped to publish Marianne Moore's *Poems* (1921), and H. D.'s first piece of literary criticism in August 1916 was an appreciation of Moore's work (Marek 1995). Moore's 'Fiction or Nature' in *Close Up* (September 1933) describes the first American showing of *Mädchen in Uniform*, and her 'Lot in Sodom' in December 1933 is an imagistic review of the film (Moore 1933a, 1933b). Her well-known opposition to self-revelation in her poetry and her famous constant revisions and rhetorical conciseness are *not* a marked feature of her cinema writing. Like other women modernist cinema critics, she autobiographically takes the standpoint of a common viewer: 'As I was coming out of the playhouse I overheard an incorrigible movie unenthusiast say, "It has richness of imagination enough to last you a year and makes you want to see a film every week". I agree' (Moore 1933a, p. 319).

Close Up ceased publication in December 1933 due to a combination of events: the death of its financial supporter, Bryher's father; H. D.'s analysis with Freud; and Macpherson's travels with Norman Douglas. Not all *Close Up*'s subscribers were avid modernists, as a letter from a

Viola B. Jordan of New Jersey revealed in the March 1928 issue: 'Every time I get the magazine I have a sinking feeling in the pit of my stomach. I say to myself, more grouches, snobbishness and sly hittings at America and its MONEY. And its ART and its PEOPLE, and its general all round BIGNESS. I am quite fed up on it and I do not read anything modern any more' (Jordan 1928, p. 74).

Viola's hatred of 'grouches and snobbishness' was shared by the modernist women contributors to *Close Up*. Unlike the more didactic, argumentative style of many male contributors, in women's writing we find an engaging personalism. Whether women writers gender film explicitly, like Dorothy Richardson in 'The Film Gone Male', or implicitly, as in H. D.'s emotional, psychoanalytic response to film, all create the critical essay as an inviting, welcoming space. All share women spectators' need to identify with women stars, and describe cinema spectatorship as a more democratically collective event. In brief, it could be argued that women modernists write the feminine by analysing cinema through a gendered lens.

VIRGINIA WOOLF AND 'THE CINEMA'

Virginia Woolf was intermittently a novelist but continually a critic. She wrote over five hundred critical reviews and essays, which often inter-weave autobiographical asides with conjectures about art, literature and life. Before beginning to write fiction, she reviewed for the *Times Literary Supplement* and other periodicals, building up an aesthetic expertise while addressing and problematising the critical tradition. Woolf took her journalism and criticism very seriously. She heavily revised essays and reviews, often completing several drafts before editing the essays for collections. Although she did not call her essays 'criticism' until 1927, the *First* and *Second Common Reader*s reveal an astonishing range of literary and cultural interests, as does Woolf's key essay 'The Cinema'. Ken Macpherson invited her to contribute to *Close Up* in 1927. She declined, suggesting that she had no available essay or free time in that specific year ('The Cinema' had already been published in 1926).

'The Cinema' is one of the first British essays to identify cinema's 'potential in modernism' (O'Pray 1996, p. 7). The essay was triggered by Woolf's interest in *The Cabinet of Dr Caligari*, directed by Robert Wiene

in Germany in 1919 (figure 40). The film depicts a story told by a madman about a psychopathic murder, and interweaves nightmare and reality. Woolf's essay is only tangentially about the film itself and focuses more on issues of the psychoanalytic and film spectatorship in general. 'The Cinema' addresses the central concerns of other women modernist film critics: how 'common viewers' experience film and film's psychic power; the relationship between film and the arts, and film's status and future. Woolf's account of the unconscious optics of film and film's future, described by Michael O'Pray as 'astonishingly prescient', is based on a clear and repeated premise that film is a new, dynamic, psychic and cognitive process (O'Pray 1996, p. 7). The eye and the brain together, Woolf suggests:

Figure 40
The Cabinet of Dr Caligari, 1919
BFI National Library

look at the King, the boat, the horse, and the brain sees at once that they have taken on a quality which does not belong to the simple photograph of real life. They have become not more beautiful, in the sense in which pictures are beautiful, but shall we call it (our vocabulary is miserably insufficient) more real, or real with a different reality from that which we perceive in daily life. (Woolf 1994, p. 349)

Woolf's image of the eye and the brain, which appears also in her essay *Walter Sickert*, in *Three Guineas* and elsewhere in her work, matches Freud's model of the unconscious (Woolf 1934). Both Woolf and Freud represent visual thinking as an archaic consciousness.

The manuscript of 'The Cinema' is in the Berg Collection, New York Public Library. The published essay appeared as 'The Cinema' in *Arts* (June 1926) and the *Nation and Athenaeum* (3 July 1926) and as 'The Movies and Reality' in *New Republic* (4 August 1926) (McNeillie 1994). The *New Republic* essay was published by prior arrangement (but without Woolf's consent) from *Nation and Athenaeum*'s page proofs. Andrew McNeillie, the editor of Woolf's essays, claims that the versions 'differ only in minor features of house style' (McNeillie 1994, p. xxvi). He is oddly disingenuous, since the differences between manuscript and each essay version might be minor in volume but do show Woolf's incremental understanding of cinematic processes. She makes a continuing effort to understand and to analyse the power of cinema and film technologies. Reading the manuscript and essays inter-textually reveals that her swift and ready acquisition of cinematic metaphors is not a rhetorical gesture but rather a detailed, sophisticated response to cinema techniques.

Gilbert Seldes reviewed Woolf's essay on 15 September 1926 in his *New Republic* column (Seldes 1926). He accused her of writing 'without knowledge of the abstract films which have been made in Paris in the last two or three years', citing Léger's *Ballet Mécanique* and Clair's *Entr'acte* as examples (Seldes 1926, pp. 95–6). Yet Leonard Woolf attended the London Film Society, and Clive Bell saw the notorious showing there of *Entr'acte* on 17 January 1926 and *Ballet Mécanique* on 14 March 1926, so Virginia certainly had indirect knowledge of both these films. In her diaries she describes her own visit to picture palaces as early as 1915 and later visits to films by Clair and Pudovkin (see Chapter 2).

The differences between manuscript and essays reveal a writer fully aware of cinema techniques. In one essay version Woolf praises character representation: 'Annas and Vronskys – there they are in the flesh' (Woolf 1994b, p. 595). In another version, she vividly adopts a more cinematic vocabulary of close-ups – 'the very quivers of his lips' – and she understands how the filming of everyday objects such as 'pebbles on the beach' can function as a visual metonymy of character emotions (Woolf 1994b, p. 351). But even in the unpublished manuscript she is already attempting an analysis of cinema process, concluding that 'we should see the violent changes of emotion produced by their collision. And that the past could be unrolled. Distance annihilated' (Woolf, 1926). In the manuscript version Woolf describes montage processes and the ways in which film makes visible hidden psychic structures, 'but possessed of a quality for which there seems to be no name' (Woolf 1926). Although there are eight film versions of *Anna Karenina* predating 1926 it is likely that she is describing the American Fox Film Company's *Anna Karenina* (1915) directed by J. Gordon Edwards.

Woolf's overriding aim throughout the essay is to imagine fully the reproductive possibilities of film, which, as she suggests in this passage, has its own agency. She argues that, while film is currently in a primitive, 'savage' state and, similarly, spectators are 'savages of the twentieth century', even primitive, 'naked men who knocked two bars of iron together' would hear 'in that clangour a foretaste of the music of Mozart' (Woolf 1994b, p. 348). Her use of musical analogies matches that of 1920s avant-garde French criticism, which frequently characterised art as a musical performance. However, Woolf's essay was originally intended for *Vogue* magazine, and she chooses to join common viewers with 'the clothes on their backs and the carpets at their feet' in order to watch 'the King shaking hands with a football team' (Woolf 1994b, p. 348).

Woolf wants film to trigger spectators' unconscious optics by moving away from a mimetic representation of emotions (Benjamin 1972): 'We should see these emotions mingling together and affecting each other. We should see violent changes of emotion produced by their collision' (Woolf 1994b, p. 352). In both manuscript and published essays she envisages film not as mimetic but as offering a kind of dialectical psychic montage. Through the juxtaposition of images, film montage can suggest contradictory realities and asymmetrical emotions within the film's diegesis. As Woolf analyses these processes, she understands that if memory is figured iconically through a montage of filmic objects representing emotions, then such objects can provide just as convincing a unifying cognitive principle as any linear narrative: 'The past could be unrolled [...] We should have the continuity of human life kept before us by the repetition of some object' (Woolf 1994b, p. 352). She gives a theoretically astute account of film techniques.

If films have 'some new symbol for expressing thought' in 'some object', and 'if so much of our thinking and feeling is connected with seeing', then our unconscious memories will become conscious (Woolf 1994b, p. 351). Memory as an aspect of the unconscious does not conform to a linear notion of time, and film montage stylistically uses fractures in time. By juxtaposing emotions through montage, film offers spectators a mechanism by which they can activate memory (Woolf 1994b, p. 351). Film's fluid representations can catch thought processes, 'which can be rendered visible to the eye without the help of words' (Woolf 1994b, p. 351). Cinema should refuse mimeticism, especially the direct representation of literary texts, because 'the results have been disastrous to both' (Woolf 1994b, p. 350). Woolf challenges cinema's dependency on literature and calls instead for cinema to emancipate itself from narrative, otherwise spectators will feel 'that is no more Anna Karenina than it is Queen Victoria!' (Woolf 1994b, p. 350). The true meaning of a film does not derive from its narrative content but rather from the processes by which film more abstractly connects with a spectator's conscious and unconscious thoughts and memories. Woolf envisions that film will transform consciousness through processes far removed from existing literary forms:

> The most fantastic contrasts could be flashed before us with
> a speed which the writer can only toil after in vain; the
> dream architecture of arches and battlements, of cascades
> falling and fountains rising, which sometimes visits us in
> sleep or shapes itself in half-darkened rooms, could be
> realized before our waking eyes. (Woolf 1994b, p. 595)

Woolf's description of film as a cognitive source of psychic transformations is a pioneering, radical theme. She argues that the power of cinema lies in its anti-mimetic power and that spectators experience a dynamic visual process which releases buried memories and dreams. Crucially, in terms of a woman spectator, film best sutures the spectator, Woolf suggests, through cinematic processes which catch our layered Imaginary. Her theme is close to Lichtenberg Ettinger's account of reading for the feminine in the visual arts (see Chapter 1). Where film feminists in the 1970s distrusted the power of the visual image because film constructed a masculine gaze, Lichtenberg Ettinger, more positively, argues that archaic memories (of the maternal body) may in photographic art gain a borderline visibility (Mulvey 1975; Lichtenberg Ettinger 1994a). Significantly, Woolf's account of cinema presages Eisenstein's theory of montage, the way in which filmic collisions can create spectator identifications. Eisenstein's theorisation of his montage practice, 'The Dramaturgy of Film Form', was published in *Close Up* in September 1929, three years after Woolf's essay (Eisenstein 1988a, pp. 161–80). What Woolf is describing very clearly is what Eisenstein later refers to as 'overtonal montage', which can connect scenes, Woolf suggests, by means of 'something abstract, something moving' (Woolf 1994b, p. 351). She acutely understands that spectators are sutured into film by means of cinematic associations, montage and repetitions. Only a cinema providing such pleasures, she believes, can prevent films being marred by literary associations.

In 'Woolf's "The Cinema" and Film Forums of the Twenties', her expert analysis of early twentieth-century film, Leslie Hankins argues that Woolf plays devil's advocate in 'The Cinema' (Hankins 1993). Hankins claims that Woolf deliberately hides her belief in literature's superior picture-making power. Woolf's belief, Hankins argues, appears as a powerful subtext in the essay. While Hankins quite rightly points to Woolf's continual tussles with the tensions between art and literature in general, the changes in manuscript and essays reveal Woolf's growing understanding that film can produce very different, but not necessarily inferior, meanings to those produced by literature. At first she describes the emotions engendered by cinema merely as a pointless residue from literature: 'Some residue of visual emotion which is of no use either to painter or poet may still await the cinema' (Woolf 1994b, p. 594). But in the second version she subtly hints at a more positive use of this residue: 'There must be some residue of visual emotion not seized by artist or painter-poet which may await the cinema' (Woolf 1994b, p. 351).

Cutting much of her overly qualifying vocabulary of 'may still' and 'perhaps' between manuscript and published versions Woolf seems to be aware that cinema has a viable, independent aesthetic. Cinema can expose our unconscious memories and our unacknowledged emotions. Woolf's 'The Cinema' is a sophisticated analysis of how cinematic processes, in particular film's use of dialectical montage, interpellate spectators. Like her sister modernists, she is engagingly self-reflexive, placing her own experiences into her writing to entice a common reader. Reader and narrator are 'we', as in 'we have time to open the whole of our mind wide to beauty' (Woolf 1994b, p. 349). Woolf's essay is an exploratory exposition, moving at a reader's speed from point to point eclectically and juxtaposing the avant-garde *The Cabinet of Dr Caligari* with a popular newsreel of the Grand National.

Woolf's discursive engagement with common viewers is a vivid feature of women's modernism shared by Colette, H. D., Bryher and Richardson, and contrasts markedly with the splenetic acerbity of many male modernist critics. Michael Kaufmann, in a comparative study of Virginia Woolf and T. S. Eliot's literary reviews, notes a similar gender disparity. Where Eliot, Kaufmann argues, imagines the mind as a rational chemical process – 'if the critic has performed his laboratory work well, his understanding will be evidence of appreciation' – Woolf adopts 'an unassuming critical persona in her TLS reviews' (Eliot 1918, p. 113; Kaufmann 1997, p. 140). The cinema modernism which Woolf and her sister modernists were creating for their readers involved a democratic, communal learning experience rather than the scientific 'laws' set out in the dogmatic pedagogy of male critics such as Eliot and Macpherson. Women's cinema writing explores a far wider range of visual emotions and feelings in dialogue with spectators and cinema practice.

CONCLUSION

Unlike painting, cinema has a particular relationship to the everyday world, defined not by the arrangement of space and volume in a static plane, but through a technology of identifications, dreams and desires. Cinema functions in both epistemological and ontological ways in the same moment. That is to say, the ways in which a film shows us the world, its epistemology, create what a film wants us to know about the world, our ontology. This is the theme of Laura Mulvey's now classic essay 'Visual Pleasure and Narrative Cinema' (Mulvey 1975). Film's ability to manipulate our desires as represented by actors is determined, Mulvey claimed, by film's epistemology, its technologies of reproduction, specifically the male gaze of the camera and male looks within the diegesis. Mulvey argued that our ontologies, what we believe about our world, if dictated to us by classic Hollywood epistemology, can only provide limited identifications, such as Hollywood's stereotypical views of women. Subsequent cinema theory built up a detailed history of further examples of episte-mological controls particularly Hollywood's technological controls of our psyches (Penley 1988).

In criticism's overburdened attention to film epistemologies, our ontologies, our beliefs and recognitions of ourselves in the values projected by others and our memories, have suffered a lack of critical attention. Yet, in very simple terms, what exists and does not exist is also determined by existing ontologies or what we believe we see and what we want to see. As David Hockney suggests, 'we see with memory', in the sense that twentieth-century perceptual analysis has proved that at any given moment we can see only a small amount and we supply additional visual details from our memories of earlier visual events (Hockney 2001, p. 256). And memories are always gendered. This more complex suture between ontologies and cinema epistemologies is the particular focus of modernist women writers. The cinema writing of Colette, H. D., Bryher, Richardson and Woolf addresses those tensions of gendered modernism: the relationship between aesthetics and everyday spectators, particularly women spectators and screen representations. While early cinema itself was fascinated by everyday banalities, in short films like Lumière's *The Demolition of a Wall*, modernist women gave aesthetic dignity to desires dismissed as banal (usually women's filmic identifications) by Ken Macpherson and other male critics.

Modernist women strove to override the presumption of a cultural distance between everyday audiences and avant-garde cinema. While the everyday details of Dublin life, including the attraction of cinema, do illustrate *Ulysses*, for example, the modernist writers Joyce, T. S. Eliot and Ezra Pound tried to form an organic theory of art, drawing on classical and Romantic literatures more than on popular culture. Women modernists, on the other hand, prefer to describe women audiences' identifications, and favour self-reflections over critical objectifications. Like the new sciences of modernity, modernist women's writing suggests a quantum wholeness in which the physical apparatus of the cinema and the conceptual apparatus of the spectator share an active engagement with visual memory. As Colette suggests, 'don't tell me! I don't want to know how it ends!' (Colette 1980, p. 29).

But in the writings of Ken Macpherson and Herbert Read, for example, the common viewer is much less visible. The film critic

Siegfried Kracauer does touch on modernist women's concerns, with his focus on cinema as an oppositional public forum and in his sometimes hesitant, less normative rhetoric (Kracauer 1960). Miriam Hansen even argues that Kracauer's democratic view of cultural life is 'inseparably linked to the surrender of the self-identical masculine subject' (Hansen 1995, p. 378). But Kracauer never explicitly genders his descriptions of cinema's transformation of subjectivity, and his aspirations involve in the main an erosion of bourgeois identity. The cinema writings of Colette, H. D. and others show that modernist techniques can be used towards more progressive ends. By heightening their personal, even idiosyncratic subjective responses to film and often revealing their anxiety of authorship, modernist women produce criticism that is not prescriptive but very engaging.

Such writing adopts what Drucilla Cornell calls a complicated interaction with the unconscious (through enactment) close to the embodied experiences of women cinema-goers (Cornell 1995). One useful example of Cornell's ideas in practice in literature is the poetry of Adrienne Rich, who, Harriet Davidson suggests, creates a similar inter-action as a kind of witnessing: 'the moment of testimony or witness which moves from the image to a dynamic with the audience' (Davidson 1998). The act of witnessing, for example, H. D.'s 'witnessing' of *Joan of Arc*, unsettles the boundary between critic and viewer, between screen and spectator, by creating an ontology (what we believe we see) through a subjective process:

> it is something one feels, that you feel, that the baker's boy,
> that the tennis champion, that the army colonel, that the
> crocodile of English and Dutch and mixed German-Swiss
> (come here to learn French) feels. We are numb and beaten.
> We won't go a second time. The voice behind me that says
> wistfully, taken unawares, 'I wish it was one of those good
> American light things' even has its place in critical
> consciousness. (H. D. 1928b, p. 23)

H. D. shares her fellow spectators' refusal to see Carl Dreyer's film *Joan of Arc* again, and critic and common viewer gain a new knowledge of themselves from the shared situation of a gendered spectatorship.

Because such an anxiety of authorship reveals knowledge to be situated and perspectival, it could be argued that the connections which modernist women make between self-reflection, everyday experience and the aesthetic create a feminist standpoint. In recent decades, debates about feminist standpoint theory have dominated much of feminist theory. A number of classic, influential approaches include Dorothy Smith's construction of an 'everyday world' in sociology and Patricia Hill Collins' Black feminist standpoint (Smith 1987; Collins 1990). Although criticism of standpoint theory has mounted, most forcibly from Susan Hekman in her view that it 'denies the life world is, like every other human activity, discursively constituted', feminists agree that we must speak from somewhere and that somewhere is particular, not universal, shaped by relationships and embracing the everyday (Hekman 1997, p. 341).

In this sense H. D.'s essay 'Joan of Arc' could be said to take a feminist standpoint. The essay is contextual, describing H. D.'s assumed interaction with an everyday audience. It combines personal revelation with a sense of aesthetic and historical urgency. H. D. creates a 'witnessing subjectivity', in Davidson's terms; witnessing her own confusion about cinema identifications, as well as meditating on knowledge, which gives her readers access to more reflective and gendered visual identities (Davidson 1998, p. 30). Such declarations of subjectivity are a recurring motif in modernist women's criticism. The border between viewer and critic is crossed and the everyday lives of women viewers are incorporated into aesthetics. Without reifying an essentialist gender binary in critical writing, it does seem to be the case that it is modernist women critics in the main who vivify aesthetic desires coded as feminine: identifications with stars, the use of film as therapy, describing audiences as socially constituted and gendered. Modernist women critics replace the prescriptive critical gaze by addressing a collective constituency of active cinema subjects, and in doing so engender cinema modernism.

MEMORY, PHOTOGRAPHY AND MODERNISM: VIRGINIA WOOLF'S *THREE GUINEAS*

INTRODUCTION

In recent years questions of memory and the visual have become critical in cultural studies of modernity. What Richard Terdiman termed modernity's 'memory crisis', or the anxiety about memory which pervades late nineteenth- and early twentieth-century self-conceptions and social practices, is foregrounded most powerfully in representations (Terdiman 1993). Photography has a particular purchase on this larger story of visual modernities because it more evidently reveals ideological, familial and historical pressures. If we consider the entire continuum of photographic practices, including amateur photographs, then photographs are fundamentally implicated in the making of modern identities by bringing together public and private realms of memory in the defining trope of modernity – specularity. While, as Patrick Hutton claims, our recent interest in memory and the visual might be more to do with a postmodern obsession with images, and memory means different things at different times, the study of modernist women's photographic memories can tell us something about modernist subjectivities and the specifics of female subjectivity within modernity (Hutton 1993).

Virginia Woolf's *Three Guineas* goes even further than this by using photographic memories to counter patriarchal fascism. Her use of photographs resonated with her readers: 'P.S. The war has already given us two delightful footnotes to *Three Guineas*. 1, the announcement by the B.B.C. on the day that war was declared that the King and his Household had donned military uniforms, and 2, the picture of the King broadcasting on Xmas day wearing an Admiral's uniform' (Letter to Virginia Woolf from Shena D. Simon, January 1940, in Snaith 2000, p. 163).

In their essay 'The Double Helix' Margaret R. Higonnet and Patrice L.-R. Higonnet argue that a temporal or spatial expansion of war's boundaries occurs in imagistic form in 'the landscape of the mind' (Higonnet and Higonnet 1987, p. 46). If we pursue, they suggest, 'the situation of women in relation to war, *mentalités* take their place beside ideologies, and both tend to displace diplomatic and military historiography' (Higonnet and Higonnet 1987, p. 46). While it would be wrong to assume that women's *mentalités* occupy a 'purer' space outside of official chronologies, tautologically the lived effects of history must appear in images and memories as much as in political discourses. By examining how gender or sexual difference figures in modernist visual and memory construction in narratives about war, we can see more clearly the connections between gender, memory and representations.

Virginia Woolf was particularly fascinated by the connections between memory and photographs. This fascination might stem from the ways in which photography both carries gendered memories, for example, in maternal photographs (see Chapter 2), and also illuminates a symbolic world. Woolf was highly conscious of the gap between the artificial, symbolic images of war and personal memories. Throughout her life she contrasts the accuracy of private memories of war with deceitful public history:

> No one who has taken stock of his own impressions since 4
> August 1914, can possibly believe that history as it is written
> closely resembles history as it is lived; but as we are for the
> most part quiescent, and, if sceptical ourselves, content to
> believe that the rest of mankind believes, we have no right to
> complain if we are fobbed off once more with historians'
> histories. (Woolf 1988, p. 3)

My aim in this chapter is, by examining the role of photography in Virginia Woolf's *Three Guineas*, to demonstrate one major way in which photographs and visual memories can reveal a gendered subjectivity. I specifically discuss the differing textual mechanisms by means of which Woolf counters a masculine, patriarchal world represented by five published newspaper photographs – a general, 'heralds', university professors, a judge and an archbishop – with a feminine 'affect' of the narrator's visual memories of photographs of fascist atrocities, sent to British supporters during the Spanish Civil War by the Republican government, which are not reproduced in the text.

In her edition of *Three Guineas*, Michèle Barrett suggests that the function of the published photographs is to ridicule 'patriarchal, hierarchical dress codes', and she usefully argues that the photographs are 'closely drawn into Woolf's underlying theme' of the symbolic function of dress (Barrett 1993, p. xxxi). However, Barrett overlooks Woolf's descriptions of the absent photographs, which act in dialectical tension with the five visible photographs. It is the absent photographs, or rather the narrator's memory of these photographs, which in a major way shape the narrative of *Three Guineas* and its dense visual plenitude. John Berger suggests that photo-narratives (like *Three Guineas*) reassemble differing aspects of subjectivity in a radial rather than linear manner (Berger 1997). Renaissance memory diagrams, which interested Woolf, were also often radial (Fernald 1999). Woolf too uses a 'radial' method to subvert a masculine photographic narrative of public events with the affect and self-reflexivity of her narrator's visual memories. The battle between Woolf's memorial descriptions of absent photographs and the published photographs pinpoints her political aim in *Three Guineas*: to link the patriarchal Othering of women, particularly our bodies, and fascism. It is as if her differential photographic constructions encapsulate her aesthetic battle with the symbolic.

In brief, my hypothesis is that the relevance of Woolf's *Three Guineas* for an expanded understanding of the aesthetics of modernism has something to do with the text's imagistic interpellation of the body by photography, which creates a specifically female modernist memory. In Woolf's writing we find traces of a different form of memory, one drawing on corporeal affect, much like Frigga Haug's contemporary liminal memory (which occupies the space between ideology and alternative experiences), and which, by making the reader into a witness, opens up, as Shoshana Felman suggests, 'the imaginative capability of perceiving history – what is happening to others – in one's own body' (Haug 2000; Felman and Laub 1992, p. 108).

The relationship between visual memories and the symbolic is a complex psychoanalytic process, the focus of a vast range of contemporary film, literary and photographic studies. In terms of the *photographic* symbolic, Christian Metz argues that photographs are part objects, memory fetishes acting as both index and icon of what *was*, and are therefore much closer to their referents than is film (Metz 1985). *Three Guineas* displays photographs as both index and icon: narrator memories of absent photographs of the Spanish Civil War, memories to which the narrator continually returns, together with published photographs of the public, patriarchal world, a world which Woolf attacks in the argument of the text. Roger Poole, in '"We All Put Up with You Virginia": Irreceivable Wisdom about War', mistakenly argues that Woolf's descriptions of the atrocity photographs from the Spanish government have the kind of 'false objectivity about them that Swift displays in *A Modest Proposal*' (Poole 1991, p. 98). In my view, Woolf describes the absent photographs with such unmotivated vividness that, rather than a Swiftian intellectual irony, the photographs produce a powerful emotional response in both Woolf and her reader.

The published photographs, of lawyers, church leaders, academics and the army, are fetishes of the symbolic, which Woolf counters with her written inner memories of the absent, dead bodies of Spanish women and children. These she introduces very early, at the beginning of section one. Paradoxically, the public photographs become timeless dead icons of patriarchy, while the narrator's repeated mnemonic of the absent photographs of the Spanish dead becomes a lively vehicle, enabling Woolf to develop her attack on patriarchy. The Spanish photographs index experiences unacknowledged by patriarchal culture. While these photographs are not gendered in essence, although they do feature the domestic and children, the narrator's memory and her own bodily responses to the photographs are marked by gender difference. The recurring memories of the photographs in *Three Guineas* both produce sexual difference and represent its ideological effects.

The published photographs are copies of some of the newspaper photographs which Woolf collected, together with press cuttings, quotations and letters, in three scrapbooks dating from the early 1930s. Like their five visible companions, the absent photographs also have a dialectical relationship with these scrapbooks, which contain a great deal of material about the Spanish Civil War, including the pamphlet *The Martyrdom of Madrid*, a lengthy eyewitness account by Louis Delaprée written during 19–20 November 1936, about the bombing of Madrid. In the pamphlet's 'Scenes and *spectacles*' (my emphasis), Delaprée movingly depicts horrific images of destruction: 'How could one forget the image of that child lying dead on the breast of a dead woman, in the middle of a pool of black blood' (Woolf 1931–7, p. 16). Delaprée might equally be describing a photographic image, in which blood, because red, would necessarily become black in a black-and-white print. Woolf's unexposed black-and-white memory pictures of dead bodies and ruined houses act as an epigrammatic mnemonic of the theme of *Three Guineas*, a prose picture of the indissoluble link between the physical violence of fascism and patriarchal tyranny to women and children in the private home.

READING *THREE GUINEAS*

In the public newspaper photographs, which are a visual history of institutionalised patriarchy, and her memories of absent photographs, Woolf emblematises two very different narrative modes. In her analysis of the public photographs, her own body, or rather that of the narrator, is largely absent. Indeed the narrator frequently comments on the difficulties posed by that absence. Yet the narrative of the absent photographs has an indexical contiguity both to the narrator and to the arguments she makes about women's bodies, childbirth mortality and wartime atrocities. The dominant histories in the visible photographs, to which Woolf has no physical access in the text and which are icons of masculine ideologies, are a convex mirror of her memories of women's bodily, social and economic inequalities, matched by the violence in the absent photographs. *Three Guineas* is then a dense, composite image/text which exposes and resists dominant histories with Woolf's active, alternative forms of memory. The photographs, both absent and visible, are the intellectual centre of gravity of *Three Guineas*, spaces of bodily contradictions which match her narrative work of political contestation. She shows how a long history of patriarchal controls over women's bodies leads to military fascism, and the two kinds of photographs highlight this trajectory.

Contemporaneously, and still today, *Three Guineas* is a radical, anti-patriarchal, anti-fascist and pacifist work. Woolf's argument is that war can only be prevented with gendered changes in education, employment and intellectual life. She connects fascist military oppressions with the marginalisation of women in general and creates the Outsiders' Society, the disenchanted daughters of educated men, to challenge political certainties. Adopting a triadic epistolary narrative, she gives two guineas to fictional proponents of women's educational and economic freedoms, gifts which in turn require her to give a third guinea to pacifism. These separate freedoms, Woolf understands, are completely interdependent. Fascism begins in the private, patriarchal home: 'The public and the private, the material and the spiritual, for they are inseparably connected' (Woolf 1993, p. 271).

In May 1937 Virginia and Leonard had visited France and would have seen photographs of the war. In addition Vanessa saw the unfinished *Guernica* in Picasso's studio (Dalgarno 2001). Woolf's contemporary diary is immersed in news about the Spanish Civil War. There are twenty-four references to the war, and although *Three Guineas* is in part inspired by the decision of her nephew Julian Bell to drive an ambulance, and by his subsequent death, only nine references are to him. The first entry in November 1936, 'Madrid not fallen. Chaos. Slaughter. War surrounding our island', instinctively links external European aggression with a sense of home: 'our island' (Woolf 1984, p. 32). Woolf was particularly moved by the plight of children. In June 1937 she sat on the platform at a meeting organised by the National Joint Committee for Spanish Relief in the Albert Hall in order to raise funds for the Basque refugee children, whom she describes with visual intensity: 'A long trail of fugitives – like a caravan in a desert – came through the square: Spaniards flying from Bilbao, which has fallen, I suppose. Somehow brought tears to my eyes, tho' no one seemed surprised. Children trudging along' (Woolf 1984, p. 97).

But also in her diary Woolf deliberately connects the writing of *Three Guineas* not only with emotional Spanish images but also with her body. She describes the process of writing in her customary intensely embodied rhetoric. Although at proof stage she claimed to be 'bored with the book', *Three Guineas* had been 'a spine to me all last summer' (Woolf 1984, p. 130). Like the mothers she describes in Chapter 3 of the book, whose time occupied in childbirth 'is under modern conditions – remember we are in the twentieth century now – only a fraction', *Three Guineas* was 'the mildest childbirth I have ever had' (Woolf 1993, pp. 268–9, 1984, p. 148). No book had 'ever slid from me so secretly & smoothly' (Woolf 1984, p. 149). If by March 1937 she feels that writing *Three Guineas* is like drawing 'that cart across the rough ground', equally in writing she discovers self-embodiment: 'I felt flame up in me 3 Gs' (Woolf 1984, pp. 67, 80). By October 1937 *Three Guineas* 'spurted out' of her 'like a physical volcano' (Woolf 1984, p. 112).

THE ABSENT PHOTOGRAPHS
AND MEMORY

Three Guineas is structured by nine references to 'dead bodies and ruined houses', in which the narrator's differing 'looks' trigger Woolf's individuated political analysis of patriarchy. Her first account of the absent photographs is worth quoting in full:

> Here then on the table before us are photographs. The Spanish Government sends them with patient pertinacity about twice a week. They are not pleasant photographs to look upon. They are photographs of dead bodies for the most part. This morning's collection contains the photograph of what might be a man's body, or a woman's; it is so mutilated that it might, on the other hand, be the body of a pig. But those certainly are dead children, and that undoubtedly is the section of a house. A bomb has torn open the side; there is still a bird-cage hanging in what was presumably the sitting-room, but the rest of the house looks like nothing so much as a bunch of spillikins suspended in mid air.
>
> Those photographs are not an argument; they are simply a crude statement of fact addressed to the eye. But the eye is connected with the brain; the brain with the nervous system. That system sends its messages in a flash through every past memory and present feeling. When we look at those photographs some fusion takes place within us; however different the education, the traditions behind us, our sensations are the same, and they are violent. (Woolf 1993, p. 125)

The absent photograph functions as a transactional act of memory between narrator and spectator. Woolf achieves this transaction by means of specific, vivid details. In the absent photograph the ruined houses resemble a child's game of 'spillikins' (in which a collection of thin pieces of wood is thrown into a heap and players must pull off as many as possible without disturbing the rest, in which case the turn passes to another player). The 'certain' bodies are those of children, and the houses still retain 'a bird-cage', itself often a compelling metonymic referent of Victorian women's private seclusions (Woolf 1993, p. 125). In addition, the narrator chooses to examine these photographs on a domestic table, not in the public spheres of street or library. This tea-table image Woolf takes up with similar intent in a later anti-war essay, 'Thoughts on Peace in an Air Raid' (Woolf 1961a). As Cooper, Munich and Squier argue, the essay 'dismantles the dualistic figuration of war itself. In locating her concept of "mental fight" at the tea table [...] Woolf redefines the front' (Cooper, Munich and Squier 1989, p. 22). While Emily Dalgarno is right to point out that domestic photography utilises familiar class and gender codes and that the casualties of war 'posed a new problem for the viewer', certainly by its very absence, and by its anonymity, such a photographic memory becomes a generic picture (Dalgarno 2001, p. 151). Such an image directly engages readers/spectators. Hopefully none of us will be bombed but certainly many of us have played spillikins. The imagery in the absent photograph encourages us to connect our private histories to those horrific public events. The children's anonymity in the memory pictures draws in any spectator who loves children. Woolf's final peroration at the close of *Three Guineas* connects the public world of war with the private world of women: 'the tyrannies and servilities of the one are the tyrannies and servilities of the other' (Woolf 1993, p. 270). It is compelling precisely because she has textually anticipated such a connection through her carefully structured descriptions of the absent dead.

Woolf subsequently abbreviates the detailed account into a single phrasal mnemonic occurring at nine further points in the text: either 'the photograph of ruined houses and dead bodies' (p. 138), or 'pictures of dead bodies and ruined houses' (p. 154), or 'photographs of more dead bodies, of more ruined houses' (p. 162). The first passage, and its subsequent mnemonics, turn images of violence into memorials, traces of past violence and, through their sheer repetition, a sense of violence to come. In some ways, of course, the absent photographs are themselves instruments of war, because Woolf is describing propaganda sent overseas by the Spanish Republican government. All propaganda images aim to mobilise support through the display of totemistic emblems (Mitchell 1994). But the narrator's memory of the photographs diffuses any originary instrumental propaganda by means of repeated qualifiers and an intricate interweaving of the visual into the verbal. Woolf's work with these photographs is a genuine mnemonic. The emotions triggered by memory of the photographs demand a level of political action far greater than 'an hour spent listening to speeches' (Woolf 1993, p. 126).

The next 'memory' connects British patriarchal institutions directly with fascism, as Woolf traces the 'connections' between 'the sartorial splendours of the educated man and the photograph of ruined houses and dead bodies' (Woolf 1993, pp. 137–8). Each memory scene builds heuristically on another, displaying both personal and public images of patriarchy and alternatives to those images in response to the 'dead bodies and ruined houses'. Each further memory of the photographs enables Woolf to envision more radical reforms for women: 'Also consider these photographs: they are pictures of dead bodies and ruined houses. Surely in view of these questions and pictures you must consider very carefully before you begin to rebuild your college what is the aim of education [...] Now since history and biography – the only evidence available to an outsider – seem to prove that the old education', the narrator claims, breeds no 'hatred of war', then the new college must be 'an experimental college' (Woolf 1993, pp. 154–5). Each memory of the absent image gives Woolf the strength to move forward into a more complex social agenda: 'the experimental college'. To interpret a photograph is always to give it a past and a future.

Subsequent memories move the argument even further by switching Woolf's vision from a delimiting screen of championing equal opportunities, because the masculine professional agenda only makes people 'lose their senses' (Woolf 1993, p. 197). Remembering the photographs encourages her to imagine new cultural and intellectual liberties in the Outsiders' Society. The photographic memories are a performative process in which aspects of patriarchal culture and subject formation can be screened, refocused and subverted. It is the photographic memories, not the published photographs, which mark each privileged moment in the narrator's disengagement from dominant culture. Woolf's key tactical manoeuvre in unifying this political work of deconstruction is to use her body. The narrator's bodily responses to the absent photographs is a compelling motif. No longer are the images prescripted propaganda; instead they impact directly on the narrator's body, fusing 'past memory and present feeling' (Woolf 1993, p. 125). The images connect the eye 'with the brain, the brain with the nervous system' (Woolf 1993, p. 125). Erin G. Carlston, in *Thinking Fascism*, agrees that *Three Guineas'* absent photographs mediate between mind and body, but argues that this mediation provides 'an emotional shortcut through rational argument' (Carlston 1998, p. 159). In my reading of the text, the absent photographs, or memory pictures, are not an emotional *short cut* but a complex mnemonic, dramatically triggering Woolf's feminist epistemological opposition to the logic of capitalism.

KINDS OF MEMORIES

Some light can be thrown on Woolf's very physical activity of memory and writing by turning to Frances Yates' germinal account of classical and Renaissance visual mnemonics in *The Art of Memory* (Yates 1966). Her study is now widely drawn on in contemporary memory studies (Hutton 1993). I cite it here to show the marked similarities between Yates' and Woolf's bodily and domestic memories. Yates vividly describes the general principles of mnemonic learning, in which the first step is to implant into memory both the content and sequence of an argument by visually encoding rhetorical sections onto features of buildings. Although she is discussing the use of memories of buildings as a grander philosophical project encapsulating classical and Renaissance cosmologies, her understanding that 'inner techniques depend on visual impressions of almost incredible intensity' matches Woolf's need to reveal the human cost of fascism through repeated images of bodies and buildings (Yates 1966, p. 4). As Yates argues, such acts of memory are like inner writing and are likely to be much more successful if the imagined building is disfigured, as in Woolf's mental pictures of ruined houses. In these ways Woolf resembles a classical rhetorician as she moves in her argument from point to point by means of reiterated memories of ruined buildings.

Freud also represents memory facts optically. In *The Interpretation of Dreams*, he describes sequences of the unconscious as camera images which photograph mnemonic traces; in a case of female paranoia, he gives an account of a young woman's belief that she was being constantly photographed with the click of a camera shutter, which Freud identified as a displacement of the clitoris (Freud 1966). It was precisely his turn to the visibility of the unconscious from a concept of an 'invisible' mnemonic which Luce Irigaray attacks as 'the look becoming vision' (Irigaray 1993, pp. 154–5). A tissue of invisible memories is lost,

Irigaray claims, as soon as 'a sort of photograph puts them into the world' (Irigaray 1993, p. 155). Of course 'photograph', for both Freud and Irigaray, is a metaphor, whereas Woolf refers to an unconscious memory of photographs which have a different ontological status. I should add, however, that when researching the most complete archive of photographs of the Spanish Civil War in the Marx Memorial Library, London, I found no photographs resembling those described by Woolf. What is at issue in these diverse reflections on memory and the visual is the significance of the invisibility of memory significations. Sight destroys the invisibility of things and therefore destroys possible affect. The affect of the Spanish Civil War photographs is far more effectively captured in Woolf's memory traces than as published photographs, because memory traces represent ongoing states or processes, not static, frozen images.

In 'Between Memory and History: Les Lieux de Mémoire', the French historian Pierre Nora describes how 'unstudied reflexes' of the body can crystallise *lieux de mémoire*, places of memory, reflexes which very much resemble the narrator's bodily synapses in Woolf's *Three Guineas* (Nora 1989). Nora attributes his concept to his reading of Yates. There are many rich and sophisticated critiques of Nora's project, and Peter Carrier gives a significant account (Carrier 2000). I focus here on those images of Nora's which specifically match Woolf's. His now classic opposition between history's 'spectacular symbols' and memory's materialisation (in 'images' and 'the unstudied reflexes of the body') has been rightly described by Marianne Hirsch and others as 'reified', but is a very pertinent model of the figurative tensions in *Three Guineas* between published and absent photographs. Nora's essay constitutes a theoretical introduction to his ambitious collaborative work *Realms of Memory: The Construction of the French Past*, a three-volume collection of 130 essays by over a hundred historians, undertaken between 1984 and 1992 to show how 'issues of identity, memory and patrimony' supersede 'any more monolithic understanding of history' (Parish 1999, p. 7). Acts of memory or commemoration may be as, or more, significant than the political or historical events being commemorated. Nora opposes two kinds of memory: a 'dictatorial memory' that 'ceaselessly reinvents tradition' as a history of 'the undifferentiated time of heroes', and 'real memory', which is 'affective, magical' and ties us to an 'eternal present' (Nora 1989, p. 8).

Nora's distinction between history and memory closely resembles the elaborately gendered account of historical representations of sexual difference and time which Julia Kristeva develops in her essay 'Women's Time' (Kristeva 1982). 'Masculinity', Kristeva argues, is represented in history, which celebrates logical connections and linearity (the symbolic), to which Kristeva opposes 'feminine' time, which is commemorative, monumental and cyclical: 'Female subjectivity would seem to provide a specific measure that essentially retains *repetition* and *eternity* from among the multiple modalities of time known through the history of civilization' (Kristeva 1982, p. 34). Kristeva's 'feminine' memory which is repetitious and comparative matches Nora's idea that *lieux de mémoire* contain an eternal present. He focuses on issues of the embodiment of history. 'True' memory is crystallised in 'the body's inherent self-knowledge', represented in his concept *lieux de mémoire*, which he describes, in a very Woolfian image, as 'shells on the shore when the sea of living memory has receded' (Nora 1989, pp. 12–13). Memory is 'spaces, gestures, images and objects', which are nourishing recollections, in opposition to recorded history, which constructs itself in 'spectacular but empty symbols' (Nora 1989, p. 9). Historians can activate *lieux de mémoire* to 'immortalize death', just as Woolf does with the absent photographs (Nora 1989, p. 19).

Images in *lieux de mémoire* closely resemble Woolf's photo albums and the absent photographs of *Three Guineas* because all share a 'hybrid and mutant' optics of memory (Nora 1989, p. 19). For Nora, traditional history is too exterior, too obsessed with rituals which, paradoxically, mark a 'society without ritual' (Nora 1989, p. 12). His binary division between recorded history and memory is reified, but matches Woolf's binary, equally complex account of the public and remembered photography in *Three Guineas*. Indeed Nora's project encapsulates the very schema of *Three Guineas*: Woolf's attack on dead, symbolic history in the visible photographs, from which women are physically remote; and her endorsement of alternative, if invisible, memories through her bodily 'reflexes' and contiguity to the absent photographs. She describes history in the public photographs as an empty performance of patriarchal glorification which is culturally privileged. Women are not constituted by this historical pageant. In some senses Woolf is constantly negotiating identities for women through 'memory work' in opposition to this public history. Gender shapes the social imaginary of the narrator: '"we" – a whole made up of body, brain and spirit, influenced by memory and tradition – must still differ in some essential respects from "you" whose body, brain and spirit have been so differently trained' (Woolf 1993, pp. 132–3). This search for diversity in historical writing is a constant theme in her career. As Melba Cuddy-Keane points out, Woolf's 'The Journal of Mistress Joan Martyn' shows her as early as 1906 'representing history as a dialogic relation between the historical text and the historian's understanding' (Cuddy-Keane 1997, p. 66). Sandra M. Gilbert and Susan Gubar argue that Woolf dramatises a contrast between public and private histories in a number of works, including *Mrs Dalloway*: 'Just as the Big Ben history is associated with the public world, masculinity, technology, and the war, this alternative record is embodied in the private, the feminine, the natural' (Gilbert and Gubar 1994, pp. 23–4).

The attempt to revivify the dead, or what Nora calls the immortalising of death in *lieux de mémoire,* is of course a recurring theme in Woolf's fiction, most notably in *To the Lighthouse* and Lily's portrait of the dead Mrs Ramsay. Woolf's continual project, throughout her fiction, is to suggest that family memories are somehow at the core of our identities and histories, particularly at the core of women's identities. The implied photographs speak of domestic destruction, 'ruined houses' and the impact of fascism on the home and on the family. Rosemary Summer points to a similar example of Woolf's photographic imagination in the 'Time Passes' sequence of *To the Lighthouse*. The sequence resembles, Summer argues, 'time-lapse photography which enables the reader to see entropy in process, invisible to the human eye' (Summer 1999, p. 17).

PHOTOGRAPHS AND THE BODY

The published photographs tell another story. They appear to offer cropped, snatched images of public life, immune to deeper readings. Woolf's textual commentary on each photograph, together with her uneasy physical distancing from each image in the text, highlights their public abstraction. But, like their absent companions, the published photographs also carry a deeper visual plenitude. Jane Marcus cites Elizabeth Robins, the American actress, writer and suffragette, as a source for Woolf's 'provocative but correct portraits of the powerful in *Three Guineas*' (Marcus 1988, p. 144). Marcus points out that in

Ancilla's Share, published in 1924, Robins makes a vivid association between the social function of symbolic dress and patriarchal values. Woolf goes further in *Three Guineas* to suggest the emptiness of symbolic history itself, and that this emptiness represents a society entirely absorbed in its work of hyper-reality.

The five public portraits resemble Nora's 'history' at its most static. Unlike the reciprocal movements of memory from absent photo-graph to narrator and to reader, pinpointed by Woolf's description of the absent photographs' frequent circulation 'about twice a week', the public photographs stand immobile (Woolf 1993, p. 125). The first image in *Three Guineas*, of a general (Lord Baden-Powell), is a full frontal, individual shot showing the primacy of symbolic signs: the general's array of medals (figure 41) (Stavely 1998). The image seems unmediated. The second image, of heralds, also emphasises the surface detail of uniforms (a subsequent letter to Woolf identifies the heralds as 'trumpeters in, I think, the full dress of the Horse Guards') (figure 42) (Freeman 2000, p. 55). The third and fourth images, 'a university procession' and 'a judge', are wide-angle rather than medium-shot; Alice Stavely identifies them as Earl Baldwin and Lord Hewart respectively (figures 43 and 44) (Stavely 1998). Neither photograph is a cohesive or integrated composition and the effect of wide-angle is to shape perspective so as to impose a particular viewpoint on the spectator. Finally, the photograph of the archbishop William Cosmo Gordon Lang is similarly monumental, utilising a low camera angle (figure 45). The archbishop's crook is given a greater iconographic import by the parallelism of a staff held by a figure at the rear of the photograph. In addition, the archbishop's public isolation has a visual referent in the photograph's brushed-out background.

The photographs are grotesque, excessive performances of people trying to deny the effects of change. In every conceivable way these photographs match Pierre Nora's characterisation of history as 'ceaselessly reinventing tradition' to 'an undifferen-tiated time of heroes' (Nora 1989, p. 8). As he suggests, history can only represent the past with spectacular symbols full of empty 'medallions and

Figure 41
A general from
Three Guineas
(published 1938)
By permission of the
Society of Authors for
the Virginia Woolf Estate

Figure 42
'Heralds' from
Three Guineas
(published 1938)
By permission of the
Society of Authors for
the Virginia Woolf Estate

Figure 43
A university
procession from
Three Guineas
(published 1938)
By permission of the
Society of Authors for
the Virginia Woolf Estate

monuments' (Nora 1989, p. 9). Woolf's attack on masculine performance rituals in *Three Guineas* is mirrored in the attack in *A Room of One's Own* on masculine classificatory systems in the British Museum Library, and both may owe something to Leonard's rituals. The Leonard Woolf Archive in the University of Sussex contains his obsessive lists, including ones of all music he listened to between 1939 and 1969, file cards of cacti with dates of flowering, four books of daily weather observations 1942–66, annual car mileages 1927–66, and (my favourite) dates of turning the central heating off and on 1959–69.

Such artificial memory is displaced in *Three Guineas* by the lack of amplifying or antipodal subtitles for the published photographs. All commentary is located tangentially in the text, in which the narrator positions herself as the representative voice of all dissenting daughters. The verbal language of the text and the pictorial language of the photographs are deeply antagonistic. Where the photographs represent an excess of immobility, the narrator takes differing descriptive vantage points, which often resemble the camera angles of the modernist photographers Alexander Rodchenko and Moholy-Nagy in a shared exploration of the visual and political potential of overhead views (Roberts 1998).

Just as the daughters of public men have been forced to be invisible in public life, so too the narrator, their collective voice, is physically remote from each photograph. From her angle 'your world [...] undoubtedly looks queer' (Woolf 1993, p. 133). The narrator can only 'enter on tiptoe'; she has a 'bird's-eye view of the outside of things' that 'is not altogether encouraging' (Woolf 1993, pp. 133, 138). As the narrator acutely points out, political memory should involve embodiment: 'To prevent war we must try to penetrate deeper beneath the skin' (Woolf 1993, p. 141). Watching the university procession is no easier: how 'strange' this world appears 'from our vantage point' of inequality, since such processions are observed as 'so remote' (Woolf 1993, p. 142). A contemporary letter to Woolf by an Ernest Huxley beautifully encapsulates her points where he argues that women 'always look at life from a different angle than a man does, they are exceedingly childish and intolerant in their views' (Huxley 2000, p. 118). The narrator's displacement is not the same as Woolf's later abjection of her own body, or displacement, in the famous mirror scene in 'A Sketch of the Past'. Rather in *Three Guineas*, she is attempting to contest a *patriarchal* displacement of women with the narrator's very embodied reactions to a differing politics of the Spanish Republic. At best women can only go 'trapesing along at the tail end of the procession' (Woolf 1993, p. 184). As against the absent photographs, whose contingent, affective scenes electrify Woolf's bodily synapses, the public photographs lack affect. Portraits and spectator do not exchange looks, cannot exchange memories.

Woolf makes her sexual politics very clear not only by deconstructing the public photographs in the text but also by physically displacing the narrator's body from the world she observes. The masculine 'body' is openly diseased. Patriarchy's infantile fixation is 'an egg we called it; a germ. We smelt it in the atmosphere' (Woolf 1993, p. 255). Similarly 'fathers in public, massed together in societies, in professions, were even more subject to the fatal disease' (Woolf 1993, p. 266). The sequence of public photographs in *Three Guineas* in part matches Woolf's method of ordering and mounting newspaper photographs in the scrapbooks, with some distinct and interesting omissions. She does not transfer from scrapbook to text two very powerful photographs: one, dated 12 August 1935, of a fascist with a resplendent skull on his flying jacket, and one of 'Major Fey', a powerful, helmeted German soldier. Instead she ends *Three Guineas* with a scourging verbal portrait of fascism, imaginatively utilising some of the pictorial presence of the scrapbook photographs:

> Man himself, the quintessence of virility, the perfect type of which all the others are imperfect adumbrations. He is a man certainly. His eyes are glazed; his eyes glare. His body, which is braced in an unnatural position, is tightly cased in a uniform. Upon the breast of that uniform are sewn several medals and other mystic symbols. His hand is upon a sword. He is called in German and Italian Führer or Duce; in our own language Tyrant or Dictator. And behind him lie ruined houses and dead bodies. (Woolf 1993, p. 270)

This verbal montage, like John Heartfield's several photo montages of the Führer, is a hybrid portrait. The image resembles the photographic cover of *Quack, Quack*, Leonard Woolf's attack on European fascism and fascism's philosophical antecedents in the writings of Spengler and others

(L. Woolf 1935). *Quack, Quack*'s cover shows both Hitler and Mussolini in full uniforms resplendent with medals and in fascist salute. Virginia thought *Quack, Quack* 'a very spirited attack upon human nature as it is at present' (Woolf 1979, p. 388). Her choice of a verbal portrait over direct photographic evidence is, I feel, an ethical strategy, adopted to prevent us identifying with the often compelling quality of fascist imagery. She manipulates the verbal description to highlight metaphorically the main theme of *Three Guineas*. Just as the fascist is 'unnatural', 'glazed' and 'tightly cased', so in turn he tightly cases women's bodies in the bird-cages of ruined domesticity. Woolf's text stares back into the glazed gaze of fascism, denying this disturbing image any published, vivid visibility.

IMAGE/TEXT AS ESSAY

The Otherness of the published portraits to Woolf's scene of looking, in opposition to the close physical relationship between her, her interpellated reader and the absent photographs, makes *Three Guineas* a profoundly innovative image/text. The two media of language and image are very different in kind. Language progresses in a linear order through time, whereas photographs are apprehended in a more immediate manner (Eisinger 1995). Woolf solves the problem of irreconcilability by not assuming (as her critics so frequently do) that either words or pictures are inherently more important than the other. *Three Guineas* is both photographic and an address to the absence of photographs. Image/texts, W. J. T. Mitchell argues in *Picture Theory*, break with the formal generic frontiers of narrative in their textual heterogeneity, their 'multiple boundaries and frames' (Mitchell 1994, p. 190). In Mitchell's view, image/texts (and his examples range from the poems of William Blake to the films of Spike Lee) are a highly charged form because the 'text frames elements that do intervene between the reader and the image' (Mitchell 1994, p. 173). Image/texts 'construct a region of the unknown [...] both prior to and adjacent to memory', and the mixture of image and analysis constitutes what Mitchell calls an 'image/text problematic' or a dialectical relation of picture and discourse (Mitchell 1994, p. 120). The real question to ask, when confronted by such image/texts, Mitchell suggests, 'is not "what is the difference (or similarity) between the words and the images?" but "what difference do the differences (and similarities) make?"' (Mitchell 1994, p. 15). The difference which the differences between verbal and visual evidence make matters a great deal to Woolf. *Three Guineas* dramatises the image/text differences as the medium of its analytical attack on fascist patriarchy. In this way *Three Guineas* breaks with the generic conventions that tend to govern essays that are purely narratives.

It is true, of course that narrative essays are not completely consistent. As Graham Good points out in *The Observing Self*, an overview of the essay genre, essays emerged in the late sixteenth century *outside* of existing organisations of knowledge (Good 1988). Connections in essays, he suggests, are 'often made through things, rather than being linked directly in a continuous argument', and the essay's 'hybrid of art and science' is frequently 'an act of personal witness' (Good 1988, p. 7). But *Three Guineas*' composition by field and collaborative narrative of the visual and the verbal bears witness to social issues in more dynamic ways than conventional essays. For example, in Adorno's classic, definitive account of the essay, 'The Essay as Form', although he admits the 'essay's affinity to the visual image' and 'the interrelation of nature and culture', he significantly denies that the essay can break 'out of culture into nature', or address lived reality, because 'the essay honours nature by confirming that it no longer exists for human beings' (Adorno 1984a, pp. 170, 167, 159). Woolf's essays, on the other hand, have permeable boundaries. She frequently fictionalises in her essays, inventing 'real' lives, characters who may carry her voice but who jump frequently 'from fact to fiction' (Brosnan 1997, p. 138). Similarly, in her fiction, she flows in and out of interior monologue and exterior description, producing a 'certain permeability of self and other' (Nicholls 1995, p. 265).

Three Guineas shows how patriarchy ravages both the public and the private, both the symbolic body and individuals' bodies, symbolised by a lack of narrator relation to the portraits and her emotional testimony to the pictures of murdered children. Woolf's choice of *Three Guineas* as her title, over her working titles *Men Are Like That* and *Letters to an Englishman*, reveals her discomfort with direct statement and preference for metaphor and metonymy. Her recognition that militaristic history and patriarchal identity construction in the family work profoundly in tandem manifests itself in *Three Guineas*' conjunction of memory 'pictures' and referential symbols of patriarchy. In 'Uses of Photography', a response to

Susan Sontag's *On Photography*, John Berger describes how photographs come to replace memory but also contain memory traces of subjectivity (Berger 1972). Crucially, in terms of *Three Guineas*, he links memory photographs with justice. Like Woolf, Berger believes that memory, and memory's photographic referents, imply 'a certain act of redemption', since what is remembered about political history is saved from nothingness (Berger 1972, p. 54).

CONCLUSION

Woolf discusses in detail the referents of both published and 'private' photographs in order to do justice to women's economic and social invisibility. The repeated images in which women are absent in the present, public world, and masculine military genocide has created an absent, dead world, are the constitutive core of *Three Guineas*' account of history and memory. Woolf's contiguous relation to the absent photographs and her bodily distance from the public photographs indexically constructs the main theme of *Three Guineas*: her attack on the symbolic blindness of patriarchal traditions. The photographs are not simply adjuncts reflecting her textual feminism. The important feature of *Three Guineas* is the narrator's embodiment or lack of embodiment in relation to photographic testimony, and what such relationships can suggest about visual memories and history. As Gilles Deleuze argues in *Proust and Signs*, such affect has meaning by holding onto the notion of difference at the level of the body (Deleuze 1972). For him, the role of affect is to give sensations that act directly on the body. Works of art (he discusses the paintings of Francis Bacon) reveal the force of affect and restore a self-awareness to the body: 'Reminiscences are metaphors of life; metaphors are reminiscences of art' (Deleuze 1972, p. 54).

It is the exchange between the bodily affects of narrator memory and public representations in *Three Guineas* which arguably offer a fresh representation of modernity's gendered consciousness. Woolf's radial juxtapositions of the testimonies of personal affects with the alienating public photographs counters the brutalising effect of masculine modernity. Her deep knowledge of photography – her constant photographic practice and photo album construction, and the continued experience of being photographed throughout her life – inspired her to choose photography as a generative medium in *Three Guineas*. The interaction of photographs and narrative produces a more complex multiple text, able to recast the problematics of patriarchy. Woolf had a very firm grasp of how photography can conceptualise the self against history, as both 'I' and 'Not-I'. Her emotional investment in photography's multiple powers was shared by other modernist women. As I have argued, in the years leading up to *Three Guineas*, 'photography, a male bastion before 1880, emerged as a career option and avocation for women', who often, as Jane Gover explains, 'shared a willingness to flaunt social standards and expectations' (Gover 1988, pp. 17, 35; and see Chapter 1). Modernist women's photography, in a continuum from the amateur to the professional, from popular culture to high art, 'was less competitive and more communal' (Davidov 1998, p. 78). In addition, like Woolf, many modernist women were drawn to the power of photographic narratives. For example, *Dorothea Lange Looks at the American Country Woman* similarly sutures women and place in photographic stories which interweave image and text (Davidov 1998, p. 215). Modernist women photographers shared Woolf's focus on the personal in a 'form of self-representation ... a special language for expressing themselves' (Gover 1988, p. 133).

Rather than privileging, as critics frequently do, Woolf's narrative political analysis and seeing *Three Guineas*' published photographs as simply graphic documentation of this, what struck me most about *Three Guineas* is Woolf's physical as well as photographic testimony. By juxtaposing the language of the body with two differing referents – the visible public icons and the absent, private visual memories – her matrix of experiential fragments connects past with present in an uncontestable testimony. Although Picasso, Braque and other modernist artists did create matrices of paint and other materials, as W. J. T. Mitchell points out, the impulse to reject mixed media and 'to purify media is one of the central Utopian gestures of modernism', which Woolf expertly disavows with her multi-generic work of feminist modernism (Mitchell 1994, p. 5). The photographs, both visible and implied, together with her experiential responses to both kinds of photographs, drain power from patriarchal representations in order to suggest the reversibility of patriarchal structures. As Woolf incisively concludes, 'we can best help you to prevent war not by repeating your words and following your methods but by finding new words and creating new methods' (Woolf 1993, p. 272).

7 AFTERWORD AND WOOLF'S ESSAYS ON MODERNISM

The relationship between cultural modernity and modernist visual cultures and literature is complex and contested. In *English Art 1860–1914* the editors, David Peters Corbett and Lara Perry, argue that, in art history, there are two competing readings of nineteenth- and twentieth-century art, drawing on two different understandings of this relationship (Corbett and Perry 2000). On the one hand modernism is seen as a purely formal development leading to abstract expressionism. The other reading argues that modernism's subject matter *is* modernity: the representation of urban and technological experience and 'the spectacular surface of modern life' (Corbett and Perry 2000, p. 2). From this second perspective, the formal appearance of an art work alone does not define its quality, but rather a work becomes significant if it responds to modern conditions, the major one being technological advances including cinema and photography.

Virginia Woolf, Vanessa Bell, H. D. and Dorothy Richardson took a marked interest in different ways of looking at modernity utilising the new technologies of photography and cinema. Women modernists were fascinated by the relationships between aesthetic developments and the way in which the new technologies could offer new depictions of themselves and their visible worlds. Sanford Schwarz argues that modernist writers' new attention to decentred subjectivities resulted from this fascination, which came with a refusal of positivist rules of representation: 'They maintained that intellectual formulations are simply practical instruments for arranging the sensory flux in a convenient manner' (Schwarz 1988, p. 17). Schwarz's description captures the essence of domestic photography. Photography offered modernist women a 'practical instrument' with which to experiment with different representations of their place in the flux of modern life.

In her introduction to *Virginia Woolf in the Age of Mechanical*

Reproduction, Pamela Caughie summarises Woolf's position as a modernist writer specifically in relation to technologies of modernity such as photography, the cinema and the gramophone (Caughie 2000). Caughie suggests that Woolf explores the aesthetic implications of the new mass media both in narrative techniques and in critical essays. It is this theme which I have tried to develop in *Modernist Women and Visual Cultures* by juxtaposing the insights of cultural and psycho-biographic histories with detailed close readings of visual texts. My argument has been that Woolf's modernism, like that of H. D. and Dorothy Richardson, is in urgent and experimental dialogue with the technologies of modernity, particularly the vocabulary and representative effects of domestic photography.

Characteristics of the photographic event match some aesthetic features of modernism. For example, both domestic photographers and modernist artists are concerned with surface representations, in particular with moments encapsulating wider social or familial relations. Camera technologies offered new visual possibilities, such as multiple points of view and scoping strategies. H. D. directly utilises photography in her novel *Bid Me To Live*, in which the character Julia comes to understand her life and the lives of those around her through photographic representations: 'They seemed to be superimposed on one another like a stack of photographic negatives. Hold them up to the light and you get in reverse light-and-shade. Julia and Bela seated on that same chintz-covered couch, a composite' (H. D. 1984, p. 89). The language of photography provides H. D., as it did Woolf, with terms for describing relationships in modernity. Photography could capture the daily experience of a gendered life. It could also capture the biographical past in a fresh modernist syntax.

The version of modernism which emerges from studying domestic photography is very different from the grand narratives of literary criticism such as Malcolm Bradbury and James McFarlane's classic *Modernism 1890–1930*. In this collection, Bradbury argues that modernists aim to create 'a pattern and wholeness which makes art into an order standing outside and beyond the human muddle, a transcendent object' (Bradbury and Fletcher 1976, p. 407). Here modernism is presented as a unified order defined by its detachment from daily life. But, by paying attention to a writer's more domestic, local aesthetics, modernism could better be described as a cultural field. As Pierre Bourdieu suggests, 'the literary or artistic field is a *field of forces*, but it is also a *field of struggles* tending to transform or conserve this field of forces' (Bourdieu 1993, p. 30). The struggles between biographical pressures and 'significant form' in the photographs of Vanessa Bell are a good example of 'a cultural field', and provide an alternative way of thinking about the aesthetic resources of women's modernism to Bradbury's 'transcendent object' (see Chapter 3). To shift attention from high art to domestic visual technologies registers the significance of gender by attending less to the panoptic overview and more to the space of everyday practices.

Domestic photography offers a different model of spectatorship from that of the specular flâneur presupposed in modernist art such as Manet's *A Bar at the Folies-Bergère*. A woman photographing her family and friends stands in a non-invasive relationship with her subjects (Davidov 1998). The conventions of domestic photography involve physical proximity in narratives of friendship. This particularity of a female spectator is highlighted in feminist art criticism. In *Vision and Difference* Griselda Pollock argues that women's art practice 'is itself *a site for the inscription of sexual difference*' (Pollock 1988, p. 81). The depiction of domestic spaces by artists Berthe Morisot and Mary Cassatt does not of necessity, Pollock argues, 'involve restriction or lack' or 'reinscribe the patriarchal construction of woman' (Pollock 1988, p. 84). This is due to their female spectatorship, in which the spaces of femininity are defined by 'a different kind of viewing' (Pollock 1988, p. 84). Pollock's account takes us beyond a simple, polarised model of the masculine specular flâneur posed against a feminine intimate portrait, for example, Morisot's *Psyche*, and towards a more complex understanding of the private sphere and its technologies of representation.

Pollock's critique encapsulates my theme: that women modernists utilise photography in their work as a scopic tool to refashion the specularity of modernity. For example, one of Virginia Woolf's diary descriptions of her compositional modernist aims suggests a visual experiment. On Monday 26 January 1920 she famously:

> arrived at some idea of a new form for a new novel. Suppose one thing should open out of another – as in An Unwritten Novel – only not for 10 pages but 200 or so – doesn't that give the looseness & lightness I want: doesnt that get closer & yet keep form & speed, & enclose everything, everything? My

> doubt is how far it will (include) enclose the human heart –
> Am I sufficiently mistress of my dialogue to net it there? For I
> figure that the approach will be entirely different this time; no
> scaffolding; scarcely a brick to be seen; all crepuscular, but
> the heart, the passion, humour, everything as bright as fire in
> the mist […] I must still grope & experiment but this
> afternoon I had a gleam of light. (Woolf 1978c, pp. 13–14)

The new form, Woolf's modernist project, is rendered as a process of capturing subjectivity ('the human heart') by means of 'light'. She envisions her writing method as a problem of 'light' and 'speed' rather than as a slow, cumulative process of narrative 'scaffolding'. She gives a significant title to her new form, 'an unwritten novel'. The diary's editor, Anne Olivier Bell, refers the title to Woolf's short story 'An Unwritten Novel' (Woolf 2001a). In this tale the narrator watches an unknown woman sitting opposite in a train compartment. The narrator imaginatively builds a whole romance about the stranger's life, only to be disabused sharply of her filmic conjecture that the woman is a lonely spinster when the woman is met by her son at journey's end. Critics have applied the term 'unwritten novel' to Woolf's fictional techniques in general, claiming that both the diary entry and the short story represent her attempts to describe new fictional representations of consciousness (Boone 1998).

   While Emily Dalgarno suggests that 'An Unwritten Novel' explores the *limits* of the gaze, the fact that Woolf specifically draws on a terminology of vision is a significant feature of her story, and this terminology could as well refer to the visual technologies of cinema and photography as to new narrative fictional means of recording a reality which is always elusive (Dalgarno 2001). For example, the narrator of 'An Unwritten Novel' records the elderly women's gestures and behaviour in close-up and medium-shot as if using a camera: 'Then she shuddered, and then she made the awkward angular movement that I had seen before' (Woolf 2001a, p. 19). At a later point in the narrative in a seaside town (which the story's editor, David Bradshaw, suggests is Eastbourne), the narrator's eye pans like a camera: 'Everything has meaning – placards leaning against doorways – names above shop-windows – red fruit in baskets – women's heads in the hairdresser's' (Bradshaw 2001, p. 102; Woolf 2001a, p. 23).

   The dramatic expansion of new technologies of vision in the decades before 1920 had encouraged writers to use metaphors of speed, light and framing. Ruth Miller considers that Woolf's continual attention to issues of framing in her fiction derives from her interest in painting and from the influence of Bell, Fry and post-Impressionism (Miller 1993). In addition, Miller suggests, the frame is an archetype of the marginal. But the frame is also a feature of Woolf's snapshot photographs, which are often reproduced in her albums with very clear white margins. Albums often frame observed scenes into generic or thematic groups, much as Woolf's use of scenic organisation does in her short fictions. The emphasis on sight in her writing has been taken as evidence of the extent to which she was influenced by painting, but one could argue that such an emphasis is equally bound up with her experience of domestic photography.

Woolf's essays in the 1920s specifically about modernism, 'Modern Fiction' (1925), the revised version of 'Modern Novels' (1919), 'The Narrow Bridge of Art' (1927) and 'Phases of Fiction' (1929), share this concern with perspective. Like snapshots, the essays' momentary reflections often connect by focusing on objects. As Graham Good argues, to some extent the essay form is still marginal within the discipline of literature (Good 1988). Essays can encompass a personalised, scopic witnessing of events, often Woolf's preferred form of address. In essays the particular has priority over the general. She borrowed the title 'Common Reader' for her essays from Dr Johnson, and describes a common reader reading literature as if creating a photo album: 'out of whatever odds and ends he can come by, some kind of whole – a portrait of a man, a sketch of an age' (Woolf 1994a, p. 19).

Woolf's much-discussed essay 'Modern Fiction' is a good example of her use of photographic tropes of illumination and reflection (Woolf 1994c). In her seemingly unstructured view of contemporary writing, she applies scopic devices to a commentary on literary features, centring on a much-quoted call for her contemporaries to turn from the 'softly padded first-class railway carriage' of the novels of H. G. Wells and Arnold Bennett to 'myriad impressions – trivial, fantastic, evanescent' (Woolf 1994c, pp. 159–60). She begins the essay with a clear statement that 'the modern practice of the art is somehow an improvement upon the old' (Woolf 1994c, p. 157). Her contemporary writers, 'Mr Wells, Mr Bennett and Mr Galsworthy', with their 'craftsmanship' and 'plethora' of 'ideas and facts', obscure modernist improvements (Woolf 1994c, pp. 158–9). She opposes two views of contemporary literature: the 'materialist' industry of Wells, Bennett and Galsworthy and the perceptions of modernists such as James Joyce. Where the materialist articulates a total-ising mastery of social representation, in 'the work of several young writers' life is not controlled by structures but is apprehended through techniques of vision and associated symbolic mechanisms of perspective. Woolf describes modernity scopically: 'life is not a series of gig lamps symmetrically arranged; life is a luminous halo, a semi-transparent envelope [...] let us trace the pattern, however disconnected and incoherent in appearance, which each sight or incident scores upon the consciousness' (Woolf 1994c, pp. 160–1). She strains towards a photo-graphic effect of soft focus, using a modernist pictorial syntax which focuses on the ephemeral and the provisional.

Similarly Woolf's 'The Narrow Bridge of Art' evokes differing perspectives and filmic views. She suggests that the future novel will contain 'the stimulus of sight, the effect on us of the shape of trees or the play of colour', like a series of impressions from an avant-garde film (Woolf 1958a, p. 23). In this essay and in 'Phases of Fiction' Woolf, in a wide-ranging, impressionistic survey of historical examples of the English novel, begins with the 'truth-tellers' Defoe and Swift and ends with James and Proust (Woolf 1958b, p. 95). She imagines 'a whole series of thoughts, sensations, ideas, memories which were apparently sleeping on the walls of the mind' (Woolf 1958b, p. 124). Turning her mind into a camera, she pans through the history of literature in one continuous take. Like a photographer intently bent over a developing tray, 'the longer the novelist pores over his analysis, the more he becomes conscious of something that forever escapes. And it is this double vision that makes the work of Proust to us in our generation so spherical' (Woolf 1958b, p. 139). The visual complexities of modernist literature are most explicit, she argues, in the work of Proust, where 'we come upon a flight of imagery – beautiful, coloured, visual, as if the mind, having carried its powers as far as possible in analysis, suddenly rose in the air and from a station high up gave us a different view of the same object in terms of metaphor' (Woolf 1958b, pp. 125–6). Woolf describes Proust's use of metaphor as like a film which switches to an aerial long-shot to enable spectators to see juxtapositions of characters and events within a frame.

Woolf's interest in visual perspectives in her critical essays matches her turn to the new representational devices of cinema and photography elsewhere in her work. Unlike other representational forms, photography has a unique way of representing objects and people as indices of the inner feelings of a viewer or subject (Benjamin 1972). Whereas literary tropes can often seem arbitrary, photographs and the visual language of photography – its structures of looking – are material (but not a Bennett-like materialism). That is to say, photography's techniques of representation can enable writers to figure *material* objects as images of the particular gender and cultural screens which mediate structures of looking. By means of optical references, Woolf and other modernist women could include a number of perspectives, as well as their own biographies, within critical and fictional narratives, and expose the unconscious fantasies shaping such perspectives. Photographic images enable writers to reveal the constitution of gendered subjects in descriptions of oppositional looks, such as the differing looks of the narrator in *Three Guineas*. *Modernist Women and Visual Cultures* has focused on these modernist experiments, which, by means of photographic referents, evoke a gendered consciousness in differing narrative forms. The family photo album is probably the first image/text which most people encounter. Woolf's and Bell's constant attention to such aesthetic versions of familial relations reveals their continual interest in the ways in which visual fields represent absence and presence and unconscious optics, and also in the ways in which photographic images can disrupt a familiar gendered narrative.

A crucial moment from my own past figured some of these issues to me. Shortly before I undertook my first weeks of research on Virginia Woolf's photo albums, my stepmother visited, bringing old family photographs, including a photograph of me, perhaps aged two, in my bath. The photograph is somewhat out of focus, as were almost all of my father's early attempts, and taken with a Kodak 2A camera, one of the same camera models used by Virginia Woolf. The coincidence I took as a sign of wonder, clear proof that my research would be fruitful.

In my bath photograph I am supported by a ghostly hand, my mother's hand, which gave me a third image of my mother to add to the existing two photographs of her I owned. My mother died aged forty-nine when I was thirteen, the same ages as Julia Stephen and Virginia Woolf at Julia's death. Scenes from 'A Sketch of the Past' always have an incredible resonance for me. Inevitably such autobiographical identifications became part of the project of writing *Modernist Women and Visual Cultures*. My critical work, like Woolf's, is an obvious example of a need to acknowledge and move beyond the quintessential primary loss we all experience: the death or the disappearance of the mother. At some point during my research I came to understand that Virginia Woolf's mother was a ghostly revenant not only in Woolf's writing, as critics uniformly argue, but also in her photography and continual turn to photographic referents. And, hopefully, a focus on Woolf's use of domestic images can counter a purist concept of modernist aesthetics, by allowing us to cross the borderline of aesthetics into some of the specific, gendered, cultural and familial issues of modernity.

BIBLIOGRAPHY

Abel, Elizabeth (1989) *Virginia Woolf and the Fictions of Psychoanalysis*, Chicago: University of Chicago Press.
Abel, Richard (1975) 'The Contribution of the French Literary Avant-Garde to Film Theory and Criticism
    (1907–1924)', *Cinema Journal*, 14:3, pp. 19–40.
Adorno, Theodor (1984a) 'The Essay as Form', *New German Critique*, 22, pp. 151–71.
Adorno, Theodor (1984b) *Aesthetic Theory*, trans. C. Lenhevedt, London: Routledge and Kegan Paul.
Adorno, Theodor and Horkheimer, M. (1973) *Dialectics of Enlightenment*, London: Allen Lane.
Anderson, Elizabeth (1993) *Value in Ethics and Economics*, Cambridge MA: Harvard University Press.
Anderson, Linda (2001) *Autobiography*, London: Routledge.
Anscombe, Isabelle (1981) *Omega and After*, London: Thames and Hudson.
Architectural Review (1930) 'Third Prize', 68, p. 242.
Armstrong, Carol (1996) 'Cupid's Pencil of Light: Julia Margaret Cameron and the Maternalization of
    Photography', *October*, 76, pp. 115–41.
Armstrong, Nancy (1998) 'Modernism's Iconophobia and What it Did to Gender', *Modernism/Modernity*, 5:12,
    pp. 47–74.
Armstrong, Nancy (1999) *Fiction in the Age of Photography*, Cambridge MA: Harvard University Press.
Baldassari, Anne (1997) *Picasso and Photography: The Dark Mirror*, Paris: Flammarion.
Barr, Charles (ed.) (1986) *All Our Yesterdays: Ninety Years of British Cinema*, London: BFI.
Barrett, Michèle (1993) 'Introduction', in *A Room of One's Own and Three Guineas*, ed. M. Barrett,
    Harmondsworth: Penguin.
Barthes, Roland (1977) *Image-Music-Text*, New York: Hill and Wang.
Barthes, Roland (1981) *Camera Lucida*, trans. R. Howard, New York: Hill and Wang.
Barthes, Roland (1982) 'The Photographic Message', in *A Barthes Reader*, ed. S. Sontag, London:
    Jonathan Cape.
Bazin, André (1971) *What is Cinema? Vols 1 and 2*, Berkeley: University of California Press.
Beer, Gillian (2000) *Wave, Atom, Dinosaur: Woolf's Science*, London: Virginia Woolf Society of Great Britain.
Bell, Clive (1914) *Art*, London: Chatto.
Bell, Quentin (1996) *Virginia Woolf*, London: Pimlico.
Bell, Quentin and Garnett, Angelica (eds) (1981) *Vanessa Bell's Family Album*, London: Jill Norman and
    Hobhouse.
Bell, Vanessa (1896) *Album 1A*, London: Tate Gallery Archives.
Bell, Vanessa (1935) *Album 5*, London: Tate Gallery Archives.
Bell, Vanessa (1993) 'Notes on Bloomsbury', in *The Bloomsbury Group*, ed. S. P. Rosenbaum, London:
    Croom Helm.
Bell, Vanessa (1997) *Sketches in Pen and Ink: A Bloomsbury Notebook*, ed. L. Giachero, London: Hogarth Press.
Benjamin, Jessica (1998) *Shadow of the Other: Intersubjectivity and Gender in Psychoanalysis*, London:
    Routledge.
Benjamin, Walter (1972) 'A Short History of Photography', *Screen*, 13:1, pp. 5–26.
Benjamin, Walter (1973) *Illuminations*, London: Fontana.
Benjamin, Walter (1983) *Passagen-Work*, ed. R. Tiedemann, Frankfurt: Suhrkamp.
Benstock, Shari (1986) *Women of the Left Bank: Paris 1900–1940*, Austin: University of Texas Press.
Benstock, Shari (1989) 'Expatriate Modernism: Writing on the Cultural Rim', in *Women's Writing
    in Exile*, eds M. L. Broc and A. Ingram, Chapel Hill: University of North Carolina Press.
Berg, C., Durieux, F. and Lernout, G. (eds) (1995) *The Turn of the Century: Modernism and
    Modernity in Literature and the Arts*, New York: Walter de Gruyer.
Berger, John (1972) *Selected Essays and Articles: The Look of Things* Harmondsworth: Penguin.
Berger, John (1997) 'Ways of Remembering', in *The Camerawork Essays*, ed. J. Evans, London: Rivers Oram
    Press.
Berger, John and Mohr, Jean (1995) *Another Way of Seeing*, New York: Vintage.
Bergson, Henri (1949) *The Creative Mind*, New York: Citadel Press.
Bergson, Henri (1991) *Matter and Memory*, New York: Zone Books.

Berman, Marshall (1982) *All That is Solid Melts into Air: The Experience of Modernity*, New York: Simon and Schuster.

Betts, Ernest (1929) 'Why Talkies are Unsound', *Close Up*, 4:4, pp. 22–4.

Boebel, Degny (1997) 'The Sun Born in a Woman: H. D. 's Transformations of a Masculinist Icon in "The Dancer"', in *Unmanning Modernism: Gendered Re-Readings*, eds E. J. Harrison and S. Peterson, Knoxville: University of Tennessee Press.

Bond, Ralph (1930) 'Dovjenko on the Sound Film', *Close Up*, 7:4, pp. 273–5.

Boone, Joseph Allen (1998) *Libidinal Currents: Sexuality and the Shaping of Modernism*, Chicago: University of Chicago Press.

Bornstein, George (1991) *Representing Modernist Texts: Editing as Interpretation*, Ann Arbor: University of Michigan Press.

Bourdieu, Pierre (1990) *Photography: A Middle-Brow Art*, Cambridge: Polity.

Bourdieu, Pierre (1993) *The Field of Cultural Production: Essays on Art and Literature*, Cambridge: Polity.

Bradbury, Malcolm and Fletcher, John (1976) 'The Introverted Novel', in *Modernism 1890–1930*, eds M. Bradbury and J. McFarlane, Harmondsworth: Penguin.

Bradbury, Malcolm and McFarlane, James (eds) (1976) *Modernism 1890–1930*, Harmondsworth: Penguin.

Bradley, A. C. (1959) *Oxford Lectures on Poetry*, London: Macmillan.

Bradshaw, David (2001) 'Explanatory Notes', in *Virginia Woolf: The Mark on the Wall and Other Short Fiction*, ed. D. Bradshaw, Oxford: Oxford University Press.

Braidotti, Rosi (1991) *Patterns of Dissonance*, Cambridge: Polity.

Brenan, Gerald (1975) 'South from Grenada', in *The Bloomsbury Group*, ed. S. P. Rosenbaum, London: Croom Helm.

Brosnan, Leila (1997) *Reading Virginia Woolf's Essays and Journalism*, Edinburgh: Edinburgh University Press.

Bryher (1927) 'G. W. Pabst: A Survey', *Close Up*: 6, pp. 56–61.

Bryher (1928a) 'Defence of Hollywood', *Close Up*, 2:2, pp. 44–51.

Bryher (1928b) 'What Can I Do?', *Close Up*, 2:3, pp. 21–5.

Bryher (1928c) 'An Interview: Anita Loos', *Close Up*, 2:4, pp. 12–15.

Bryher (1928d) 'Films for Children', *Close Up*, 3:2, pp. 16–20.

Bryher (1929a) *Film Problems of Soviet Russia*, Territet: Pool.

Bryher (1929b) 'A Private Showing of *Cosmos*', *Close Up*, 4:5, pp. 42–5.

Bryher (1932) 'West and East of the Atlantic', *Close Up*, 9:2, pp. 131–3.

Bryher (1933) 'What Shall You Do in the War?', *Close Up*, 10:2, pp. 188–92.

Bryher (1963) *The Heart to Artemis*, London: Collins.

Bürger, Peter (1984) *The Theory of the Avant-Garde*, trans. M. Shaw, Manchester: Manchester University Press.

Burgin, Victor (1982) 'Looking at Photographs', in *Thinking Photography*, V. Burgin, London: Macmillan.

Burgin, Victor (1992) 'Perverse Spaces', in *Sexuality and Space*, ed. B. Colomina, Princeton NJ: Princeton Architectural Press.

Burnwick, Frederick and Douglas, Paul (1992) *The Crisis in Modernism: Bergson and the Vitalist Controversy*, Cambridge: Cambridge University Press.

Butler, Christopher (1994) *Early Modernism: Literature, Music and Painting in Europe 1900–1916*, Oxford: Oxford University Press.

Butler, Judith (1993) *Bodies that Matter*, London: Routledge.

Byrne, Charlotte (1998) *Lewis Carroll*, London: British Council.

Caffin, Charles (1997) 'Clarence H. White in *Camera Work*, 23, 1908', in *Camera Work*, eds S. Philippi and U. Kieseyer, New York: Taschen.

Cameron, Julia Margaret (1996) *Annals of my Glass House*, Seattle: University of Washington Press.

Campbell, Jan (2000) *Arguing with the Phallus: Feminist, Queer and Postcolonial Theory: A Psychoanalytic Contribution*, London: Zed Books.

Carlston, Erin G. (1998) *Thinking Fascism: Sapphic Modernism and Fascist Modernity*, Stanford: Stanford University Press.

Carnap, Rudolf (1995) 'Space', in *Poetics of Space*, ed. S. Yates, Albuquerque: University of New Mexico Press.

Carrier, Peter (2000) 'Places, Politics and the Archiving of Contemporary Memory', in *Memory and Methodology*, ed. S. Radstone, New York: Berg.

Carter, Huntly (1930) *New Spirit in the Cinema*, London: Harold Shayler.

Castle, Hugh (1930) 'Old Moore's Fourth Dimension', *Close Up*, 6:1, pp. 19–26.

Caughie, Pamela (2000) 'Introduction', in *Virginia Woolf in the Age of Mechanical Reproduction*, ed. P. Caughie, New York: Garland.

Caws, Mary Ann (1990) *Women of Bloomsbury: Virginia, Vanessa and Carrington*, London: Routledge.

Cherry, Deborah (2000) *Beyond the Frame: Feminism and Visual Culture, Britain 1850–1900*, London: Routledge.

Chodorow, Nancy (1978) *The Reproduction of Mothering: The Sociology of Gender*, Berkeley: University of California Press.

Cixous, Hélène (1974) 'The Character of "Character"', *New Literary History*, 5:2, pp. 383–402.

Cixous, Hélène (1975) 'The Laugh of the Medusa', *Signs*, 1:4, pp. 875–93.

Clarke, Graham (1997) *The Photograph*, Oxford: Oxford University Press.

Coburn, Alvin Langdon (1997) 'The Relation of Time to Art', in *Camera Work*, eds S. Philippi and U. Kieseyer, New York: Taschen.

Coe, Brian and Gates, Paul (1977) *The Snapshot Photograph*, London: Ash and Grant.

Cohen, Phil (1997) 'Laboring Under Whiteness', in *Displacing Whiteness: Essays in Social and Cultural Criticism*, ed. R. Frankenberg, Durham NC: Duke University Press.

Colette (1980) *Colette at the Movies: Criticism and Screenplays*, eds A. Virmaux and O. Virmaux, trans. S. W. R. Smith, New York: Frederick Ungar.

Collecott, Diana (1987) 'Images at the Crossroads: The "H. D. Scrapbook"', in *H. D.: Woman and Poet*, ed. M. King, Orono: National Poetry Foundation, University of Maine.

Collins, Patricia Hill (1990) *Black Feminist Thought*, London: Unwin Hyman.

Cooper, Helen, Munich, Adrienne and Squier, Susan (1989) 'Arms and the Woman: the Con(tra)ception of the War Text', in *Arms and the Woman: War, Gender and Literary Representation*, eds H. Cooper, A. Munich and S. Squier, Chapel Hill: University of North Carolina Press.

Corbett, David Peters and Perry, Lara (2000) 'Introduction', in *English Art 1860–1914: Modern Artists and Identity*, eds D. P. Corbett and L. Perry, Manchester: Manchester University Press.

Cornell, Drucilla (1995) 'What is Ethical Feminism', in *Feminist Contentions*, eds S. Benhabib et al., London: Routledge.

Corrigan, Paul (1983) 'Film Entertainment as Ideology and Pleasure: Towards a History of Audiences', in *British Cinema History*, eds J. Curran and V. Porter, London: Weidenfeld and Nicolson.

Crary, Jonathan (1990) *Techniques of the Observer: On Vision and Modernity in the Nineteenth Century*, Cambridge MA: MIT Press.

Crimp, Douglas (1992) 'The Museum's Old/The Library's New', in *The Contest of Meaning*, ed. R. Bolton, Cambridge MA: MIT Press.

Cripps, Thomas (1970) 'Paul Robeson and Black Identity in American Movies', *Massachusetts Review*, summer, pp. 468–85.

Cuddy-Keane, Melba (1997) 'Virginia Woolf and the Varieties of Historicist Experience', in *Virginia Woolf and the Essay*, eds B. C. Rosenberg and J. Dubino, Basingstoke: Macmillan.

Dalgarno, Emily (2001) *Virginia Woolf and the Visible World*, Cambridge: Cambridge University Press.

da Silva, Takei N. (1990) *Modernism and Virginia Woolf*, London: Windsor Publications.

Davidov, Judith F. (1998) *Women's Camera Work: Self/Body/Other in American Visual Culture*, Durham NC: Duke University Press.

Davidson, Harriett (1998) 'Poetry: Witness Feminism', unpublished paper delivered at Rutgers Institute for Research on Women, February.

DeKoven, Marianne (1989) 'Gendered Doubleness and the "Origins" of Modernist Form', *Tulsa Studies in Women's Literature*, 8:1, pp. 19–42.

DeKoven, Marianne (1991) *Rich and Strange: Gender, History, Modernism*, Princeton NJ: Princeton University Press.

DeKoven, Marianne (1999) 'Modernism and Gender', in *The Cambridge Companion to Modernism*, ed. M. Levenson, Cambridge: Cambridge University Press.

Deleuze, Gilles (1972) *Proust and Signs*, trans. R. Howard, New York: George Braziller.

Deleuze, Gilles (1983) 'Plato and the Simulacrum', *October*, 16, pp. 45–56.

Dettmar, Kevin J. H. (1992) *Rereading the New: A Backward Glance at Modernism*, Ann Arbor: University of Michigan Press.

Dick, Susan (ed.) (1985) *The Complete Shorter Fiction of Virginia Woolf*, London: Hogarth Press.

Dick, Susan (ed.) (1989) *The Complete Shorter Fiction of Virginia Woolf*, 2nd edn, San Diego: Harcourt.

Dimock, George (2000) 'Edward Weston's Anti-Puritanism', *History of Photography*, 24:1, pp. 65–74.

Dobb, Henry (1929) 'Landseer's Lions and Kate Greenaway', *Close Up*, 4:2, pp. 71–2.

Duberman, Martin (1989) *Paul Robeson*, London: Bodley Head.

Duffy, Julia and Davis, Lloyd (1995) 'Demythologizing Facts and Photographs in *Three Guineas*', in *Photo-Textualities: Reading Photographs and Literature*, ed. M. Bryant, Newark: University of Delaware Press.

DuPlessis, Rachel Blau (1985) *Writing Beyond the Ending: Narrative Strategies of Twentieth-Century Women Writers*, Bloomington: Indiana University Press.

Dusinberre, Deke (1996) 'The Avant-garde Attitude in the Thirties', in *The British Avant-Garde Film 1926–1995*, ed. M. O'Pray, Luton: University of Luton Press.

Edmunds, Susan (1994) *Out of Line: History, Psychoanalysis and Montage in H. D.'s Long Poems*, Stanford: Stanford University Press.

Eisenstein, Sergei M. (1929) 'The New Language of Cinematography', *Close Up*, 4:5, pp. 10–13.

Eisenstein, Sergei M. (1930a) 'The Fourth Dimension in the Kino: Part I', *Close Up*, 6:3, pp. 253–68.

Eisenstein, Sergei M. (1930b) 'The Fourth Dimension in the Kino: Part II', *Close Up*, 6:4, pp. 253–68.

Eisenstein, Sergei M. (1931a) 'The Dinamic Square Part I', *Close Up*, 8:1, pp. 2–16.

Eisenstein, Sergei M. (1931b) 'The Principles of Film Form', *Close Up*, 8:3, pp. 167–82.

Eisenstein, Sergei M. (1943) *The Film Sense*, London: Faber.

Eisenstein, Sergei M. (1988a) 'The Dramaturgy of Film Form', in *S. M. Eisenstein: Selected Works: Vol. 1, Writings 1922–34*, ed. and trans. R. Taylor, London: BFI.

Eisenstein, Sergei M. (1988b) *S. M. Eisenstein: Selected Works: Vol. 1, Writings 1922–34*, ed. and trans. R. Taylor, London: BFI.

Eisinger, Joel (1995) *Trace and Transformation: American Criticism of Photography in the Modernist Period*, Albuquerque: University of New Mexico Press.

Eliot, T. S. (1918) 'Studies in Contemporary Criticism', *Egoist*, 5:9, pp. 113–14.

Elliott, Bridget and Wallace, Jo-Ann (1994) *Women Artists and Writers: Modernist (Im)positions*, London: Routledge.

Elliott, Eric (1928) *Anatomy of a Motion Picture Art*, Territet: Pool.

Evans, Jessica (ed.) (1997) *The Camerawork Essays: Context and Meaning in Photography*, London: Rivers Oram Press.

Evans, Jessica and Hall, Stuart (eds) (1999) *Visual Culture: The Reader*, London: Sage.

Eysteinsson, Astradur (1990) *The Concept of Modernism*, Ithaca NY: Cornell University Press.

Falkenheim, Jacqueline V. (1980) *Roger Fry and the Beginnings of Formalist Art Criticism*, Ann Arbor: UMI Research Press.

Farwell, Beatrice (1977) *The Cult of Images: Baudelaire and the Nineteenth-Century Media Explosion*, Santa Barbara: USCB Art Museum.

Faulkner, Peter (1977) *Modernism*, London: Methuen.

Felman, Shoshana and Laub, Dori (1992) *Testimony: Crises of Witnessing in Literature, Psychoanalysis and History*, London: Routledge.

Felski, Rita (1995) *The Gender of Modernity*, Cambridge MA: Harvard University Press.

Fernald, Anne E. (1999) 'The Memory Palace of Virginia Woolf', in *Virginia Woolf: Reading the Renaissance*, ed. S. Greene, Athens OH: Ohio University Press.

Film Art (1933–7) London: BFI Archives.

Film Society Programmes (1925–39) rpt 1972, New York: Arno Press.

Fineberg, Jonathan (1997) *The Innocent Eye: Children's Art and the Modern Artist*, Princeton NJ: Princeton University Press.

Flanner, Janet (1972) *Paris Was Yesterday 1925–1939*, New York: Viking Press.

Flesher, Erika (1997) 'Picturing the Truth in Fiction: Revisionary Biography and the Illustrative Portraits for *Orlando*', in *Virginia Woolf and the Arts: Selected Papers from the Sixth Annual Conference on Virginia Woolf*, eds D. F. Gillespie and L. Hankins, New York: Pace University Press.

Fokkema, Douwe E. (1984) *Literary History Modernism and Postmodernism*, Amsterdam: John Benjamins.

Frawley, Maria (1997) 'Modernism and Maternity: Alice Meynell and the Politics of Motherhood', in *Unmanning Modernism*, eds E. J. Harrison and S. Peterson, Knoxville: University of Tennessee Press.

Freeman, David (2000) 'Letter to Virginia Woolf dated 12. 7. 1938', in '*Three Guineas* Letters', ed. A. Snaith, *Woolf Studies Annual*, 6, p. 55.

Freud, Sigmund (1899) 'Screen Memories', in *The Standard Edition of the Complete Psychological Works of Sigmund Freud*, vol. 3, trans. J. Strachey, London: Hogarth Press.

Freud, Sigmund (1938) 'Childhood and Concealing Memories', in *Psychopathology of Everyday Life*, Harmondsworth: Penguin.

Freud, Sigmund (1938–9) *Moses and Monotheism*, in *The Standard Edition of the Complete Psychological Works of Sigmund Freud*, vol. 23, trans. J. Strachey, London: Hogarth Press.

Freud, Sigmund (1953) *The Interpretation of Dreams*, in *The Standard Edition of the Complete Psychological Works of Sigmund Freud*, vols IV and V, trans. J. Strachey, London: Hogarth Press.

Freud, Sigmund (1961) *Beyond the Pleasure Principle*, Harmondsworth: Penguin.

Freud, Sigmund (1966) 'A Case of Paranoia Running Counter to the Psychoanalytic Theory of the Disease', in *The Standard Edition of the Complete Psychological Works of Sigmund Freud*, vol. XII, trans. J. Strachey, London: Hogarth Press.

Freud, Sigmund and Breur, Joseph (1974) *Studies on Hysteria*, Harmondsworth: Penguin.

Freund, Gisèle (1974) *The World in My Camera*, trans. J. Guicharnaud, New York: Dial.

Friedberg, Anne (1983) *Writing About Cinema 'Close Up' 1927–1933*, Ann Arbor: University Microfilms International.

Friedberg, Anne (1993) *Window Shopping: Cinema and the Postmodern*, Berkeley: University of California Press.

Friedman, Susan Stanford (1987) 'Modernism of the "Scattered Remnant": Race and Politics in H. D.'s Development', in *Feminist Issues in Literary Scholarship*, ed. S. Benstock, Bloomington: Indiana University Press.

Friedman, Susan Stanford (1990) 'H. D. : Introduction', in *The Gender of Modernism*, ed. B. Kime Scott, Bloomington: Indiana University Press.

Fry, Roger (1919) 'The Artist's Vision', *Athenaeum*, 11 July, p. 594.

Fry, Roger (1921) *Vision and Design*, London: Chatto and Windus.

Fry, Roger (1922) 'Independent Gallery', *New Statesman*, 3 June, pp. 237–8.

Fry, Roger (1996) *The Roger Fry Reader*, ed. C. Reed, Chicago: University of Chicago Press.

Giddens, Anthony (1991) *Modernity and Self-Identity*, Cambridge: Polity.

Gilbert, Sandra M. and Gubar, Susan (1988a) *No Man's Land. Vol. 1: The War of the Words*, New Haven CN: Yale University Press.

Gilbert, Sandra M. and Gubar, Susan (1988b) *No Man's Land. Vol. 2: Sex Changes*, New Haven CN: Yale University Press.

Gilbert, Sandra M. and Gubar, Susan (1994) *No Man's Land. Vol. 3: Letters from the Front*, New Haven CN: Yale University Press.

Giles, Steve (1993) *Theorizing Modernism: Essays in Critical Theory*, London: Routledge.

Gillespie, Diane F. (1988) *The Sisters' Arts: The Writing and Painting of Virginia Woolf and Vanessa Bell*, New York: Syracuse University Press.

Gillespie, Diane F. (1993) '"Her Kodak Pointed at his Head": Virginia Woolf and Photography', in *The Multiple Muses of Virginia Woolf*, ed. D. F. Gillespie, Columbia OH: University of Missouri Press.

Goldman, Jane (2001) *The Feminist Aesthetics of Virginia Woolf*, Cambridge: Cambridge University Press.

Good, Graham (1988) *The Observing Self: Rediscovering the Essay*, London: Routledge.

Gover, Jane C. (1988) *The Positive Image: Women Photographers in Turn of the Century America*, Albany NY: State University of New York Press.

Green, André (1993) *On Private Madness*, Madison CN: International Universities.

Gualtieri, Elena (1999) '*Three Guineas* and the Photograph: The Art of Propaganda', in *Women Writers of the 1930s*, ed. M. Joannou, Edinburgh: Edinburgh University Press.

H. D. (1927a) 'The Cinema and the Classics: Beauty', *Close Up*, 1, pp. 22–33.

H. D. (1927b) 'The Cinema and the Classics: Restraint', *Close Up*, 2, pp. 30–9.

H. D. (1927c) 'Conrad Veidt', *Close Up*, 3, pp. 34–44.

H. D. (1927d) 'The Cinema and the Classics: The Mask and the Movietone', *Close Up*, 5, pp. 18–31.

H. D. (1928a) 'Expiation', *Close Up*, 2:5, pp. 38–49.

H. D. (1928b) 'Joan of Arc', *Close Up*, 3:1, pp. 15–23.

H. D. (1928c) 'Russian Films', *Close Up*, 3:3, pp. 18–29.

H. D. (1929) 'An Appreciation', *Close Up*, 4:3, pp. 56–68.

H. D. (1984) *Bid Me To Live*, London: Virago.

H. D. (1990a) 'Notes on Thought and Vision', in *The Gender of Modernism*, ed. B. Kime Scott, Bloomington: Indiana University Press.

H. D. (1990b) 'The Borderline Pamphlet', in *The Gender of Modernism*, ed. B. Kime Scott, Bloomington: Indiana University Press.

Habermas, Jürgen (1983) 'Modernity – An Incomplete Project', in *Postmodern Culture*, ed. H. Foster, London: Pluto Press.

Hall, Stuart (1991) 'Reconstruction Work: Images of Post-War Black Settlement', in *Family Snaps*, eds J. Spence and P. Holland, London: Virago.

Hamilton, Violet (1996) *Annals of My Glass House: Photographs by Julia Margaret Cameron*, Seattle: University of Washington Press.

Hankins, Leslie (1993) 'Woolf's "The Cinema" and Film Forums of the Twenties', in *The Multiple Muses of Virginia Woolf*, ed. D. F. Gillespie, Columbia: University of Missouri Press.

Hankins, Leslie (2001) 'Reel Publishing: Virginia Woolf and the Hogarth Essays Film Pamphlets', unpublished paper, Eleventh Annual Conference on Virginia Woolf: 'Voyages Out, Voyages Home', 13–16 June, Bangor University.

Hansen, Miriam B. (1987) 'Benjamin, Cinema and Experience: The Blue Flower in the Land of Technology', *New German Critique*, 40, pp. 179–224.

Hansen, Miriam B. (1995) 'America, Paris, the Alps: Kracauer (and Benjamin) on Cinema and Modernity', in *Cinema and the Invention of Modern Life*, eds L. Charney and V. R. Schwartz, Berkeley: University of California.

Hanssen, L. (1995) 'Een Kamer(a) voor jezelf: op weg naar een androgyne verbeelding', *Obscuur*, 2:2, pp. 6–10.

Harrison, Charles (1999) 'Degas' *Bathers* and Other People', *Modernism/Modernity*, 6:3, pp. 57–91.

Hartmann, Sadakichi (1997) 'The Exhibition of Children's Drawings', in *Camera Work*, eds S. Philippi and U. Kieseyer, New York: Taschen.

Haug, Frigga (2000) 'Memory Work: The Key to Women's Anxiety', in *Memory and Methodology*, ed. S. Radstone, New York: Berg.

Hekman, Susan (1997) 'Truth and Method: Feminist Standpoint Theory Revisited', *Signs*, 22:2, pp. 341–65.

Herring, Robert (1928) 'Film Imagery: Eisenstein', *Close Up*, 3:6, pp. 20–30.

Herring, Robert (1930) 'The Whiteman Front', *Close Up*, 7:1, pp. 52–62.

Hertz, Neil (1985) 'Dora's Secrets, Freud's Techniques', in *Dora's Case: Freud, Hysteria, Feminism*, eds C. Bernheimer and C. Kahane, London: Virago.

Higonnet, Margaret and Higonnet, Patrice L-R. (1987) 'The Double Helix', in *Behind the Lines: Gender and the Two World Wars*, eds M. R. Higonnet, J. Jenson, S. Michel and M. C. Weitz, New Haven CN: Yale University Press.

Hiller, Susan (ed.) (1991) *The Myth of Primitivism*, London: Routledge.

Hillis, Miller (1983) 'Mr. Carmichael and Lily Briscoe: The Rhythm of Creativity in *To The Lighthouse*', in *Modernism Reconsidered*, eds R. Kiely and J. Hildebidle, Cambridge MA: Harvard University Press.

Hirsch, Elizabeth A. (1986) '"New Eyes": H. D., Modernism and the Psychoanalysis of Seeing', *Literature and Psychology*, 33, pp. 1–10.

Hirsch, Marianne (1997) *Family Frames: Photography, Narrative and Postmemory*, Cambridge MA: Harvard University Press.

Hirschler, Erica E. (2001) *A Studio of Her Own: Women Artists in Boston 1870-1940*, Boston: Museum of Fine Art Publications.

Hockney, David (2001) *Secret Knowledge*, London: Thames and Hudson.

Hoffman, Frederick J., Allen, Charles and Ulrich, Carolyn F. (1946) *The Little Magazine: A History and Bibliography*, Princeton NJ: Princeton University Press.

Howard, J. (1990) *Whisper of the Muse: The World of Julia Margaret Cameron*, London: Colnaghi.

Humm, Maggie (1986) *Feminist Criticism: Women as Contemporary Critics*, Brighton: Harvester Press.

Humm, Maggie (1991) *Border Traffic: Strategies of Contemporary Women Writers*, Manchester: Manchester University Press.

Humm, Maggie (1997) *Feminism and Film*, Edinburgh: Edinburgh University Press.

Humm, Maggie (2000) 'Virginia Woolf's Photography and the Monk's House Albums', in *Virginia Woolf in the Age of Mechanical Reproduction*, ed. P. Caughie, New York: Garland.

Humm, Maggie (2002) *Virginia Woolf, Photography and Modernism*, Southport: Virginia Woolf Society of Great Britain.

Hutton, Patrick (1993) *History as an Art of Memory*, Burlington: University of Vermont.

Huxley, Ernest (2000) 'A Letter to Virginia Woolf dated June 1939', in '*Three Guineas* Letters', ed. A. Snaith, *Woolf Studies Annual*, 6, pp. 114–34.

Huyssen, Andreas (1986) *After the Great Divide: Modernism, Mass Culture, Postmodernism*, Bloomington: Indiana University Press.

Irigaray, Luce (1974) *Speculum de l'autre femme*, Paris: Editions Minuit.

Irigaray, Luce (1993) *An Ethics of Sexual Difference*, Ithaca NY: Cornell University Press.

Jacobus, Mary (1995) *First Things: The Maternal Imaginary in Literature, Art and Psychoanalysis*, London: Routledge.

Jardine, Alice A. (1985) *Gynesis: Configurations of Women and Modernity*, Ithaca NY: Cornell University Press.

Jenks, Chris (ed.) (1995) *Visual Culture*, London: Routledge.

Johnson, George M. (1997) 'A Haunted House: Ghostly Presences in Woolf's Essays and Early Fiction', in *Virginia Woolf and the Essay*, eds B. C. Rosenberg and J. Dubino, Basingstoke: Macmillan.

Johnston, Sheila (1999) 'Italian Neo-Realism', in *The Cinema Book*, 2nd edn, London: BFI.

Jordan, Viola B. (1928) 'Letter', *Close Up*, 3:1, p. 74.

Joyce, James (1922) *Ulysses*, Paris: Shakespeare and Company.

Kaufmann, Michael (1997) 'Virginia Woolf's TLS Reviews and Eliotic Modernism', in *Virginia Woolf and the Essay*, eds B. C. Rosenberg and J. Dubino, Basingstoke: Macmillan.

Kloepfer, Deborah Kelly (1989) *The Unspeakable Mother: Forbidden Discourse in Jean Rhys and H. D.*, Ithaca NY: Cornell University Press.

Knowles, Nancy (1999) 'A Community of Women Looking at Men: The Photographs in Virginia Woolf's *Three Guineas*', in *Virginia Woolf and Communities: Selected Papers from the Eighth Annual Conference on Virginia Woolf*, eds J. McViker and L. Davis, New York: Pace University Press.

Kofman, Sarah (1990) *Freud and Fiction*, trans. S. Wykes, Cambridge: Polity.

Kofman, Sarah (1998) *Camera Obscura: Of Ideology*, London: Athlone Press.

Kracauer, Siegfried (1960) *Theory of Film: The Redemption of Physical Reality*, Oxford: Oxford University Press.

Kracauer, Siegfried (1994) *The Mass Ornament*, ed. and trans. T. Y. Levin, Cambridge MA: Harvard University Press.

Krell, David Farrell (1990) *Of Memory, Reminiscence and Writing: On the Verge*, Bloomington: Indiana University Press.

Kristeva, Julia (1980) *Desire in Language: A Semiotic Approach to Literature and Art*, Oxford: Blackwell.

Kristeva, Julia (1982) 'Women's Time', in *Feminist Theory*, eds N. O. Keohane, M. Z. Rosaldo and B. C. Gelpi, Brighton: Harvester Press.

Kristeva, Julia (1992) 'Stabat Mater', in *The Kristeva Reader*, ed. T. Moi, Oxford: Blackwell.

Kumar, Shiv K. (1957) 'Virginia Woolf and Bergson's Durée', *Research Bulletin of the University of Panjab*, xxiv:vi, pp. 11–13.

Lacan, Jacques (1978) *The Four Fundamental Concepts of Psychoanalysis*, ed. J.-A. Miller, trans. A. Sheridan, New York: W. W. Norton.

Laity, Cassandra (1996) *H. D. and the Victorian Fin de Siècle*, Cambridge: Cambridge University Press.

Lang, Berel (1962) 'Significance of Form: The Dilemma of Roger Fry's Aesthetics', *Journal of Aesthetics and Art Criticism*, 21:2, pp. 167–76.

Lawder, Standish D. (1975) *The Cubist Cinema*, New York: New York University Press.

Lee, Hermione (1996) *Virginia Woolf*, London: Chatto and Windus.

Lefebvre, Henri (1983) 'Modernity and Modernism', in *Modernism and Modernity*, eds B. H. D. Buchloh, Serge Guilbaut and David Solkin, Vancouver: Press of Nova Scotia College of Art and Design.

Lenauer, Jean (1929) 'The Sound Film: Salvation of Cinema', *Close Up*, 4:4, pp. 18–21.

Levenson, Michael (ed.) (1999) *The Cambridge Companion to Modernism*, Cambridge: Cambridge University Press.

Levin, Harry (1966) *Refractions: Essays in Comparative Literature*, Oxford: Oxford University Press.

Levinas, Emmanuel (1996) *Basic Philosophical Writings*, eds A. T. Paperzak, S. Critchley and R. Bernasion, Bloomington: Indiana University Press.

Leyda, Jay (1960) *Kino*, New York: Macmillan.

Lichtenberg Ettinger, Bracha (1992) 'Matrix and Metamorphosis', *Differences*, 4:3, pp. 176–208.

Lichtenberg Ettinger, Bracha (1994a) 'The With-in-Visible Screen', in *Inside the Visible*, ed. C. de Zegher, Cambridge MA: MIT Press.

Lichtenberg Ettinger, Bracha (1994b) 'The Almost-Missed Encounters as Eroticised Aerials of the Psyche', *Third Text*, 28/29, pp. 47–60.

Lichtenberg Ettinger, Bracha (1994c) 'The Becoming Threshold of Matrixial Borderlines', in *Travellers Tales*, eds G. Robertson, M. Mash, L. Tickner, J. Bird, B. Curtis and T. Putnam, London: Routledge.

Lichtenberg Ettinger, Bracha (1995) *The Matrixial Gaze*, Leeds: Feminist Arts and Histories Network.

Locket, M. (1932) 'Children at the Pictures', *Sight and Sound*, 1:1, pp. 27–8.

Lodge, David (1977) *Modes of Modern Writing: Metaphor, Metonymy and the Typology of Modern Literature*, London: Edward Arnold.

Lothrop, E. S. (1982) *A Century of Cameras*, Dobbs Ferry NY: Morgan and Morgan.

Low, Barbara (1927) 'Mind-Growth or Mind-Mechanization? The Cinema in Education', *Close Up*, 1:3, pp. 44–52.

Low, Rachael (1971) *The History of the British Film 1918–1929*, London: George Allen and Unwin.

Luckhurst, Nicola (2001) 'Photoportraits: Gisèle Freund and Virginia Woolf', in *Virginia Woolf in Camera*, N. Luckhurst and M. Ravache, London: Cecil Woolf.

Lyons, Nathan (1966) *Toward a Social Landscape*, New York: Horizon Press.

Lyotard, J.-F. (1984) *The Postmodern Condition: A Report on Knowledge*, trans. G. Bennington and B. Massumi, Minneapolis: University of Minnesota Press.

Lyotard, J.-F. (1990) *Heidegger and 'the Jews'*, trans. A. Michel and M. S. Roberts, Minneapolis: University of Minnesota Press.

MacCarthy, Desmond (1943) 'The Art Quake of 1910', *Listener*, February, pp. 124–5.

McConkey, Kenneth (2000) 'A Walk in the Park: Memory and Rococo Revivalism in the 1890s', in *English Art 1860–1914: Modern Artists and Identity*, eds D. P. Corbett and L. Perry, Manchester: Manchester University Press.

McNeillie, Andrew (1994) 'Editorial Note', in *The Essays of Virginia Woolf: Vol. 4, 1925–28*, ed. A. McNeillie, London: Hogarth Press.

Macpherson, Don (ed.) (1980) *Traditions of Independence*, London: BFI.

Macpherson, Kenneth (1927a) 'As Is', *Close Up*, 1:1, pp. 1–15.

Macpherson, Kenneth (1927b) 'As Is', *Close Up*, 1:2, August, pp. 5–17.

Macpherson, Kenneth (1929a) 'As Is', *Close Up*, 4:4, pp. 5–10.

Macpherson, Kenneth (1929b) 'As Is', *Close Up*, 5:2, pp. 85–90.

Macpherson, Kenneth (1930) 'An Introduction to "The Fourth Dimension in the Kino Part I"', *Close Up*, 6:3, pp. 175–84.

Mao, Douglas (1998) *Solid Objects: Modernism and the Test of Production*, Princeton NJ: Princeton University Press.

Marcus, Jane (1987) *Virginia Woolf and the Languages of Patriarchy*, Bloomington: Indiana University Press.

Marcus, Jane (1988) *Art and Anger: Reading Like a Woman*, Columbus: Ohio State University Press.

Marcus, Laura (1998) 'Introduction', in *Close Up 1927–1933: Cinema and Modernism*, eds J. Donald, A. Friedberg and L. Marcus, London: Cassell.

Marek, Jayne E. (1995) *Women Editing Modernism*, Lexington: University Press of Kentucky.

Marler, Regina (ed.) (1993) *Selected Letters of Vanessa Bell*, London: Bloomsbury.

Marshall, Barbara (1994) *Engendering Modernity: Feminism, Social Theory and Social Change*, Boston: North Eastern University Press.

Mavor, Carol (1996) *Pleasures Taken: Performances of Sexuality and Loss in Victorian Photographs*, London: I. B. Tauris.

Meisel, Perry (1987) *The Myth of the Modern: A Study in British Literature and Criticism after 1850*, New Haven CN: Yale University Press.

Mercurius (1930a) 'Reality and Fantasy', *Architectural Review*, July, p. 29.

Mercurius (1930b) 'Art, Fact and Abstraction', *Architectural Review*, November, p. 258.

Meskimmon, Marsha (1997) *Engendering the City: Women Artists and Urban Space*, London: Scarlet Press.

Metz, Christian (1982) *The Imaginary Signifier*, Bloomington: Indiana University Press.

Metz, Christian (1985) 'Photography and Fetish', *October*, 34, pp. 81–90.

Meynell, Alice (1930) *Essays*, London: Burns, Oates and Waterbourne.

Miller, Ruth C. (1993) *Virginia Woolf: The Frames of Art and Life*, London: Macmillan.

Millett, Kate (1970) *Sexual Politics*, New York: Doubleday.

Mitchell, W. J. T. (1994) *Picture Theory*, Chicago: University of Chicago Press.

Moholy-Nagy, Lásló (1995) 'Space', in *Poetics of Space*, ed. S. Yates, Albuquerque: University of New Mexico Press.

Monnier, Adrienne (1976) *The Very Rich Hours of Adrienne Monnier*, trans. and intro. R. McDougall, New York: Charles Scribner's Sons.

Montagu, Ivor (1980a) 'The Film Society, London', in *Traditions of Independence*, ed.D. Macpherson, London: BFI.

Montagu, Ivor (1980b) 'Film Censorship', in *Traditions of Independence*, ed. D. Macpherson, London: BFI.

Moore, G. E. (1903) 'The Refutation of Idealism', *Mind*, 12:48, pp. 433–53.

Moore, Marianne (1933a) 'Fiction or Nature', *Close Up*, 10:3, pp. 260–5.

Moore, Marianne (1933b) 'Lot in Sodom', *Close Up*, 10:4, pp. 318–19.

Morphet, Richard (1999) 'Image and Theme in Bloomsbury Art', in *The Art of Bloomsbury*, ed. R. Shone, London: Tate Gallery.

Mulvey, Laura (1975) 'Visual Pleasure and Narrative Cinema', *Screen*, 16:3, pp. 6–19.

Mulvey, Laura (1996) *Fetishism and Curiosity*, London: BFI.

National Trust (1995) *Monk's House*, London: National Trust.

Nava, Mica (1994) 'Modernity's Disavowal: Women, the City and the Department Store', in *Modern Times: Reflections on a Century of English Modernity*, eds M. Nava and A. O'Shea, London: Routledge.

Naylor, Gillian (ed.) (1990) *Bloomsbury: The Artists, Authors and Designers by Themselves*, London: Pyramid.

Neumaier, Diane (1995) *Reframings: New American Feminist Photographies*, Philadelphia: Temple University Press.

Neverow, Vara (1999) 'Thinking Back through Our Mothers, Thinking in Common: Virginia Woolf's Photographic Imagination and the Community of Narrators in *Jacob's Room*, *A Room of One's Own*, and *Three Guineas*', in *Virginia Woolf and Communities: Selected Papers From the Eighth Annual Conference on Virginia Woolf*, eds J. McVicker and L. Davis, New York: Pace University Press.

Nicholls, Peter (1995) *Modernism: A Literary Guide*, London: Macmillan.

Nochlin, Linda (1988) *Women, Art and Power and Other Essays*, New York: Thames and Hudson.

Nora, Pierre (1989) 'Between Memory and History: Les Lieux de Mémoire', *Representations*, 26, pp. 7–25.

O'Pray, Michael (ed.) (1996) *The British Avant-Garde Film 1926–1995*, Luton: University of Luton Press.

Orton, Fred and Pollock, Griselda (1996) *Avant-Gardes and Partisans Reviewed*, Manchester: Manchester University Press.

Parish, Richard (1999) 'Recalling of Things French', *Times Higher Education Supplement*, 16 April, p. 27.

Parsons, Deborah C. (2000) *Streetwalking the Metropolis*, Oxford: Oxford University Press.

Penley, Constance (ed.) (1988) *Feminism and Film Theory*, London: Routledge.

Perry, Gillian (1995) *Women Artists and the Parisian Avant-Garde: Modernism and 'Feminine' Art 1900 to the late 1920s*, Manchester: Manchester University Press.

Phelan, Peggy (1993) *Unmarked: The Politics of Performance*, London: Routledge.

Pollock, Griselda (1988) *Vision and Difference: Femininity, Feminism and the Histories of Art*, London: Routledge.

Pollock, Griselda (1994a) 'Inscriptions in the Feminine', in *Inside the Visible*, ed. C. de Zegher, Cambridge MA: MIT Press.

Pollock, Griselda (1994b) 'Territories of Desire: Reconsiderations of an African Childhood', in *Travellers' Tales*, eds G. Robertson, M. Mash, L. Tickner, J. Bird, B. Curtis and T. Putnam, London: Routledge.

Pollock, Griselda (1995) 'After the Reapers: Gleaning the Past, the Feminine and Another Future, from the Work of Bracha Lichtenberg Ettinger', in *Halala-Autistwork*, J.-F. Lyotard, C. Buci-Glucksmann and G. Pollock, Aix-en-Provence: Arfiac.

Pollock, Griselda (1999) *Differencing the Canon: Feminist Desire and the Writing of Art's Histories*, London: Routledge.

Poole, Roger (1991) '"We All Put Up With You, Virginia": Irreceivable Wisdom about War', in *Virginia Woolf and War: Fiction, Reality and Myth*, ed. M. Hussey, New York: Syracuse University Press.

Powell, Tristram (1973) 'Preface', in *Victorian Photographs of Famous Men and Fair Women by Julia Margaret Cameron*, eds V. Woolf and R. Fry, London: Hogarth Press.

Prettejohn, Elizabeth (1999) 'Out of the Nineteenth Century: Roger Fry's Early Art Criticism 1900–1906', in *Art Made Modern: Roger Fry's Vision of Art*, ed. C. Green, London: Merrell Holberton and Courtauld Gallery.

Price, Reynolds (1992) 'Afterword', in *Sally Mann: Immediate Family*, Sally Mann, Oxford: Phaidon.

Proust, Marcel (1996) *In Search of Lost Time: Vol. I, Swann's Way*, New York: Vintage.

Quick, Jonathan R. (1985) 'Virginia Woolf, Roger Fry and Post-Impressionism', *Massachusetts Review*, 26:4, pp. 547–70.

Quinones, Ricardo (1985) *Mapping Literary Modernism*, Princeton NJ: Princeton University Press.

Radford, Jean (1991) *Dorothy Richardson*, Bloomington: Indiana University Press.

Rado, Lisa (1994) *Rereading Modernism: New Directions in Feminist Criticism*, New York: Garland.

Read, Herbert (1932) 'Towards a Film Aesthetic', *Cinema Quarterly*, 1:1, pp. 7–11.

Reed, Christopher (1993) 'Through Formalism: Feminism and Virginia Woolf's Relation to Bloomsbury Aesthetics', in *The Multiple Muses of Virginia Woolf*, ed. D. F. Gillespie, Columbia: University of Missouri Press.

Reed, Christopher (2000) 'Housework vs Heroism or the Individual against the Avant-garde: An Argument for Bloomsbury's Significance', unpublished paper, Bloomsbury and Modernism Conference, 22 January, London: Tate Gallery.

Rich, Adrienne (1976) *Of Woman Born*, New York: W. W. Norton.

Richardson, Dorothy (1927) 'Continuous Performance', *Close Up*, 1, pp. 34–7.

Richardson, Dorothy – (1928a) 'Continuous Performance VIII – [*Animal Impudens…*]', *Close Up*, 2:3, pp. 51–5.

Richardson, Dorothy (1928b) 'Continuous Performance XII – The Cinema in Arcady', *Close Up*, 3:1, pp. 52–7.

Richardson, Dorothy (1928c) 'Continuous Performance IX – The Thoroughly Popular Film', *Close Up*, 2:4, pp. 44–50.

Richardson, Dorothy (1928d) 'Continuous Performance VII – The Front Rows', *Close Up*, 2:1, pp. 59–64.

Richardson, Dorothy (1928e) 'Films for Children', *Close Up*, 3:2, pp. 21–7.

Richardson, Dorothy (1929a) 'Continuous Performance – Dialogue in Dixie', *Close Up*, 5:3, pp. 211–18.

Richardson, Dorothy (1929b) 'Continuous Performance – Almost Persuaded', *Close Up*, 4:6, pp. 31–7.

Richardson, Dorothy (1929c) 'Continuous Performance – Pictures and Films', *Close Up*, 4:1, pp. 51–7.

Richardson, Dorothy (1930) 'The Censorship Petition', *Close Up*, 6:1, pp. 7–11.

Richardson, Dorothy (1932) 'Continuous Performance – The Film Gone Male', *Close Up*, 9:1, pp. 36–8.

Richardson, Dorothy (1979) *Pilgrimage*, London: Virago.

Rickels, Laurence (1988) *Aberrations of Mourning*, Detroit: Wayne State University Press.
Roberts, John (1998) *The Art of Interruption: Realism, Photography, and the Everyday*, Manchester: Manchester University Press.
Roberts, Pam (1997) 'Alfred Stieglitz, 219 Gallery and Camera Work', in *Camera Work*, eds S. Philippi and U. Kieseyer, New York: Taschen.
Robins, Anna Gruetzner (1997) *Modern Art in Britain 1910–1914*, London: Merrell Holberton.
Rose, Jacqueline (1994) *The Case of Peter Pan*, London: Macmillan.
Rosenblum, Naomi (2000) *A History of Women Photographers*, New York: Abbeville Press.
Rotha, Paul (1930) 'The Revival of Naturalism', *Close Up*, 7:1, pp. 21–32.
Rotha, Paul (1932) 'Approach to a New Cinema', *Cinema Quarterly*, 1:1, pp. 18–28.
Rotha, Paul (1949) *The Film till Now: A Survey of World Cinema*, London: Vision Press.
Rowbotham, Sheila (1983) *Dreams and Dilemmas*, London: Virago.
Rugg, Linda (1997) *Picturing Ourselves: Photography and Autobiography*, Chicago: University of Chicago Press.
Russell, Bertrand (1959) *My Philosophical Development*, London: Allen and Unwin.
Saalschutz, L. (1929) 'The Film in its Relation to the Unconscious', *Close Up*, 5:1, pp. 31–8.
Sachs, Hanns (1928) 'Film Psychology', *Close Up*, 3:5, pp. 8–15.
Schaffer, Talia (1994) 'Posing Orlando', *Genders*, 19, pp. 26–63.
Schorer, Mark (1961) *Modern British Fiction*, Oxford: Oxford University Press.
Schwarz, Daniel R. (1997) *Reconfiguring Modernism: Explorations in the Relationship Between Modern Art and Modern Literature*, New York: St Martin's Press.
Schwarz, Sanford (1988) *The Matrix of Modernism: Pound, Eliot and Early Twentieth Century Thought*, Princeton NJ: Princeton University Press.
Seiberling, Grace (1986) *Amateurs, Photography and the Mid-Victorian Imagination*, Chicago: University of Chicago Press.
Seldes, Gilbert (1926) 'The Abstract Movie', *New Republic*, 15 September, pp. 95–6.
Shone, Richard (1976) *Bloomsbury Portraits*, Oxford: Phaidon.
Shute, Nerina (1929) 'Paul Robeson's Talkie Search', *Film Weekly*, 2:45, p. 11.
Sichel, Kim (1999) *Germaine Krull: Photographer of Modernity*, Cambridge MA: MIT Press.
Silver, Brenda R. (1992) 'What's Woolf Got to Do with It? Or the Perils of Popularity', *Modern Fiction Studies*, 38:1, pp. 21–61.
Silverman, Kaja (1988) *The Acoustic Mirror: The Female Voice in Psychoanalysis and Cinema*, Bloomington: Indiana University Press.
Silverman, Kaja (1996) *The Threshold of the Visible World*, London: Routledge.
Smith, Dorothy (1987) *The Everyday World as Problematic: A Feminist Sociology*, Boston: North Eastern University Press.
Smith, Lindsay (1998) *The Politics of Focus: Women, Children and Nineteenth-Century Photography*, Manchester: Manchester University Press.
Smith, Sidonie (1993) *Subjectivity, Identity and the Body: Women's Autobiographical Practices in the Twentieth Century*, Bloomington: Indiana University Press.
Snaith, Anna (2000) '*Three Guineas* Letters', *Woolf Studies Annual*, 6, pp. 17–168.
Snyder, Joel (1980) 'Picturing Vision', in *The Language of Images*, ed. W. J. T. Mitchell, Chicago: University of Chicago Press.
Solomon-Godeau, Abigail (1991) *Photography at the Dock: Essays on Photographic History, Institutions and Practices*, Minneapolis: University of Minnesota Press
Sontag, Susan (1989) *On Photography*, New York: Anchor Books.
Spalding, Frances (1983) *Vanessa Bell*, London: Weidenfeld and Nicolson.
Spence, Jo (1991) 'Shame-Work: Thoughts on Family Snaps and Fractured Identities', in *Family Snaps: The Meanings of Domestic Photography*, eds J. Spence and P. Holland, London: Virago.
Spence, Jo and Holland, Pat (eds) (1991) *Family Snaps: The Meanings of Domestic Photography*, London: Virago.
Stavely, Alice (1998) 'Name that Face', *Virginia Woolf Miscellany*, 51, pp. 4–5.
Stein, Gertrude (1927a) 'Mrs Emerson', *Close Up*, 2, pp. 23–9.
Stein, Gertrude (1927b) 'Three Sitting Here I', *Close Up*, 3, pp. 17–28.
Stein, Gertrude (1927c) 'Three Sitting Here II', *Close Up*, 4, pp. 17–25.
Stein, Gertrude (1935) *Lectures in America*, New York: Random House.
Stein, Gertrude (1937) *Everybody's Autobiography*, New York: Random House.
Stein, Gertrude (1967) *Writings and Lectures 1911–1945*, ed. P. Meyorowitz, London: Peter Owen.
Stein, Gertrude (1997) 'Matisse and Picasso', in *Camera Work*, eds S. Philippi and U. Kieseyer, New York: Taschen.
Steiner, George (1975) *After Babel*, Oxford: Oxford University Press.
Steiner, Wendy (1987) 'Postmodern Portraits', *Art Journal*, 46:3, pp. 173–7.
Stephen, Leslie (1874) *Hours in a Library*, London: Smith Elder.
Stephen, Leslie (1895) *Photograph Album*, Northampton MA: Mortimer Rare Book Room, Smith College.
Stephen, Leslie (1977) *Sir Leslie Stephen's Mausoleum Book*, ed. A. Bell, Oxford: Clarendon Press.
Stieglitz, Alfred (1997a) 'The New Color Photography', in *Camera Work*, eds S. Philippi and U. Kieseyer, New York: Taschen.

Stieglitz, Alfred (1997b) 'Editorial', in *Camera Work*, eds S. Philippi and U. Kieseyer, New York: Taschen.

Stimpson, Catharine (1986) 'The Somagrams of Gertrude Stein', in *Critical Essays on Gertrude Stein*, ed. M. J. Hoffman, Boston: G. K. Hall.

Stokes, Philip (1992) 'The Family Photograph Album: So Great a Cloud of Witnesses', in *The Portrait in Photography*, ed. G. Clarke, London: Reaktion Books.

Summer, Rosemary (1999) 'An Experiment in Fiction: "The Thing that Exists when We Aren't There"', *Virginia Woolf Bulletin*, 1, pp. 17–19.

Szarkowski, John (1973) *Looking at Photographs*, New York: Museum of Modern Art.

Tagg, John (1988) *The Burden of Representation: Essays on Photography and Histories*, London: Macmillan.

Terdiman, Richard (1993) *Present Past: Modernity and the Memory Crisis*, Ithaca NY: Cornell University Press.

Thompson, Kristin (1985) *Exploring Entertainment: America in the World Film Market 1907–1934*, London: BFI.

Tickner, Lisa (2000) *Modern Life and Modern Subjects: British Art in the Early Twentieth Century*, New Haven CN: Yale University Press.

Tillyard, S. K. (1988) *The Impact of Modernism 1900–1920*, London: Routledge.

Todd, Dorothy and Mortimer, Raymond (1977) *The New Interior Decoration*, New York: Da Capo Press.

Vanacker, S. (1997) 'Autobiography and Orality: The Work of Modernist Women Writers', in *Women's Lives/Women's Times: New Essays on Autobiography*, eds T. L. Broughton and L. Anderson, Albany NY: State University of New York Press.

Virmaux, Alain and Virmaux, Odette (1980) 'Introduction', in *Colette at the Movies: Criticism and Screenplays*, eds A. Virmaux and O. Virmaux, trans. S. W. R. Smith, New York: Frederick Ungar.

Walton, Jean (1997) 'Nightmare of the Uncoordinated White Folk: Race, Psychoanalysis and *Borderline*', *Discourse*, 19:2, pp. 88–109.

Walton, Jean (1999) 'White Neurotics, Black Primitives, and the Queer Matrix of *Borderline*', in *Outtakes: Essays on Queer Theory and Film*, ed. E. Hanson, Durham NC: Duke University Press.

Watney, Simon (1980) *English Post-Impressionism*, London: Studio Vista.

Watney, Simon (1983) 'The Connoisseur as Gourmet', in *Formations of Pleasure*, ed. Formations Editorial Collective, London: Routledge and Kegan Paul.

Watson, Julia (1992) 'Unspeakable Differences: The Politics of Gender in Lesbian and Heterosexual Women's Autobiographies', in *De/Colonizing the Subject: The Politics of Gender in Women's Autobiographies*, eds S. Smith and J. Watson, Minneapolis: University of Minnesota Press.

White, Eric W. (1931) *Walking Shadows*, London: Hogarth Press.

Williams, Val (1991) 'Carefully Creating an Idyll: Vanessa Bell and Snapshot Photography 1907–46', in *Family Snaps: The Meanings of Domestic Photography*, eds J. Spence and P. Holland, London: Virago.

Williams, Val (1994) *The Other Observers: Women Photographers in Britain 1900 to the Present*, London: Virago.

Wilson, Elizabeth (2001) *The Contradictions of Culture: Cities, Culture, Women*, London: Sage.

Wilson, Norma (1932) 'The Spectator', *Cinema Quarterly*, 1:1, pp. 3–6.

Woolf, Leonard (1935) *Quack, Quack*, London: Hogarth Press.

Woolf, Virginia (1926) 'The Movies', manuscript, Berg Collection, New York Public Library.

Woolf, Virginia (1927) *To the Lighthouse*, London: Hogarth Press.

Woolf, Virginia (1929) *A Room of One's Own*, London: Hogarth Press.

Woolf, Virginia (1931–7) *Virginia Woolf Manuscripts from the Monk's House Papers*. Press cuttings and extracts collected or copied by Virginia Woolf relating to *Three Guineas*, 16F, 3 vols, Brighton: University of Sussex Press.

Woolf, Virginia (1934) *Walter Sickert: A Conversation*, London: Hogarth Press.

Woolf, Virginia (1953) *A Writer's Diary*, London: Hogarth Press.

Woolf, Virginia (1958a) 'The Narrow Bridge of Art', in *Granite and Rainbow: Essays by Virginia Woolf*, ed. L. Woolf, London: Hogarth Press.

Woolf, Virginia (1958b) 'Phases of Fiction', in *Granite and Rainbow: Essays by Virginia Woolf*, ed. L. Woolf, London: Hogarth Press.

Woolf, Virginia (1961a) 'Thoughts on Peace in an Air Raid', in *The Death of the Moth and Other Essays*, V. Woolf, Harmondsworth: Penguin.

Woolf, Virginia (1961b) *The Death of the Moth and Other Essays*, Harmondsworth: Penguin.

Woolf, Virginia (1966–7) *Collected Essays*, ed. L. Woolf, London: Chatto and Windus.

Woolf, Virginia (1975a) 'Recent Paintings by Vanessa Bell', in *The Bloomsbury Group*, ed. S. P. Rosenbaum, London: Croom Helm.

Woolf, Virginia (1975b) *The Flight of the Mind: The Letters of Virginia Woolf: Vol. 1, 1888–1912*, eds N. Nicolson and J. Trautmann, New York: Harcourt Brace Jovanovich.

Woolf, Virginia (1976) *The Question of Things Happening: The Letters of Virginia Woolf: Vol. II, 1912–22*, eds N. Nicolson and J. Trautmann, London: Hogarth Press.

Woolf, Virginia (1977a) *The Diary of Virginia Woolf: Vol. 1, 1915–19*, ed. A. O. Bell, London: Hogarth Press.

Woolf, Virginia (1977b) *A Change of Perspective: Collected Letters: Vol. 3, 1923–28*, eds N. Nicolson and J. Trautmann Banks, London: Hogarth Press.

Woolf, Virginia (1978a) 'Mr Bennett and Mrs Brown', in *The Captain's Death Bed and Other Essays*, V. Woolf, New York: Harcourt Brace Jovanovich.

Woolf, Virginia (1978b) *A Reflection of the Other Person: The Letters of Virginia Woolf: Vol. 4, 1929–31*, eds N. Nicolson and J. Trautmann Banks, London: Hogarth Press.

Woolf, Virginia (1978c) *The Diary of Virginia Woolf: Vol. 2, 1920–24*, ed. A. O. Bell, London: Hogarth Press.

Woolf, Virginia (1979) *The Sickle Side of the Moon: The Letters of Virginia Woolf: Vol. 5, 1932–35*, eds N. Nicolson and J. Trautmann Banks, London: Hogarth Press.

Woolf, Virginia (1980a) *Leave the Letters Till We're Dead: The Letters of Virginia Woolf: Vol. 6, 1936–41*, eds N. Nicolson and J. Trautmann Banks, London: Hogarth Press.

Woolf, Virginia (1980b) *The Diary of Virginia Woolf: Vol. 3, 1925–30*, ed. A. O. Bell, London: Hogarth Press.

Woolf, Virginia (1982) *The Diary of Virginia Woolf: Vol. 4, 1931–35*, ed. A. O. Bell, London: Hogarth Press.

Woolf, Virginia (1984) *The Diary of Virginia Woolf: Vol. 5, 1936–41*, ed. A. O. Bell with A. McNeillie, London: Hogarth Press.

Woolf, Virginia (1985) 'A Sketch of the Past', in *Moments of Being*, ed. J. Schulkind, Brighton: University of Sussex Press.

Woolf, Virginia (1988) *The Essays of Virginia Woolf: Vol. 3, 1919–24*, ed. A. McNeillie, San Diego: Harcourt Brace Jovanovich.

Woolf, Virginia (1989) 'Portraits', in *The Complete Shorter Fiction of Virginia Woolf*, ed. S. Dick, San Diego: Harcourt.

Woolf, Virginia (1990) *A Passionate Apprentice: The Early Journals 1897–1909*, ed. Mitchell A. Leaska, San Diego: Harcourt Brace Jovanovich.

Woolf, Virginia (1993) *Three Guineas*, in *A Room of One's Own and Three Guineas*, ed. M. Barrett, Harmondsworth: Penguin.

Woolf, Virginia (1994a) 'The Common Reader', in *The Essays of Virginia Woolf: Vol. 4, 1925–28*, ed. A. McNeillie, London: Hogarth Press.

Woolf, Virginia (1994b) 'The Cinema', in *The Essays of Virginia Woolf: Vol. 4, 1925–28*, ed. A. McNeillie, London: Hogarth Press.

Woolf, Virginia (1994c) 'Modern Fiction', in *The Essays of Virginia Woolf: Vol. 4, 1925–28*, ed. A. McNeillie, London: Hogarth Press.

Woolf, Virginia (2001a) 'An Unwritten Novel', in *Virginia Woolf: The Mark on the Wall and Other Short Fiction*, ed. D. Bradshaw, Oxford: Oxford University Press.

Woolf, Virginia (2001b) 'Blue and Green', in *Virginia Woolf: The Mark on the Wall and Other Short Fiction*, ed. D. Bradshaw, Oxford: Oxford University Press.

Wollen, Peter (1978/9) 'Photography and Aesthetics', *Screen*, 19:4, pp. 9–29.

Wussow, Helen (1994) 'Virginia Woolf and the Problematic Nature of the Photographic Image', *Twentieth Century Literature*, XLII, pp. 1–14.

Wussow, Helen (1997) 'Travesties of Excellence: Julia Margaret Cameron, Lytton Strachey, Virginia Woolf, and the Photographic Image', in *Virginia Woolf and The Arts: Selected Papers from the Sixth Annual Conference on Virginia Woolf*, eds D. F. Gillespie and L. Hankins, New York: Pace University Press.

Yates, Frances A. (1966) *The Art of Memory*, London: Routledge and Kegan Paul.

Yates, Steve (1995) *Poetics of Space: A Critical Photographic Anthology*, Albuquerque: University of New Mexico Press.

INDEX